John Caird

University sermons

preached before the University of Glasgow, 1873-1898

John Caird

University sermons
preached before the University of Glasgow, 1873-1898

ISBN/EAN: 9783744745420

Printed in Europe, USA, Canada, Australia, Japan

Cover: Foto ©Lupo / pixelio.de

More available books at **www.hansebooks.com**

UNIVERSITY SERMONS

PUBLISHED BY

JAMES MACLEHOSE AND SONS, GLASGOW,

Publishers to the University.

MACMILLAN AND CO., LTD., LONDON AND NEW YORK.

London, - - *Simpkin*, *Hamilton and Co.*
Cambridge, - *Macmillan and Bowes.*
Edinburgh, - ***Douglas and Foulis.***

MDCCCXCVIII.

University Sermons

Preached before the University of Glasgow
1873–1898

By
JOHN CAIRD, D.D., LL.D.
Late Principal and Vice-Chancellor of the University of Glasgow

Glasgow
James MacLehose and Sons
Publishers to the University
1898

GLASGOW: PRINTED AT THE UNIVERSITY PRESS
BY ROBERT MACLEHOSE AND CO.

PREFATORY NOTE.

ALL the Sermons included in this volume were preached before the University, and all but the one placed first, during my brother's tenure of the office of Principal. Only two of them have previously been published: the Sermon "What is Religion?" which was printed separately, and the Sermon on "Corporate Immortality," which was contributed to the volume entitled "Scotch Sermons." I have to thank Messrs. Macmillan & Co. for allowing me to reprint it. The Sermon on "The Law of Heredity in the Spiritual Life," which is placed last, was preached on November 4th, 1894, and was the last which the Principal preached before the University. In the following Session, 1895-6, he delivered the last part of his Gifford Lectures, which I hope to publish in the course of next year.

I am indebted to Professor Jones and Mr. Robert MacLehose for much assistance in revising the proofs of this volume.

EDWARD CAIRD.

BALLIOL COLLEGE,
    October 28*th*, 1898.

CONTENTS.

	PAGE
WHAT IS RELIGION?	1
THE LIKENESS AND UNLIKENESS OF GOD'S WAYS AND MAN'S WAYS,	27
EVIL WORKING THROUGH GOOD,	52
THE NEW BIRTH,	70
THE CHRISTIAN WAY OF RECONCILING MAN WITH HIMSELF,	92
CAN RIGHTEOUSNESS BE IMPUTED?	112
IS REPENTANCE EVER IMPOSSIBLE?	133
THE REVERSAL OF NATURE'S LAW OF COMPETITION,	154
CORPORATE IMMORTALITY,	176
TRUTH AND FREEDOM,	196

CONTENTS.

	PAGE
THE GUILT AND GUILTLESSNESS OF UNBELIEF,	215
THE RELATIONS OF LOVE AND KNOWLEDGE,	240
THE MEASURE OF GREATNESS,	260
THE PROFIT OF GODLINESS,	282
THE SPIRITUAL RELATIONS OF NATURE TO MAN,	300
ART AND RELIGION,	322
THINGS NEW AND OLD,	340
THE TEMPORAL AND THE ETERNAL,	360
THE LAW OF HEREDITY IN THE SPIRITUAL LIFE,	380

UNIVERSITY SERMONS.

WHAT IS RELIGION?

"Pure religion and undefiled before God and the Father is this, To visit the fatherless and widows in their affliction, and to keep himself unspotted from the world." JAMES i. 27.

THIS text does not determine what the nature of true religion is. It treats of the expression or manifestation of religion rather than of its essence, of its proper form rather than of its spirit or principle. The persons addressed were Jewish converts to Christianity, who seem to have been disposed to attach undue importance to the external forms and observances of religious worship, and, if not to introduce into Christianity something of the elaborateness and sensuous splendour of their former faith, at any rate to identify religion too much with the exact performance of its outward rites and ceremonies. The word translated 'religion' means more properly what we understand by the terms 'worship' and 'ritual'; and the idea of the writer is, that it is not ceremonial observances but kind words and gentle deeds—sympathy, charity, purity, which constitute the true Christian ritual; in other words, that the most genuine expression of religion is to be found, not in special forms and acts of devotion, in observances which are always more or less technical and conventional, and which vary with the particular conditions of time and place; but in those moral acts which are universal as the common nature of man, and unchanging as his relations to his brother man and to God. "If any man among you," he writes, "seem to be religious, and bridleth not his tongue, but deceiveth his own heart, this man's religion is vain." 'Be you,' that is, 'never so exact in the repetition of solemn words and formulas of devotion; let accordant voices blend in chanted litanies, and sweetest hymns of praise swell up without one jarring note to heaven—a selfish heart, a slanderous tongue will vitiate all the sweetness of the song. The divinest harmony is that of loving hearts: kind thoughts and gentle words are heaven's best anthems.' "Pure religion and undefiled," he adds, is "to visit the fatherless and widows in their affliction." 'Not,' that is, 'in repairing to places conventionally holy, to temples and shrines and sacred localities, do we come nearest to God. The object of our worship has representatives on earth truer than stone temples. The poor, the weak, the friendless, the unprotected,—in the homes of these the presence of the Infinite Love and

Pity dwells; and by acts of charity and helpfulness to these, we render a tribute of devotion, dearer far than the most costly offerings laid on consecrated altars, to him who hath said, "Inasmuch as ye have done it unto one of the least of these my brethren, ye have done it unto me."' Finally, "pure religion and undefiled," the Apostle writes, is "to keep himself unspotted from the world." In other words, moral, not artificial, sanctity is the true sign of Christian purity. Not the unsoiled hands are the surest witness to the stainless soul. Avoid all contact with the ceremonially unclean; eat no meat which Church laws have tabooed; fly from the world to some secluded haunt fenced off from all profane contiguities,— not thus will you best prove your purity or preserve it unsullied. Holiness is something nobler than innocence, grander than the cowardly spotlessness of isolation. He alone can be called pure who, living where duty calls him, amidst the throng and thoroughfare of life, surrounded by its temptations, breathing the atmosphere of its sins and sorrows, yet keeps the mirror of a blameless soul, unruffled by the passions, unspotted by the vices of the world. "Pure religion and undefiled before God and the Father is this, To visit the fatherless and widows in their affliction, and to keep himself unspotted from the world."

But in thus contrasting an imperfect with a higher and truer expression of religion, the text does not give us any direct insight into what religion in itself essentially is. Morality is a better manifestation of the principle of religion than ceremonial observances, but it is not that principle itself, nor even an infallible sign of it. For while the text implies that there can be no religion without morality, it does not teach, conversely, that there can be no morality without religion. And in point of fact we know that the social and personal virtues here enumerated are not invariably the effects of religious principle. A kind, tolerant, compassionate man, or a man of unsullied and blameless life, is not necessarily one of whom we conclude that he is a man of deep religious convictions. If religion be a thing of doctrinal belief, then, notoriously, charity and purity may exist independently of correct religious notions or ideas, under a thousand diversities of creeds and dogmas. The gentle virtues are not plants that bloom only on the soil of orthodoxy. They flourish, with a wonderful disdain of ecclesiastical restrictions, on the unhallowed domain of heresy; nay, sometimes are found blossoming into a strange luxuriance on the outlying wastes of heathendom. If, again, religion be a thing of feeling rather than of intellect, of profound spiritual emotions and aspirations rather than of correct doctrinal conceptions, is there any necessary and invariable connexion betwixt religious feeling and the virtues of which the text speaks? Do we not meet everywhere in the world with men of fair and blameless lives, just, honourable, chaste, charitable, alive to the claims of society, active in all beneficent schemes and enterprises; who are yet strangers to those spiritual griefs and joys which belong to the sphere of religious experience, who have never been conscious of any profound convictions of sin, or yearnings after reconciliation with God, or ardent aspirations of faith and hope, and to whom the language of devout sentiment is a sealed book, if it seem not even a sort of jargon from which good taste recoils?

And the reason of all this is obvious. There are other than religious sources to which the virtues here spoken of may be traced. A humane and charitable life, gentle and kindly words and deeds, for instance, may be the expression merely of a kind of spontaneous or instinctive sweetness of nature, a soft, susceptible, sympathetic temperament, which, however attractive and amiable, has as little affinity to religious notions and beliefs as the fragrance of the flower or the song of the summer bird. To be capable of being touched by the sight of human sorrow, to have the ear open to the appeal of defencelessness, and to fold the orphan in pity's arms,—all this may be due only to the strength of the universal instincts of humanity implanted in our common nature, which are strong or weak more as nature than as grace determines, and which, though religion may deepen or hallow, it cannot be said to create. So again, with respect to that other side of morality which is indicated by the words, "to keep himself unspotted from the world,"—how obviously may this too have its root in other than religious causes. There is, for instance, a certain purity and elevation of character which springs simply from intellectual culture. Education, thought, liberal culture, if they do not sanctify, do at least refine; they may not change the heart, but they powerfully tend to ennoble the life. When we speak of a man, not as a Christian, but simply as 'a scholar and a gentleman,' there rises up before the mind the representation of a character in which the religious element may have no place, yet which embraces some of its most beautiful and attractive results,—that of a man not only incapable of low vice or immorality, whose self-respect would be gone if he suffered himself to be betrayed into vulgar intemperance and licentiousness, but also one who is superior to all that is mean, ignoble, ungenerous; whose word you know to be inviolable as his oath; whose honour would perchance in the hour of trial nerve him for the most painful and magnanimous sacrifices, and in the time of danger render him, though softly reared and physically weak, brave as a lion;—a man courteous in speech and bearing, considerate of the feelings of others, and though reserved to the obtrusive, and capable of being roused to almost savage sternness and scorn by the sight of falsehood and baseness, yet gentle to the timid, simple as a child to little children, tender to all weak and helpless things. Yet these and other characteristic features of the refined and highly educated nature are due to motives entirely within the sphere of what is human and finite; identical in form with the manifestations of religion, they are totally different in spirit. They are virtues, not graces; morality, not godliness or holiness.

What, then, the question recurs, is the essence of religion itself? If morality is not religion, nor even the infallible sign of its existence; if purity, charity, beneficence, integrity, if even a certain nobleness and elevation of character, though they may spring from a religious spirit, may also spring from a source far less profound, then the only way in which we can distinguish between them is by penetrating beneath the form, going deeper than the outward life, and ascertaining what the inward spirit or principle of that which we designate religion is. That which makes a man religious is some state, or attitude, or relation of his inner spiritual nature—what is sometimes called the 'state of his soul.' What then is that? Examining my own consciousness—what is that by the presence or absence of which I can determine whether or not I am a religious man?

Now the answers which have been given to this question differ in their general form (and it is to this only that we shall have time to advert) in this respect, that some make religion to consist essentially or mainly in *feeling*, whilst others make it to consist primarily in *knowledge*. In our relations to God, whether immediate, or through whatever means they begin and are carried on, there are certain feelings, emotions, aspirations, which are awakened within the devout heart; and, again, there are certain notions, ideas, doctrines, concerning God and divine things which we form or accept as true. In which of these two kinds of experience does the essence of religion lie? Is it in either as distinguished from the other, or in a combination of the two? Is religion a thing of the head or of the heart? In order to be a religious man, is the main or indispensable thing soundness of creed, or depth and intensity of feeling—a correct system of doctrines, or a devout and ardent spirit? May we hold, on the one hand, that notwithstanding much error and inaccuracy of dogmatic belief, a man may still be a genuine Christian if the fire of devout and holy feeling burn within his breast; or, on the other hand, that however cold, unimpassioned, unemotional a man's nature be, he must be regarded as a religious man if he knows and sincerely accepts all the articles of the Christian faith?

Now, of the possibility and importance of a science of theology, of sound, accurate, self-consistent religious ideas, no thoughtful man can entertain a doubt. And were we here called to treat of that subject, it would be easy to show that a theology which pretends to rest merely on pious feeling, without going on to appeal to those principles by which alone feeling can be tested and objective truth grasped and determined, is self-contradictory and futile. But whilst no man can despise theology, that science which investigates the grounds of our religious ideas, and tries to give to them systematic development and harmony—and least of all would it become one whose vocation in life it is to teach that science to do so,—yet our present enquiry respects not the value of theological knowledge in itself, but its *religious* value. The question we have to deal with is, whether, and how far, religion consists in accurate or sound theological conceptions; whether, and how far, these are 'necessary to salvation.' In the history of the Church it has been but too much the tendency to lay stress on these as the all-important and indispensable thing in religion. In our own country—partly from the peculiar intellectual genius of the nation, partly from external and historic causes—it has been in other days, and to some extent is still in our own, the tendency to confound religion with theology, and to reduce religion in its ultimate essence much to a thing of knowledge. Now, there are considerations, many and cogent, which lead us to question the correctness of this view—considerations which seem to be fatal to the assertion that the main or indispensable thing in religion is accuracy of theological opinions; or, in other words, that in its ultimate principle or essence, religion is a thing of knowledge. To some of these considerations I desire now briefly to direct your attention.

In the first place, it may be urged, that religion must be a thing attainable by all, and therefore cannot, like knowledge, be dependent on gifts and acquirements accessible only to a few. All need it; none can be saved without it. Science and philosophy are noble things. Literary and artistic culture and refinement are most desirable attainments—dignifying and beautifying life, and opening up to their possessor the springs of purest enjoyment. But they are not indispensable. It is possible to live and die without them, and there are thousands of men who must and do contrive to live tranquil, happy, and useful lives, to whom these blessings are but a name. But religion is something altogether different. It is no luxury or superfluity of life; it is itself the very life, the happiness, the salvation, of man, that without which existence is vanity and wretchedness, and death is darkness and horror, without which we cannot live, and dare not die. Its attainment cannot therefore be dependent on conditions which would render it the monopoly of a learned and cultured class, of acute or logical or philosophical minds. It must be a blessing not more accessible to these than to little children, to dull and feeble-minded and unlettered men. No one must be able to plead intellectual incapacity in excuse for irreligion—to urge that inasmuch as he has neither the leisure nor ability to follow out a process of historic proof, to verify the logical accuracy of terms and definitions, to weigh elaborate arguments and investigate subtle trains of reasoning, religion is not a thing for him. But if sound theological opinions be of the essence of religion, then, it would seem, this excuse would be valid. For not only does the proof of the genuineness and divine authority of the Scripture documents demand, in order to its appreciation, the exercise of rare gifts of historic criticism, metaphysical insight, logical acumen,—not only is it impossible, without powers possessed only by the educated and disciplined mind, to decide between rival schools and systems of theology, to determine, for instance, that Calvinism is true and Arminianism or Pelagianism false; but, it may be maintained, with some show of reason, that there is not one of those doctrines which are generally deemed essential and fundamental, which does not imply, in order to its accurate apprehension as a theological dogma, a measure of ratiocinative ability, a capacity to analyze, distinguish, compare, define, of which the vast majority of men are altogether destitute.

It may be said that no such burden is thrown on the unlettered Christian, inasmuch as the doctrines of religion are not left to be excogitated by the mind of man, but are clearly and authoritatively revealed in the Word of God. And this indeed is true; but it is not true in any sense available for the present argument, that is, so as to obviate the objection to making religion a thing of knowledge. For, the intellectual apprehension of the doctrines of Scripture cannot, it may be argued, be a matter so simple and easy, inasmuch as eighteen hundred years have been spent upon it, and yet there is not one of these doctrines about which theologians are perfectly agreed, scarcely any of them with respect to which controversies and discussions are not waged and diverse and discordant notions entertained by men equally acute and earnest-minded, all alike appealing to the authority of Scripture, and each claiming its sanction for his own particular view.

What, then, while theologians differ as to the doctrines of Scripture, is the simple-minded enquirer to do? He cannot afford to wait. There is that at stake on the possession or lack of religion which will not brook delay till terms have been defined and curious investigations settled. If the problem be not solved, it will soon and practically solve itself. He needs religion, this simple, unlettered man, as the solace of a life perhaps hard, and grim, and grey: must he wait till 'arguments from design,' 'evidences external and internal,' and the like, have run themselves clear of doubt, before one gleam of heavenly light shall gild the ruggedness of a toil-worn lot, and meanwhile resign himself to the loneliness of a world that is without God? He needs religion as his sole refuge from guilt and sin, from harassing recollections of the past, from the fears and forebodings of a troubled conscience: must he be content to wait the solution of metaphysical questions as to the extent and the terms of a scheme of redemption, before he knows whether there is mercy for him in the bosom of God, or he must go down to eternity with all his sins upon his head? Life is passing, death is coming, the lengthening shadows and the waning sun are warning him that soon his little day of trial shall have run its course; he needs religion to cheer the pathway to the grave, to strip death of its terrors, and shed around life's closing hours the brightness of immortality: must he wait, perplexed by the vain effort to discover which of the many conflicting systems of doctrine is true, till 'the shadow that keeps the key of all the creeds' has silenced and solved his difficulties for ever?

Now, the answer which, with many, I would be disposed to give to all such questions is, No! he need not wait. For, for one thing, experience irresistibly proves that religion may exist in all its reality and purity in minds in which intelligence is yet undeveloped, in minds in which its vigour has become enfeebled, in minds in which it is, all through life, defective and uncultured. Is the spirit of religion not there where the little child breathes forth from stammering lips, at a mother's knee, its first prayer of wonder and awe and reverence to the great Father in Heaven? Yet need we ask, if this be religion, whether it is a religion that is independent of all theological lore? Is the essence of religion not there where the weak, worn sufferer lies stretched on the bed of pain, incapable of the faintest approach to consecutive thought or intellectual effort, bereft of every other power save the power to love and pray, clinging with dying hands to the Christian's cross of hope? Or, have we never witnessed the unmistakable influence of religion in the life of many a humble follower of Christ—the influence of a faith which he could neither define nor defend; yet which made him strong for duty and submissive in trial, which softened care and sweetened joy, shed an atmosphere of dignity around coarse toils and rude, unpolished ways, and lifted him by converse with an infinite ideal above the narrow influences of a contracted sphere of life?

Nor do we merely know from experience that the fact is so, but, further, the reason for it is plain. Of all things good and fair and holy there is a spiritual cognizance which precedes and is independent of that knowledge which the understanding conveys. By the understanding, for instance, a man may master the theory of music, or, by observance of technical rules, learn to reproduce the finest productions of genius with a certain wooden fidelity; but the spirit of music may dwell in the soul which has never heard of its terms, and strains of unpremeditated art may not seldom be heard ringing from lowly lips, which, lacking indeed that refinement that culture gives, may yet prove the presence of a soul in sympathy with sweet sounds—a genuine inspiration of song—a sense and feeling of harmony which no science of periods and intervals could confer. It may tax, again, the most subtle intellect to investigate the theory of beauty, or to apprehend the laws by which we judge of the presence of the beautiful in nature, and the criteria by which we test the value of the productions of art. But it is not by any such intellectual canons of beauty that we detect and delight in her presence. When you gaze on the green earth in the garniture of her summer glory, and meadow and woodland are gay with flowers, and soft lights and flickering shadows play on the surface of river and stream; or when you behold from afar the summit of some old mountain rising grand and silent before you from amidst the surrounding rampart of hills, now perchance glorified by the gorgeous hues of sunset, and anon as the radiance slowly passes away and the grey shadows creep around it, fading into weird indistinctness, till night closes over it, and it is lost to your view;—in the contemplation of these and similar aspects of nature the discernment of her beauty or awfulness that thrills a man's spirit is not an apprehension got by any process of logical proof, it has nothing in common with the acceptance of proposition and doctrines. In proportion, indeed, to the depth and intensity of the impression which the sensitive spirit feels in the presence of nature, thought is suspended, the reasoning, inquisitive side of the mind is for the moment in abeyance; and by an organ deeper than intellectual thought, quickest often in those who are least capable of intellectual accuracy of apprehension, the revelation of material beauty flows in upon the soul.

And, in like manner, it is maintained, there is an apprehension of God and divine things that is independent of that which comes to us in the form of propositions and doctrines, and which may be possessed in fullest measure by the man who could not define or prove a single article of a theological creed. The investigation of the evidences, the analysis and systematic development of the doctrines of religion, may indeed furnish fit occupation for the highest intellects; but it is by no such process that the essence of religion wins its way into the soul. It comes upon the spirit not as a proposition which it has proved, but as a living reality which it immediately and intuitively perceives,—as a heavenly melody falling on the ear, as the splendour of an infinite loveliness breaking on the eye of faith. The believer no more needs to wait for proof of the reality of God and spiritual things than the musical ear for proof of the sweetness of the song to which it listens, or the sensitive eye of the beauty of the scene on which it is gazing. When the soul is lifted up in loving trust and awe and aspiration to the Father of spirits, it no more needs a definition of divine grace than a child needs a definition of the love that is beaming on it from the parent's countenance, and which, by the instantaneous grasp of a sympathetic affection, it feels and knows. When, in contrition and sorrow and self-surrender, the penitent spirit yields itself up to Christ, its faith does not depend on a theological harmonizing of the abstract attributes of justice and mercy—on the piecing and dovetailing together of the parts of an ingenious scheme of salvation. Justice and mercy are there, indeed, but not anatomized into abstractions; they are, rather, undistinguishably blended in the fair concrete reality of the living presence of Christ. In the presence of One whose august holiness awes, while, at the same time, his pity and tenderness melt and win the heart; before whom hypocrisy and guilt cower dismayed, yet at whose feet penitence weeps its unforbidden tears; whose denunciations of sin send quailing to the heart of hardened insincerity and selfishness, yet who dies for a world's iniquities, breathing a prayer for mercy on his murderers,—in that wondrous Presence, type at once of inexorable rectitude and of boundless pitifulness, of perfect purity, and of illimitable love, the soul needs no long-drawn argument to see how mercy and truth can meet together, righteousness and peace kiss each other. Thus have we seen that, not only from the consideration that religion is for all might we presume that its essence cannot lie in that knowledge the capacity for which is confined to a limited class of minds; but, further, that in point of fact, it is not so limited, experience proving that theological knowledge is not the measure of piety; and, finally, that there is a capacity of the soul, by which, apart from accurate doctrinal notions, the truths of religion may be apprehended and appropriated.

There is but one other thought pointing to the same conclusion to which I shall advert. There is springing up in many devout minds the conviction that the principle of Christian fellowship cannot be an intellectual one, that that which makes Christians one must be something deeper and more comprehensive than agreement in a long-drawn system of doctrines. Religion is eminently social. It is essentially the deepest bond of union between man and man. Whatever that be which makes a man a Christian, it should unite him to all Christians, to all good and religious men. No matter what our natural or acquired diversities, no matter what our deep hereditary distinctions, our individual or national genius and temperament, our age, or country, or class, our habits of thought and ways of looking at things, religion is that which should lift us above such distinctions, and bring us into perfect accordance and unity of spirit. At its first preaching Christianity broke upon a divided and distracted world,—torn asunder by wars, broken up by sharp nationalities, in which the spirit of caste, of social and religious exclusiveness had struck deep root, and in which nation was severed from nation, class from class, and man from man, often by an intellectual and moral gulf which it seemed impossible to bridge over. And yet to all these discordant elements Christianity proclaimed itself the all-uniting principle. "Ye are all one in Christ Jesus." In Christ "there is neither Greek nor Jew, circumcision nor uncircumcision, Barbarian, Scythian, bond nor free : but Christ is all, and in all." The descendant of Abraham, the heir of the covenant, the Jew steeped in national and religious exclusivism, a stranger to the softening influences of art and letters; the Greek, with his hereditary love of freedom and art, his worship of sensuous beauty, his delight in poetry and speculation ; the Alexandrian philosopher, imbued with the notions of a strange and fantastic metaphysic, half allegory, half science ; the Roman statesman or soldier, with his national reverence for law and order, his hard practical wisdom, his arrogant disdain, yet contemptuous tolerance of the religions of the subject nations ; the rude barbarian from the banks of the Danube or the Rhine, his temperament savage as the primeval forests in which he roamed, his religious ideas the reflexion of the bloody rites that were practised amidst them:—to each and all of these alike, divided in spirit by barriers more impassable than mountains and seas, remote in thought, feeling, mental character from each other as the inhabitants of different worlds, the preachers of the Cross could proclaim,—' Believe in Jesus Christ, and in the deepest centre of your spiritual being you will become one.' "There is one body and one Spirit, even as ye are called in one hope of your calling."

And still the announcement is the same. Christianity is the all-uniting element,—that which has power to solve all distinctions, to heal all divisions, to bind together in loving fellowship minds the most heterogeneous, to breathe harmony and peace over a distracted world. Open your spirit to its benign influence, and with every other Christian spirit you will see eye to eye, and feel heart to heart.

But if this be so, it is obvious that the bond of a union so comprehensive cannot be an intellectual one. We cannot, of course, make an absolute division between the intelligence and the heart, between thought and feeling, but it cannot be purely intellectual agreement that makes all Christians one; for amongst minds so many and so differently constituted, unanimity would seem to be impossible. Accepting in common the Bible as the inspired record of the Divine mind, the religious conceptions, the doctrinal notions and systems which different minds extract from the Bible, will of necessity vary more or less with the varying character and culture which they bring to the study of it. And so it is always. Step off the ground of positive fact, or of demonstrative science, and there is no subject on which the thoughts of men can be employed— literary, philosophical, political, or other—in which the attempt to secure absolute and universal agreement would not be the wildest chimæra. Truth, indeed, is one; and there might be hope of unanimity if each man could see truth with a mind perfectly developed and free from all external bias or conditions foreign to its own pure light. But men do not so see it. They see it with minds of different temperaments and degrees of intelligence;—some contemplative, some practical, some ratiocinative, some sentimental; some with the temperament of the mystic, others of the logician; some with weak, confused, illogical minds, others with minds of different measures of breadth and culture: and it is impossible that the aspect which truth assumes to each and all of these should be precisely the same. Moreover, the principles according to which men think, the mould into which their opinions are cast, depend greatly on their early and hereditary associations, on the age and country they live in, on the intellectual atmosphere in which they have been accustomed to breathe. They cannot shake off these, or, save in a limited measure, rise above them. The thinkers of the Middle Ages could not see truth with the eyes of an early church Father, nor we of our day with those of a scholastic doctor or philosopher. The passionate East cannot shape its views into the same forms with the more calm, reserved, and self-contained West. Often it is impossible for the practical, common-sense English mind to build a bridge between itself and the scientific German mind, moving in the region of pure ideas, or the mind of the brilliant, superficially-clear, sentimental Frenchman. The national genius is something that is bred in the bone, which grows with our growth, and clings to us in all our thinkings. And if all these causes and conditions so act on men's minds as to produce great variety in their views on other and secular subjects, it is in vain to expect that they should not have, more or less, the same result in their views on religious subjects.

But there is another and different road to unity. The irresistible conviction is winning its way into all candid and tolerant minds that the essential spirit of religion may exist under wide theological divergencies; and that though good men may differ, and differ greatly, in doctrinal forms of belief, there is something deeper which unites them. The essence of religion is something more catholic than its creeds. The theological schools to which they belonged were very far apart, but who can doubt that between the religion of St. Bernard and Thomas à Kempis and Savonarola and Fénelon and Pascal, on the one hand, and the religion of Cranmer and Latimer and Jeremy Taylor and Hooker and Leighton, on the other, there was a deep and essential harmony? In modern times could dogmatic differences be wider than those which separated Newman from Arnold, or the author of *The Christian Year* from Frederick Robertson, or all of these from Chalmers and M'Cheyne; yet, can we hesitate to think that there is a something profounder than ecclesiastical and dogmatic differences, in which as religious, as Christian men, these good men were really at one? And could we get at that something,—call it spiritual life, godliness, holiness, self-abnegation, surrender of the soul to God, or, better still, love and loyalty to Christ as the one only Redeemer and Lord of the spirit,—could we, I say, pierce deeper than the notions of the understanding to that strange, sweet, all-subduing temper and habit of spirit, that climate and atmosphere of heaven in a human breast, would not the essence of religion lie in that, and not in the superficial distinctions which kept these men apart?

I cannot prosecute this subject any further at present. But in conclusion let me dwell for a moment longer on the thought we have reached. Yes! it is here and nowhere else that the essence of religion lies:—not ecclesiastical order, not theological soundness, not even morality and purity of life, but love and loyalty to Christ. Theology is indeed the noblest of sciences. The human intellect has no higher employment than that of searching into its great problems, and trying to give clearness and systematic connexion to our ideas of God and divine things. But perhaps it is those who have studied and laboured most in this high province who are least disposed to exaggerate the religious importance of their work. Conscious of the immense difficulties that attend their enquiries at every step, knowing how hard it is for man's imperfect reason to grapple with them, how many are the causes of misapprehension and error, and how possible it is for the most conscientious enquirers to reach different conclusions,—aware of all this, perhaps it is those who have thought most and deepest on such subjects who shrink most from dogmatism and confident assertion. Perhaps there are those here who will sympathize with me when I say that, as life advances, a more modest, a calmer, sweeter, more tolerant spirit begins to infuse itself into a man's mind. He begins to attach less and less importance to the points which divide sects and churches from each other, to think that few of them are worth a breach of charity,—at any rate, to be convinced that it is not on these that the relation of the soul to God and eternity depends. Seeing in all churches men whose sweet and saintly lives breathe the very spirit of Christ, and of whom it is impossible to doubt that to Christ they are dear; shall he refuse to recognize those whom his Lord has received, or turn away with unchristian hardness and exclusiveness from men whom he may soon have to meet in heaven? No! whenever in the heat of party feeling, amid the weary strifes and rivalries of sects and churches, we are tempted to indulge the spirit of theological or ecclesiastical exclusiveness, or to feel for intellectual error the indignation and hostility that should be reserved for sin, there is one thought that may well bring us to a better mind. Let us recall to mind the good and holy men of different sects and churches who once were with us and are now in the presence of Christ; and ask whether the points which divided them here, and about which, it may be, they contended and wrangled so hotly, can keep them asunder there, in that deeper, diviner life into which they have entered. Let us think, too, if it be ours to join one day their blissful society, whether we shall carry with us much of our ecclesiastical partizanships or our theological jealousies into the still, sweet rest of heaven. Travellers as we are amidst the mists and shadows of this life, it is not wonderful, perhaps, that in its dim and deceptive light, we should sometimes mistake a friend for a foe, or turn away from a brother as if he were a stranger and an alien. But "the night is far spent, the day is at hand"; not distant is the hour when the sun of our souls shall rise full-orbed on our waiting eyes, and the mists shall disappear and the shadows shall flee away for ever; and then—then at last, if not now, we shall recognize in every soul that has ever loved and lived for Christ, the face of a brother and a friend.

THE LIKENESS AND UNLIKENESS OF GOD'S WAYS AND MAN'S WAYS.

> "Let the wicked forsake his way, and the unrighteous man his thoughts: and let him return unto the Lord, and he will have mercy upon him; and to our God, for he will abundantly pardon. For my thoughts are not your thoughts, neither are your ways my ways, saith the Lord." ISAIAH lv. 7, 8.

THE consideration that God's nature is unlike to ours, that his thoughts are not as man's thoughts, his ways not as man's ways, is here adduced as a reason why a sinful being should have all the more hope for mercy at his hands. Yet there is a point of view from which we must hold the very opposite of this proposition to be the truth. Neither morality nor religion would be possible if, deeper than any dissimilarity, there were not a real and essential likeness between God's nature and ours. Morality is not obedience to an arbitrary authority, but sympathy with the principle or spirit of God's law. Religion is the communion of the soul with God, but betwixt beings absolutely unlike there could be no communion. It is just because God's nature is essentially one with ours—his that of the Father of spirits, ours that of spirits made in his own image after his own likeness; it is because what we call thought, intelligence, mind, is in essence the same in God and in us—in him the infinite thought or reason, in us that of beings to whom the inspiration of the Almighty hath given understanding; it is, finally, because when I say "God is love," I can ascribe to him as that which constitutes the deepest essence of his nature that same feeling which binds human hearts together, and, as by a hidden yet all-powerful solvent, melts their separateness into unity;—in one word, it is because in the profoundest sense of the words, God's thoughts *are* as our thoughts, and God's ways as our ways, that we can understand the revelation he has given of his will, and enter into that spiritual fellowship with him in which true religion consists.

And this, too, is the uniform representation of Scripture. The very words of the text which at first sight appear to deny, are based upon the fact that the nature of God and the nature of man are essentially alike. It declares that God's thoughts are not as man's, but the word 'thought' would have no more meaning to me than the words 'red' or 'green' to a man born blind, if it were not that I have the key to it in the principle of thought or intelligence within me, and that when anything is asserted or denied of the thoughts of God, the proposition is intelligible only because it tacitly implies that thought in God is essentially the same with that which I call thought in me. Moreover, with respect to this very matter of divine forgiveness of which the text treats, and which it seems to represent as altogether different from human forgiveness, the Bible is full of representations which imply the very reverse. When it is declared that "As a father pitieth his children, so the Lord pitieth them that fear him"; when it is said, "If ye then, being evil, know how to give good gifts unto your children; how much more shall your heavenly Father give the Holy Spirit to them that ask him"; when we are told to pray, "Forgive us our debts, as we forgive our debtors"; and when our Lord sets forth as the type of that love and tenderness which in our furthest aberrations from goodness, God bears to us, the love which no ingratitude has been able to exhaust, no depth of infamy render hopeless of its object, the mingled sorrow and pity and joy of an earthly father over his prodigal yet penitent child,— what have we in all this if not the assurance that we *may* know God by human analogies, that if we would learn what love and pity and forgiveness are in God's heart, we have only to look into our own; so that, even as regards that very characteristic of the divine nature of which the text treats, there is a sense in which we must not deny, but assert, that God's thoughts are as our thoughts, and God's ways as our ways.

Nevertheless there is an obvious sense in which we can perceive the words of the text to be true. Our nature may be like God's but it is not the measure of God's. Even one human being is often a mystery to another. The words and actions of one who is far in advance of us in wisdom and goodness are often unintelligible to us. It is the penalty of greatness to lose the sympathy of meaner men. A great man is indeed the exponent of the truest spirit of humanity, but for that very reason he is often misunderstood by the men among whom he lives. His motives are purer, his aims nobler, his actions determined by wider principles, his whole career in life regulated by ideas more far-reaching and comprehensive than those of ordinary men. And so, just for this very reason that he is truer to the perfect ideal of humanity than they, it may be said that his thoughts are not as their thoughts, nor his ways as their ways. Much more, obviously, may this be said of Him whose wisdom and goodness are infinite. Man is made in the image of God, but God is not the reflexion of imperfect man. There is much in us and in all our thoughts and ways which we cannot transfer to him, and if we attempt to do so, we only ascribe to the object of worship, as has often been done, our human weakness and errors, sometimes even our follies and crimes. With respect to the particular point brought before us by the text, the pardon of sin, the possibility of divine forgiveness and the ground of it, there is much in God which we must interpret by contrast with, rather than conformity to, that which is oftenest found in man. We may not say that God forgives just as man forgives, that mercy goes forth from him towards the offender in the same measure and for the same reasons as mercy from man to his offending brother. It is possible for man to be cruel where God is kind, and to be weakly lenient where God is stern. There are occasions when the culprit might hope for escape were man only his judge; there are occasions when, shrinking from the merciless censure of human judges, the sinful soul might well cry out, "Let me fall now into the hand of the Lord; for very great are his mercies: but let me not fall into the hand of man." Let us reflect on some of the reasons why, in so far as God's nature differs from man's, he might, in the first place, be supposed to be less likely, and then, in the second place, why in accordance with the doctrine of the text, he is, just because of that difference, infinitely more likely than man, to forgive the offender who craves for mercy at his hands.

In so far as God's thoughts are not as man's thoughts, it might at first sight seem less, and not more, likely that He should forgive the offender. The difference would seem to be a reason why we should have more hope of mercy at the hands of man than at the hands of God.

For one thing, God knows us more thoroughly than

any human being can. The estimate which a human censor forms of us is not based on any immediate knowledge, but is an inference from our outward conduct and bearing. But this estimate may easily be an erroneous one, inasmuch as our actions may only partially betray us, may in many ways be an inadequate or deceptive expression of character. Would any of us like that a human eye should read our thoughts and feelings, draw back the curtain of reserve, of conventional propriety, of decorous looks and regulated speech, and see our undisguised selves for a single day? Would there be nothing to abate the observer's good opinion of us, nothing revealed which neither our words nor deeds nor outward aspect betrays?

I do not speak here of concealed sins or crimes, the facts of which are unknown to the world, and which, if they were known, would brand our name with dishonour and infamy; for in so far as these things are concealed, it is obviously nothing in the nature of human actions themselves, but only the accident of their being unobserved or undetected, that makes a man seem in the eyes of men better than he is, and gains him exemption from shame and censure. But what needs more reflection is that from the very nature of the thing there is much in a man's inward character and spirit that never comes above-board, or only partially and fitfully, and which cannot form an element in the judgment of those who measure us only by overt acts. There is an inner life which no mortal eye sees, a great hidden element of character seething beneath the surface, which only the occasional outflash or unexpected outbreak betrays. There are, for instance, lurking in many a man's nature evil tendencies which lack of opportunity has kept latent. The unregulated appetite, the secret lust, the cowardice, covetousness, or malignity, the frail virtue which, if but the hour of opportunity came, would present but a feeble front to temptation, may be there within the man's breast; but the conditions that would convert inclination into action have been lacking, and like the latent disease that has not become active, or the subterranean firedamp which the flame has never reached, it lies harmless and hidden from observation.

So, again, the repressing influence of public opinion acts often as an artificial check on character, and secures, apart from inward principle, a common level of outward respectability. With a pressure silent, constant, all-pervading as that of the atmosphere enfolding us, blending with our every movement, penetrating our minutest actions, yet of which, because of its very uniformity, we are all but unconscious, public opinion acts on us with a tremendous power, so that the real man,—what we would be without its restraining force,—seldom or never comes out. Partially perhaps the disguise drops in the family circle, before our inferiors or intimates, and in the undress of private life we are seen to be more nearly what we are. But even these know not, and cannot know, the whole. There may be that in the secrecy of our being which we dare not whisper to our nearest friend—thoughts, inclinations, aims, tendencies, which no human eye has seen and no earthly scrutiny suspected. Happy they who can feel that that inmost shrine is kept as an Holy of Holies, sacred to what is pure and good and true. Happy they who feel that no unhallowed flame ever burns on its altars, that no ministering priests save those who wear the white robe of innocence and purity are ever admitted within its still and silent precincts.

Lastly on this point, it is to be noticed, that even that part of human character which expresses itself in overt acts is, in its real moral complexion, often hard to understand. The outward act is simple, but motives are mixed, complicated, intertwined of good and evil, and the most delicate observation and analysis may fail to say to what precise motives or combination of motives, and in what proportion of good or evil, an individual act may be traced. And so the rough-and-ready estimate of society is often a grossly mistaken one. It is possible for cold commendation or censure to be the fate of deeds which are really noble; and, on the other hand, many a man has lived, lauded by all admirers, whose philanthropy or patriotism or piety has had a dark thread of vanity or vulgar selfish ambition running through it. Many a man has seemed through life a model of social respectability, who—could we dissect his consciousness and get at the real anatomy of the man—would turn out to be a very poor and pitiful creature after all.

From these and other causes of concealment or inadequate knowledge, it is obvious that a brother man's perception of the evil that is in us is necessarily imperfect, and on that account it would seem his inspection and judgment of us the less hard to meet. But if there be an inspection which is intercepted by no softening veil, before which all disguise and ambiguity are gone, which sees us through and through; if there be a moral estimate which takes into account all that men are and have been and done—secrets which perhaps have never been told, burdens of guilt that have been borne for years in silent anguish, smouldering tendencies to vice, unhallowed passions straining against the leash of self-respect and social propriety, every rude, bad thought, every impure imagination, every meanness and weakness, every act of cowardly silence or sham disinterestedness—if, I say, there be a moral Judge before the broad, unshaded, piercing light of whose inspection all that we are is thus laid bare; and if betwixt him and a fellow man a sin-stained soul had its choice who should be its judge, by whose decision its fate should be determined, might we not deem it impossible to hesitate for a moment? 'I can bear,' might he not well say, 'man's inspection, but not God's; before the tribunal of a mortal there is room for hope, but what hope or help can there be for a guilty soul at the bar of the Omniscient? Let me fall into the hands of man and not into the hands of God, for his thoughts are not as man's thoughts, nor his ways as man's ways.'

There are other obvious considerations leading to the same conclusion, as, *e.g.* that God not only knows our sins more thoroughly, but judges them by an infinitely higher standard than man; or, again, that as himself erring and guilty, a fellow man might be expected to be a more lenient censor of a brother's guilt than One in whom is no possibility of error or sin; or, once more, that in many cases men judge of others with a predisposition to make light of their aberrations from rectitude, with a judgment blinded by doting affection, or by the beauty, grace, talent, brilliant reputation, social attractiveness of the culprit; whilst the Divine Censor puts all that aside, sees men just as they are, judges all men alike by the standard of absolute righteousness. And, finally, there is the consideration that, if nothing else, time softens the severity of man's censure, so that even foul acts of sensuality or other flagrant sins that may at first have roused the public conscience, may by and by be forgotten or condoned; whereas now and for ever the sins of the past, the impurities, basenesses of years long bygone stand out before the unslumbering eye of the eternal Judge in all their unsoftened reality alike with the sins of yesterday. On these considerations I cannot further insist, but they obviously lead to the same conclusion, namely, that in so far as God's thoughts differ from man's, he might be expected to be less and not more ready to forgive.

And yet, all this notwithstanding, or rather just because of all this, I go on to say, God is more forgiving than man; where the justice which only half knows the magnitude of the offence is often merciless, the justice which sees it in all its heinousness is ready to pardon; even where all hope of clemency from a mortal weak and erring as himself is gone, to Him who knows no sin, who is absolutely inaccessible to temptation, may the forlorn and guilty soul repair with the assurance that its appeal for mercy will never be heard in vain. Let us, for a moment, endeavour to see why it is so; in other words, reversing our point of view, let us attempt to show that it is just because God's thoughts and ways are not as man's, because his righteousness is infinitely exalted above man's, that therefore the unrighteous man may "return unto the Lord" with the assurance that "He will have mercy upon him, and to our God" with the confidence that "He will abundantly pardon."

In the first place, it may be observed that, contrary to what might be supposed and to what the foregoing arguments might lead us to expect, it is not in point of fact, even amongst men, the best and purest who are found to be the severest censors and judges of others. Quickness to detect and expose the weakness and frailties of a fellow man, harshness in condemning them, mercilessness in punishing them, are not the characteristics which experience would lead us to expect in a very high and noble nature. On the contrary, it is only a low type of virtue that is characterized by rigidity and sternness to the fallen; and it is not seldom the men and women whose own moral nature is weak, who are the least forbearing, the least considerate of palliating circumstances, the most inflexible in carrying out the sentence of social infamy and exclusion, when a brother or sister has been betrayed into sin. Whether it be that the secret sense of insecure virtue seeks re-assurance by assuming the attitude of immaculateness and infallibility; or that it flatters our pride to be able to look down from the pedestal of moral superiority on our weaker brethren; or that unconsciously we try to indemnify conscience for our own defects and sins, not by renouncing and forsaking them, but, which is very much easier, by taking the tone of moral indignation and severity to the sins of others,— whatever be the explanation, is it not so, that moral rigidity and sternness is often the sign of a nature that greatly needs indulgence for its own defects? On the other hand, to be gentle, pitying, forbearing to the fallen, to be averse to see or hear of human faults and vices, and when it is impossible not to see them, to be pained and grieved by them, to be considerate of every extenuating circumstance that will mitigate their culpability, to delight in the detection of some redeeming excellence even in the vilest, a soul of goodness in things evil, and to hail with joy the faintest whisper of penitence or sign of moral restoration,—is not all this the sort of conduct which, as experience teaches us, betokens, not moral apathy or indifference, but the nature which is the purest and most elevated beyond all personal sympathy with vice?

And if, thus, human goodness is the more merciful in proportion as it approaches nearer to perfection, if amongst men the highest, heavenliest spirituality is the most tolerant, the last to let go the fallen or to lose its faith in human goodness, and the possibility for the worst of better things,—might we not conclude that when goodness becomes absolutely perfect, just then will mercy reach its climax and become absolutely unlimited?

Again, in proof of the assertion that God's nature, in so far as it differs from man's, makes Him more and not less likely to forgive, consider that in God there is not, and cannot be, any personal irascibility or resentment; He can never regard a sinful soul with any feeling of vindictiveness, any desire to extract from his sufferings reparation for wrong. There are certain defective theological notions according to which the relations of sinful man to God have been represented as turning on the principle of what is called 'vindictive justice,' and the so-called 'scheme of redemption' as based on the necessity of extracting from suffering, reparation for wrong. Now, there may be a true notion which men try thus to express, but the form in which they express it is erroneous and unworthy. In God, and therefore in that moral order of the world which is the expression of his nature, there is no vindictiveness, no personal resentment; and it is the utter absence of this in his nature which makes him infinitely more forgiving than men, even the best of men ever are. For apart altogether from moral indignation or the anger of righteousness, there is in the case of injured or offended human beings another and quite different sentiment, that of the sense of personal affront, anger, wrath, resentment at the act, not as an offence against morality, but as an offence against '*me*.' The two feelings may co-exist, but they may also exist quite independently of each other, and it is possible for the latter—wounded personal feeling and desire of retaliation—to remain unabated, unappeased, even when the former—moral indignation, disapprobation of the sinfulness of the act—has ceased to be felt, or has never been felt at all. Stung by an insult or smarting under a blow, the flush of anger that suffuses the face, the fire that kindles in the flashing eye, is not all, may not be even partially the expression of disapproval of sin; but simply personal resentment, the reaction of physical pain or wounded pride against the being who has hurt us. And the instant and instinctive prompting of this feeling is to retaliate, to smite the smiter, to make the slanderer smart for it, to hurl back his taunt or reproach with insult as bitter, or, if possible, more keen and cutting, to return with interest the pain he has caused or evil he has done to us. All men are conscious more or less of the feeling which seeks satisfaction simply and apart from all other ends, in the pain, suffering, humiliation of another. In some natures, too light and emotional for permanent resentment, or too sweet and gentle to be capable of long bearing a grudge, or which have learned to restrain and quell it by higher principle, it takes no deep hold; but there are others in which it burns with the intensity of a slow fire and becomes the most insatiable of passions. Perhaps, indeed, there is no passion—love, ambition, covetousness, sensuality—that has ever taken so deep a hold of man's nature, as vindictiveness; no delight which human hearts have felt more keen and thrilling than the strange unhallowed sweetness of gratified revenge.

Human law, becoming the deputed and regulated avenger of injuries, now in most cases restrains and curbs it; but we all know how there have been stages of the moral history of mankind when it assumed even the aspect of a virtue and gathered round it an evil consecration, so that the more relentlessly and remorselessly a man pursued a wrong to the bitter end, the more he was honoured by his fellows. In the old days of bloody feud it was deemed cowardly and pusillanimous to submit to an injury or refrain from avenging it, a sacred duty to treasure up a sense of wrong, and never to rest till it could be wiped out in the blood of the wronger. If it could not be immediately avenged, it was sometimes handed down as a legacy from sire to son; all expedients of open hostility or stealthy and silent malice were deemed justifiable in such a cause; and only at last when hate and vindictiveness had had their way, when the avenger had inflicted a terrible retribution for long-past evil on the person or household of his hereditary foe, as he returned from the blackened hearth and desolated hall where he had left the wife of his enemy a widow and her children fatherless, did he feel that the old wrong had had its due.

Such acts, and perhaps even the feelings that prompted them, are no longer possible. Nevertheless, still in a modified shape the sentiment is often at work amongst us. Still personal resentment for injuries is regarded as a proper feeling, still there are insults which we deem it pusillanimous to refrain from resenting. Still there are wrongs which we say no man can be expected to forgive. Still, though they may have repented of their offences, there are men to whom we bear life-long dislikes and grudges, and whom we never can feel it in our hearts to treat as friends.

Now, conceive for a moment what a change would take place in our relations to those who offend or injure us, how far it would go to the removal of everything that hinders forgiveness, if we could eliminate from our feelings every vestige of what is due to personal irritation or resentment. Conceive a man looking on all insults, wrongs, offences with absolute, passionless indifference as regards his own personality, and contemplating them only with the pain and grief due to their moral culpability. Suppose, further, that, with a mind thus no longer agitated by personal feeling, no longer biassed by wounded self-love, he could see in the wrong or injury an evil inflicted on the wronger's own nature far greater than any inflicted on himself, the exhibition of a morally diseased spiritual state so deplorable as to swallow up every other emotion than that of profoundest sorrow and pity for his wretchedness: and so, that instead of retaliating or inflicting fresh evil upon him, or never resting till the offence should be worked out in his misery, there should arise in the injured man's breast an intense longing to cure the diseased spirit, to save him from himself and win him back to goodness—conceive such a state of mind, and though, as we depict it, it seems to imply a magnanimity and self-forgetfulness almost impossible in a being of flesh and blood, yet is it an exact representation of the heart and life of him who was God manifest in the flesh, and therefore of the relation of God to all sinful and guilty men. For what is the life of Christ on earth but the story of a long, silent, immovable patience; of absolute, life-long superiority to personal feeling, of sorely-tried yet unshaken calm and freedom of spirit amidst insults and wrongs. He could feel, he could grieve, he was not incapable of anger; but where in the record of his life shall we find *him* betrayed into one whisper of resentful or vindictive feeling for the ills he suffered at the hands of men? He moved through life exposed to almost ceaseless hostility, subjected to almost every form of injury that human hatred and cruelty could inflict—to scorn, contumely, misrepresentation of motives, treachery, ingratitude, desertion; he was subjected to foul personal indignities, disowned and deserted by the friends he most trusted, and, in his sore need, betrayed by one of them to his enemies. The tenderest, kindest, most loving Spirit that ever breathed, he lived rejected and despised of men, and he died amidst the cries and taunts of an infuriated mob. There were moments when his personal followers, amazed at his forbearance, would have unsheathed the sword in his defence, or called down heaven's artillery on his persecutors. And yet never, from first to last, can we find in his history one slightest sign of personal irritation, one transient flash of exasperated sensibility, or cry for redress of his cruel wrongs. All other feeling in his breast was swallowed up in an infinite pity and sorrow for those at whose hands he suffered. He lived their unwearied benefactor, and he died invoking, amidst the paroxysms of his agony, heaven's mercy on his murderers. And in all this he was to us the manifestation of that Being into whose nature personal irascibility can never enter, who has no personality apart from goodness— the incarnate image of that God who is long-suffering and slow to wrath, abundant in goodness and mercy, and who, exalted in the infinitude of his goodness far above the agitation of man's resentful passions, declares that as the heavens are higher than the earth, so are his thoughts above our thoughts, and his ways above our ways, and that if the wicked will forsake his way and the unrighteous man his thoughts, and return unto the Lord, He will have mercy upon him, and will abundantly pardon him.

But there is a question which here presents itself, to which, in conclusion, I must offer a word or two in reply. Grant that there is no personal irascibility or vindictiveness, no resentment prompting to revenge of personal injuries in God, and that in so far God's thoughts are not as man's thoughts; yet is there not another kind of anger, the anger of justice, moral indignation, the condemnation and hatred of sin which a good and holy nature must feel; is there not such a thing as retributive justice, the demand of outraged law for the punishment of transgressors, and the satisfaction of righteousness in seeing crime get its due? I answer, Yes, there is. Justice demands satisfaction for sin. But there are two kinds of satisfaction which justice or righteousness seeks. So long as a man remains in his sins there is the satisfaction of punishment, and that is the only possible one in his case. But a far deeper satisfaction to justice or righteousness than to punish him as a sinner, would be that he should turn from sin to goodness. Infinite justice or goodness receives a sort of compensation in the fact that a hardened sinner cannot but be miserable; but it receives a far deeper compensation in seeing his hardness softened, his impenitence passing away, and yielding to the tenderness, the sorrow, the love, the purity, the peace of a nature restored to goodness and to God. Let us consider these two kinds of satisfaction.

Apart from all personal feeling there is such a thing as moral indignation, the anger of incensed righteousness against sin and sinners, which the holiest natures must feel the more keenly, and which, in man or God, it is a right thing to feel.

There is nothing more false and immoral than the weak, sentimental tenderness with which crime and criminals are sometimes regarded. It is a spurious benignity which always recoils from severity, shrinks from the sight of pain, and would treat vice and crime as a thing to be wept over with effusive sensibility, and not to be sternly condemned and punished. The hysteric cry for remission of a criminal's sentence that occasionally bursts forth from foolish women and still more foolish men, has in it nothing of the spirit of true Christian charity. On the other hand, the feelings of scorn, disgust, and indignation which are called forth in the individual mind, or which, in flagrant cases, will agitate the spirit of a whole community, at the perpetration of acts of cruel oppression, of brutality, treachery, base and selfish cowardice, and the like, are not things to be checked or stifled, or restrained from seeking their proper satisfaction. When a hypocrite is unmasked, when a cheat or scoundrel comes to grief, when a mean slanderer or seducer of innocence is subjected to ignominious chastisement, when the perpetrator of some dishonourable trick or piece of baseness loses caste, is driven from decent society, or otherwise made to smart for it; or, again, when a selfish despot who has long repressed freedom, corrupted public morals by a life of evil splendour, and grown great on the ruins of other men's happiness, is driven in shame and dishonour from his place of power, the feeling of moral satisfaction, the sense as of a hunger for justice allayed, is an altogether wholesome feeling, and the absence of it would indicate, not a tender and benignant nature, but a nature ignobly callous, or morally diseased and distorted.

And it is impossible not to regard this feeling as having something corresponding to it in the nature of God. In God there is an immitigable abhorrence and hatred of evil, to which, in our keenest moments of aggrieved sensibility, we only faintly approximate. The easy, good-natured divinity who makes everything comfortable is not the God of the Bible. There He has a frowning as well as a smiling face, an aspect, not of feeble benignity, but of terror and wrath and relentless hostility to evil and evil doers. If mercy mean foregoing just indignation and letting off from punishment, then there is no mercy in God. He is the most merciless, relentless, inexorable of all beings. If sin and misery were disconnected, if in all the universe one selfish soul could ever escape wretchedness and live on at peace, it would be a universe over which God had ceased to rule. Wherever a sinful soul exists in all time and space, there, sooner or later, in its loneliness and restlessness and wretchedness, in its guilty anguish, as of a worm that dieth not and a fire that is not quenched, there is the proof that the justice of God demands, and will not abate aught of its terrible satisfaction.

But this is not the only satisfaction of which justice is capable. There is another and higher satisfaction than punishment which it more eagerly seeks. To justice or righteousness it is some satisfaction that a bad man should be miserable; but it is another, a nobler, a sweeter satisfaction that he should become a good man. To make a sinner righteous is an infinitely greater triumph of righteousness than to make a sinner wretched. In itself there is nothing valuable in pain or misery or torture as pain, misery, torture; God has and can have no pleasure in them; but in every holy act there is something that is inherently and essentially precious. Conceive then Eternal Righteousness seated on the throne of judgment, while I, a trembling, conscience-smitten sinner, stand before him, and ask what to him shall be the dearest satisfaction for sins and crimes that have been done against it? What is the satisfaction for the sin of the world which Infinite Goodness seeks, and which, because it is infinite, it will surely attain? The tribute of penal anguish wrung out from wretched souls, or the tribute of new-born love and sorrow and self-surrender, offered up from grateful hearts to the God who has redeemed and saved them? Is there anything in God which, if I now repent and turn with my whole heart to him, bars the way to forgiveness, makes him insist first on the satisfaction to his offended law which misery and suffering bring? Be my past life what it may—wasted, misspent, stained with the indelible traces of selfish and evil deeds—if now I break away from the past, hate it, renounce it, and in sincerest sorrow and penitence turn to offer up my soul, my life, my whole being to God, will he say: 'No, till vengeance for the past have its due, till the demand of my law for penal suffering be satisfied, mercy is impossible, I cannot forgive'? Is not such a thought a foul travesty of the nature of God, a misconception of what He, the All-good, All-loving, must regard as the sacrifice for sin that is best and truest? For what must be that sacrifice or satisfaction that is dearest to Righteousness or to the Infinite Righteous One? The misery of lost souls, the pain, and sorrow, and dismay of their moral desolation, that knows no mitigation, and the smoke of a torment that rises up for ever? Oh no, offer that to Moloch, but not to the God whom Christ has revealed. But the tear of penitence, the prayer of faith, the sighs of a contrite spirit, the love and hope that will not let go its hold on God, the confiding trust that from the depths of despair sends forth the cry, "Father, I have sinned against heaven and before thee"; the yearning after a purer, better life, that finds utterance in the prayer, "Create in me a clean heart, O God; and renew a right spirit within me. Cast me not away from thy presence, and take not thy holy spirit from me,"—

yes, I make answer, that is the sacrifice dearest to Him who despiseth not the sighing of a broken and contrite spirit, who hath said, "Come unto me, all ye that labour and are heavy laden, and I will give you rest," and whose gospel, proclaimed by the lips and sealed by the sacrifice and death of his dear Son, is but a glorious renewal of that ancient promise, "Let the wicked forsake his way, and the unrighteous man his thoughts: and let him return unto the Lord, and He will have mercy upon him; and to our God, for He will abundantly pardon."

EVIL WORKING THROUGH GOOD.

"Sin, that it might appear sin, working death in me by that which is good; that sin by the commandment might become exceeding sinful." ROMANS vii. 13.

THE antithetic form of expression in this passage is obviously intended to emphasize the unnatural and abnormal relation of the cause and effect, the means and end here spoken of. We do not wonder at evil producing evil, or good good. For a given effect we naturally look to a cause of its own kind. But the case to which the Apostle points is that of a wholesome food producing the effects of poison, of pure air and other conditions of health issuing only in disease and death. And the idea he wishes to bring out is, that it is the worst and most appalling characteristic of moral evil, of sin, that it does sometimes manifest its presence by a result of this unnatural and distorted kind. It is sad enough when men become vitiated and degraded by the operation of things that appeal directly to their evil desires and passions, when outward provocations to lust or malice or avarice or treachery or cruelty, achieve the baneful results with which they are fraught, when loose company or bad books or evil example, immoral influences of whatever sort, corrupt a man's principles and ruin his life. But there is, we are here taught, a sadder and more subtle manifestation of the power of evil than this. It is possible for sin to get hold of the very motives and instruments of goodness and to turn them to its own ends. The very light from heaven may be employed to lead men astray. The higher and better impulses of man's nature may be so played upon as to degrade instead of elevating. That which constitutes the very greatness of man's nature may bring about only its greater disorganization and render its fate more disastrous. The revelation of a law of truth and righteousness and goodness, the natural and inherent tendency of which is to awaken the conscience and kindle the spiritual aspirations, to cultivate and perfect the higher life of the soul, may be turned into the means of its deeper moral ruin. The law of God itself, instead of enlightening and quickening, may enter with the result only that the offence may abound. "The law is holy, and the commandment holy, and just, and good"; but "the commandment which was ordained to life" may prove only to be unto death. Sin that it may appear sin, that it may betray to the full extent its disastrous and destructive nature, may work death in us by that which is good.

It is then of the moral law, of that revelation of eternal truth and righteousness which awakens in us the sense of responsibility and calls us to a life of purity and holiness, that the Apostle here specially treats. But the principle involved in this special case is of wider scope. It applies, not only to moral law, but to all kinds of law, and before touching on the particular aspect of the subject here referred to, we may glance at some of the ways in which in other and lower spheres, evil is seen in its most flagrant aspect when it works either on or through what is here designated good, namely, law, order, the systematic sequence and relation of things in God's world. We find illustrations of this malversation in the laws of the material as well as of the spiritual world. A world of which law is the essential characteristic, is, for that very reason, a world in which evil can work all the more terrible havoc.

It is just in a world where law prevails that evil becomes a more potent agent of destructiveness. Sinful desires and intentions can put into operation God's physical laws, and make them the ministers and conductors of evil. They find at their command an immense array of ordered agencies and successions, ready to carry out and propagate with unfailing energy and certainty their unhallowed force. Evil is thus perpetually usurping agencies that were meant for good. The structure and functions of the body, the organic laws by which the satisfactions of the appetites and passions are procured, set themselves at work at the sensualist's will to minister to his depraved inclinations; the violent, revengeful man's criminal intention finds the beautiful interactions of the nervous system at its command, the nervous cord ready to carry down the evil volition, the muscles of the arm ready to contract, the whole physical sequences prepared to operate with prompt and unfailing regularity till the mandate of the evil will is carried into effect. And, in general, it is obvious that in a thousand ways the vast mechanism of physical law is being put into perpetual operation to give realization to evil motives and execution to evil designs. The pulsations of the air are every day we live carrying to and fro evil words, the agency of light reflecting evil looks; and earth and sea and skies, winds and tides, mechanical and chemical forces, organic processes, all nature's vast harmonious and beautiful system of sequences, are working with incessant and unfailing accuracy to enlarge the domain and extend far and wide the power of evil over God's world. Even in this outer sphere, therefore, of human activity, we have an obvious illustration of the principle involved in the words, "Sin, that it might appear sin," that its virulent character may be displayed, "working death in me by that which is good."

It is, however, the perversion of moral law which

forms the special subject of the text. It is this law which the Apostle characterizes as "holy, and just, and good," and yet which he regards as capable of becoming "the strength of sin," the means by which sin works in man's nature a deadlier ruin.

How then, we ask, is this possible? The general answer is that we are capable of a deeper ruin and wretchedness because we are moral beings, than if we had not been endowed with a moral and spiritual nature. And the particular way in which St. Paul presents this idea is that the divine law, not merely the outward moral code, but the law in the mind, wars against the law in the members, or, in other words, that it awakens in the soul a discord which it cannot heal, it stirs up an inward strife which it is powerless to allay. Conscience, the sense of what is good and right in us, may be strong enough to disquiet where it is not strong enough to rule. There are multitudes who cannot silence its rebukes, though they will not submit to its sway. Duty, righteousness, the invisible and eternal realities, the objects that appeal to man's higher nature, present themselves, in many instances, only under the form of a law which secures the assent of the reason and conscience, but has no power to subdue the passions and govern the will.

Now, for a man who is in this state of mind—and there are multitudes who are—the law of God, though in itself good, is an agent of cursing instead of blessing, a minister of death and not of life. It has put an end to the possibility of a life of mere animal instinct and enjoyment, and yet it is insufficient to bear him onward to the profound peace and blessedness of the life of the spirit. You might be happy as an animal if you were conscious of being no more than an animal, if you had in you only natural passions and instincts to which you might give unfettered and unlimited play. You may become happy as a spiritual being if you yield up your whole nature, soul, body, and spirit, in loving surrender to the will of God. But if you only get to the moral attitude which lies between these two, if the will of God be a law which commands your reason, but cannot touch and sway your affections; if, amidst the enthralling influence of animal impulses and earthly desires, your higher nature reveal itself only as the vision of a law which you are constrained to reverence but which you cannot fulfil, of an ideal you can never realize, of a possibility of goodness you have no power to reach, then are you of all beings the most miserable. Better to be a mere animal, with an animal's untroubled satisfactions, better to be a creature without reason and conscience, if reason and conscience cannot control your life; for then would you be no longer, in your selfish and sensual delights, humiliated by the ever-recurring feeling of degradation, harassed by the sense of guilt; then would you be free to revel in the lusts of the flesh without one passing pang of compunction. But as it is, your moral nature, the sense of duty and obligation, deprives you of the satisfaction of sin without bestowing on you the blessedness of the saint, renders you incapable alike of the mindless, thoughtless happiness of the animal life, and of the serener, deeper joy of the spiritual.

But on this special aspect of the subject, familiar as it is to most of us, I do not at present intend to dwell. There is another and subtler way in which the moral law, or the moral element in man's nature to which it appeals, may be so perverted as to work ruin and death, instead of life, to the soul, and that is, *by infusing a new intensity into our vices and sins.* A barren or scanty soil will grow neither good crop nor bad, but if a rich soil is left uncultured, its very fertility and richness may manifest itself by the rampant growth of noxious weeds and thorns. So it is the very richness of man's spiritual nature which, when all its hidden possibilities of moral beauty and excellence are left to run wild, infuses a special rankness and intensity into his vices. In the merely animal nature the appetites and passions are simply natural tendencies seeking their own ends; but in a being made for things infinite and eternal, the passions and appetites do not remain what they are in the animal; they draw into themselves a kind of false boundlessness stolen from his higher nature. Sensuality and selfishness, the love of the world and the things of the world, is in man, so to speak, the love of God and of goodness run wild. Evil inclinations and desires would never be so intense, would never have in them the ruinous passionate ardour and force which characterizes them, if it were not that we are ever trying to create a fictitious heaven out of them. A spiritual nature capable of finding satisfaction and happiness in what is infinite and eternal could never be happy in the pleasures of a brute, in the transient pleasures of appetite and sense, if it were not that we insensibly make these things assume an illusory reality and boundlessness, a deceptive show of that infinite joy and blessedness for which as spiritual beings we were made. The keenest joys of appetite and sense, the intensest earthly pleasures, can never be commensurate with a nature made in God's image and capable of sharing in a divine and eternal life; but finite and transient though they be, they owe their persistent attraction to this, that our imagination tricks them out with a false capacity of delight, which often no experience of failure serves to dissipate.

I may illustrate this by what sometimes occurs in our social relations. We sometimes see a man of a refined and elevated nature wreck his own peace and happiness by union with one who is immeasurably inferior, and we explain the mistaken union by saying that it was not the weak, silly, frivolous creature whom the man really loved, but a being of his own imagination, invested with ideal charms, into whom he had unconsciously transformed her. And, in this case, it may be said to be that very elevation of the man's nature which is the secret of the wreck of his happiness and the ruin of his life. In like manner may we pronounce of all men who seek their happiness in the world and the things of the world, that they are fools of their own fancy. It is the very infinitude of their nature that makes it possible for them to paint the idols of time and sense with an imaginary glory, and to waste on them a spurious and disproportionate devotion. Our lowest vices catch a false glow and fascination from the virtues they mimic;—sin thus working death in us by that which is good.

The foregoing train of thought finds, I think, some confirmation in one peculiar feature of the teaching of the writer from whom the text is taken. You may have observed that in treating of particular vices and sins, it is a characteristic method of St. Paul to place, side by side, the sin of which he speaks and a virtue or grace of which it may be said to be the counterfeit or caricature. To take but two examples of what I mean: we find him rebuking the sin of intemperance, not by a simple denunciation of it, but by contrasting the false or spurious elation of the drunkard with another and legitimate means of spiritual exaltation—

"Be not drunk," says he, "with wine, wherein is excess; but be filled with the Spirit." In other words, 'Be not intoxicated with the false elation of wine, but seek the true exaltation which comes from being filled with the Spirit of God.' Again, we find the same peculiar vein of ethical exhortation in his treatment of the sin of covetousness—"Nor trust," are his words, "in uncertain riches, but in the living God"; and again and again he recurs to the same contrast between these two passions or affections, the one the spurious, the other the genuine: devotion to money and devotion to God—"Nor covetous man, *who is an idolater*, hath any inheritance in the kingdom of Christ and of God"; "Mortify therefore your members which are upon the earth—inordinate affection, evil concupiscence, and *covetousness, which is idolatry*." And the idea which runs through these passages seems to be, that the covetous man is unconsciously trying to find in money the happiness that can only be found in God; that the passion of covetousness stands to the principle of piety or devotion to God as the counterfeit to the genuine, the fictitious to the true; and the object of the one to that of the other, as the imposing and unsubstantial imitation to the reality in which we can repose our trust. The passionate self-surrender with which so many give themselves to the pursuit of riches, he seems to teach us, is the morbid action of a nature formed for devotion to an infinite object, of which money is, to its unconscious votary, the base and miserable, but, in many respects, deceptive imitation.

Let me, in conclusion, illustrate the point of view of the text by a few words on each of these specimens of misdirected devotion.

There is a sense in which even so common a vice as drunkenness may be said to work death in us in virtue of its semblance to that which is good. It is not always the vulgar vice of coarse and sensual natures, for whom the mere brutal gratification of appetite is the sole attraction. "It is," says a well-known writer who has admirably traced the working of this passion, "it is almost as often the finer as the baser spirits of our race who are found the victims of such indulgences. Many will remember the names of the gifted of their species, the degraded men of genius who have been the victims of these deceptive influences. The half-inspired painter, poet, musician, mistook the sensation produced by stimulating the exhausted brain for something half divine, . . the intensity of feeling produced by stimulating the senses for that which is produced by vivifying the spiritual life within." In other words, intellectual results which are, when legitimate, the expression of mental ability and attainment, may be simulated by the stimulation of the senses. Quickness and brilliancy of thought, fluency of expression, ideas, fancies, images flowing as if with the unsought fervour of inspiration from the poet's pen or the orator's lip, an imagination set free from the stagnation and dulness of common life, a strange and unwonted fertility of resource, a power of sustained intellectual effort in which the mind seems for the moment emancipated from physical impediment and exhaustion,—these and such as these are intellectual experiences, due legitimately to mental culture and discipline, of which at least a temporary possession may be achieved by the influence of wine. And in this case we see that the possibility and fascination of the vice arises from the very fact of the largeness of the nature that yields to it.

But it is not merely intellectual results which can be got at by this unwholesome means. There are inward experiences which lie closer to man's spiritual life, feelings which are possible to him only in virtue of his relation to God and the world of infinite and eternal realities, which this vulgar vice may simulate. Courage, generosity, enthusiasm, patriotic ardour, readiness to do and dare all for others—it is because our nature is capable of these things that even their transient semblance can, by unhallowed means, be artificially produced. The capacity of religion, again, is the capacity to rise above ourselves and the world, to forget and cast behind us the soils and stains of guilt, to feel no longer the drag and bondage of earthly cares and troubles, to soar into a region where the interests and agitations of time are dwarfed into their inherent littleness, and, in the fulness and ecstasy of spiritual emotion, we can claim our birthright of communion with the things unseen and eternal. And even of this highest experience of religion, the vice I speak of can give us a spurious copy. It can make us forget the past, it can free us for the moment from the anguish of bitter memories, from the sense of disgrace, the pangs of remorse, the dread forebodings of the future. It can for the time lift the wretched into a rapturous elevation above care and sorrow, and transport the foul and sin-stained soul into a sham heaven of sensuous enjoyment. In all this there is indeed but a poor and shallow imitation of spiritual blessings; but it is because man has a self to forget, to lose in God, that the illusive self-forgetfulness, the counterfeit rapture, of the vice of which we speak is possible.

"Nor trust in uncertain riches, but in the living God"—it is thus that St. Paul indicates one other example of that counterfeiting of good by evil of which we speak. In this case, too, he seems to teach, vice owes its attraction to the very greatness of the nature on which it acts. The secret of the mastery which the passion of covetousness gains over so many minds, of the eager enthusiasm with which men fling themselves into the pursuit of wealth, he finds in this, that the love of money is, so to speak, a misdirected worship. The perverted imagination pictures to itself in this object a happiness practically boundless, and so secures for it an absorbing devotion, which is due only to the infinite object of reverence. The covetous man is an idolater, wasting on Mammon the capacities of trust, of homage, of absolute self-surrender, which are intended for the Living God.

Nor is it difficult to trace, here too, some of the causes of that unconscious illusion by which an object so incommensurate with man's higher nature draws it away from the infinite object for which it was made. One thing at least in man's nature which shows it was made for God is the sense of weakness and the capacity of absolute trust. One element, at any rate, of religious feeling is that which takes its rise from our experience of the fleeting, evanescent character of our own life and of all that surrounds us. "The world passeth away, and the lust thereof"; "What is your life? It is even a vapour, that appeareth for a little time, and then vanisheth away"—such words as these express a feeling, old as the history of our race, which is awakened by the fleeting, shifting character of the scene on which we look, the transiency of life, the uncertainty of its pleasures, the lack of any fixed stay, of anything real and enduring on which our hearts can rest; and this it is which impels us to seek after some reality beyond the world of shadows, some enduring and eternal rock on which, amidst the stream that bears us away, we may plant our feet.

I want, in my conscious helplessness, some presence ever near to me to which I can repair, some being or power that will give me calmness, reliance, rest, on whom with absolute security I can depend, and in whose all-embracing arms I can find, whatever betide me, a home and shelter from the storms of life.

But it is just this deep and universal craving, this capacity of boundless trust, which can find its true object only in Him who is the rock and refuge of his people in all generations, that makes it possible for me to waste on meaner objects a disproportionate devotion. If we cannot serve God and Mammon, yet Mammon furnishes to many who turn from the infinite Reality, a strange semblance of His power to protect and save. It offers itself to the imagination clothed with a kind of mimic omnipotence, as that which in all possible changes gives us a solid sense of security. Like a secret Providence, it places its votary in fancy above the fear of coming ills, and enables him to look calmly onward and say: 'I need fear no evil; this fortune I have amassed is a security in all the coming years against a thousand ills, and it gives me the certain command of a thousand sources of enjoyment. Whilst others are worn with toil and harassed by anxieties and perplexed by cares and fears, here is that which breathes peace and repose into my spirit and banishes all anxious thought from my breast.' What wonder that that which can accomplish all this, comes to be regarded with an unfounded yet absolute dependence, that it gathers round it the feelings of abject respect and homage, and that those who turn away from the soul's true object should squander on this sham divinity the treasure of a boundless trust that is due to God alone!

And so, may we not say that this vice which often exerts a more corroding and desolating influence than any other on the human spirit, all the while that it is weakening and eating out the finer and gentler affections and the nobler impulses, and spreading itself like a foul weed over the springs of human action, is yet by its false appeal to man's diviner nature, working death in us by that which is good?

We see then, let me say in conclusion, what is the point of view according to the text, in which the disastrous and deadly nature of sin is most strikingly manifested. Sin, that it might appear sin—that it might be displayed in its blackest colours—worketh death in us by that which is good. It is not by any description of the outward penalties attached to sin here or hereafter, it is not by any physical terrors appealing to a sensuous imagination, that the sacred writer seeks to convey to us a conception of the deadly nature of sin. To see it in its direst aspect, we are called simply to think of the greatness it frustrates, the splendid destiny it baulks, the glorious opportunities which it causes us to fling away. St. Paul bids us think only of wasted powers and misdirected capacities, of the ruin and wretchedness of which a soul made for God is capable when it squanders itself on things that are base and evil. In a life of sensuality and worldliness, viewed in itself, there is, he seems to teach us, nothing very deplorable. To find your happiness in meat and drink, in the pleasures of the senses, in worldly ease and comfort, would be a very harmless thing if you were made for nothing better. If your nature were of no larger range than that of the senses, your satisfaction in these things would be a spectacle as little repulsive as the contentment of browsing cattle, or the satiated hunger and lust of a beast of prey. But what in you such a life does mean is very different from this. The pity and sadness and shame of it lie in the degradation and impoverishment which it implies. It is the thought of the wealth that is thus thrown away, of the treasure infinitely more precious than any material riches, the capacities of love and aspiration and reverence that could soar so high, the possibilities of great and glorious aims and of a career of blessedness through untold ages in communion with God—all squandered, all forfeited, all sunk in the slough of a mere earthly and animal existence—it is this thought of the grandeur of the destiny God designed for us and the meanness of that which we have chosen for ourselves, which, in St. Paul's eyes, lends its most appalling aspect to a selfish and worldly life. As when we visit the scenes over which war and destructive violence have swept, and stand in contemplation of the ruins of some fair palace or stately temple, the scathed and shattered columns, the broken arches, the fragments of exquisite tracery buried in dust and foulness, the indications of the vast extent and architectural splendour that once pertained to the edifice, the impression produced on the mind is that which arises from the sense of the original grandeur and beauty which we contrast with the dishonour and desolation to which they are now reduced. So it is then, when we discern in the spirit of man the indications of an infinite origin and an infinite destiny, of a nature made for the inhabitation and communion of the Living God,—it is then that we have the direst measure of sin's destructive power, when it thus worketh death in us by that which is good.

THE NEW BIRTH.

"Marvel not that I said unto thee, Ye must be born again" (or, "from above"). JOHN iii. 7.

IT must be confessed that to many readers of Scripture in the present day the teaching of the New Testament with respect to what in theological language is termed the doctrine of 'regeneration,' sounds as strange and foreign to their own experience as did our Lord's words in the ears of Nicodemus. We are all indeed, as life wears on, conscious of many changes of thought and feeling, of opinions, tastes and principles of judgment; but, for the most part, these changes come upon us so slowly and gradually that it is only by an effort of reflection that, looking back on our former selves, we become aware of the transitions we have undergone. Seldom or never do we experience any such swift and sudden mental revolutions, any such radical transformations of character as could be represented as nothing less than a re-creation of our being, a second birth of the soul. For our Lord's incredulous auditor, indeed, the strangeness of this doctrine was partly due to misapprehension—to his understanding in a gross and physical sense what was true only in a figure. Yet the figure of a second birth would be meaningless if it did not imply a revolution in man's spiritual nature as great as if the interpretation put upon it by Nicodemus were literally true. Marvellous as would be an actual re-entrance on life with our whole past history obliterated from our consciousness; marvellous as it would be for one surrounded by the cares and responsibilities of manhood, or sinking into the feebleness of old age, to feel the shadow on the sundial of life going back and the light of life's morning once more shining on his path, yet, if the figure have any meaning, this is a marvel which must somehow reflect itself in man's spiritual life.

Could we entertain for a moment the strange fancy that some one here who is now far advanced in life should become conscious, as if by some mysterious spell passing over him, of a new freshness beginning to be infused into the springs of his physical life, so that the features on which time had graven its seemingly indelible impress were being moulded anew into the roundness and softness of childhood, and that the worn and exhausted frame was becoming animated once more by 'the buoyancy and elasticity of days long bygone,'—extravagant as such a conception may be, it would lose all its figurative significance if it did not point to a moral and spiritual regeneration, a transmutation in the inner life as radical in some point of view as a literal and physical rejuvenescence. But when we turn to our own experience, and reflect how utterly unconscious we are in ourselves or in our observation of others of any such sudden metamorphosis of mind, does it not seem an extraordinary assertion that such changes are not merely miraculous exceptions, but the uniform condition of the religious life; and in listening to such a doctrine are we not tempted to sympathize, in some measure, with the wonder and incredulity of our Lord's auditor?

But, besides the difficulty of finding in our experience anything corresponding to such a sudden and revolutionary change, there is for many minds the further difficulty in the arbitrary and inexplicable character that seems to be ascribed to it. It seems to remove religion and the religious life from the domain of intelligible order and sequence into that of arbitrariness and unaccountable mystery, and even to attribute to the dealing of God with the human spirit a kind of caprice and fitfulness foreign to infinite wisdom and goodness. Ignorance and superstition revel in the region of magic and mystery, and find nothing to revolt them in the ascription to their divinities of the waywardness and capriciousness of arbitrary power. But, with the advancing spiritual life of the world, men are led more and more to seek their proofs of God and of divine action, not in sudden and unaccountable marvels or capricious displays of supernatural power, but in the manifestations of wisdom and beneficence in intelligible relations and sequences; and both the intelligence and the moral sense recoil from ascribing to the object of supreme reverence in its dealings with human souls the uncertainty and capricious action, not to say the arbitrary favouritism, of an irresponsible potentate.

Yet does not some such element of arbitrariness, it may be asked, seem to form an essential feature of the doctrine before us? Could there be for the common mind any more vivid image of inscrutable and unaccountable force than that by which in the narrative before us the agency in regeneration is depicted? What, to the ordinary eye at least, is so fitful, wayward, incalculable as the action of the restless wind? Who can for a single day or hour foresee or with certainty pronounce what its course shall be? As we think of it, sometimes breathing in softness, sometimes rushing in storm; now gently fanning the summer fields, or wandering over woodland and meadow and glade with a force that scarce suffices to sway the tiniest floweret on its stalk, or to ripple the surface of the running brook; anon sweeping with wild impetuosity over land

and sea, bowing the trees of the forest or lashing the ocean into fury; sinking into a quiescence which leaves one spot or region of the earth parched, cloudless, rainless, till the soil cracks and the plants wither; yet bringing to other lands the fertilizing influence of refreshing gales and showers,—what natural phenomena are, to the common eye, so indicative of the very spirit of arbitrariness as those of the wind that "bloweth where it listeth"? And when we are told that here we have the fittest type of that renewing agency without which there is no salvation, no possibility of spiritual life for man, are we not disposed with our Lord's auditor to marvel, or at least to think very natural the hesitancy which was expressed in the exclamation, "How can these things be?"

And then, lastly, comes the fundamental question which ever arises when we think of the relation of the infinite will and power to the will and actions of men, Can the doctrine of regeneration be reconciled with human responsibility and freedom? In trying to save our own souls and the souls of others, are we not arrested at the very outset by the assertion that spiritual renewal or reformation is absolutely dependent on an inscrutable and omnipotent agency, without whose quickening touch not the feeblest pulsation of spiritual life, of penitence or faith or love, can begin to stir in the human breast, and yet which is as absolutely beyond our control as the mighty forces of nature, as the heaving of the ocean or the flashing of the lightning, or the coming and going of the wind that "bloweth where it listeth"? If every aspiration and effort after goodness, every volition and action of the religious life, be due to an unseen but infinite presence and power acting on us and in us, so that it is God that worketh in us to will and do of his good pleasure, is not our consciousness of individual activity only a dream and an illusion? If Paul may plant and Apollos water, but God alone giveth the increase, if *with* this agency the feeblest efforts to do good are armed with the force of omnipotence, and *without* it the strength of reason, the force of argument, the eloquence of an apostle or an angel from heaven would be as ineffectual as the stammering lips of folly and ignorance to move and convert men's hearts to goodness, does it not follow that, in the spiritual life, human effort counts for as little in shaping its own destiny as that of the clay in the hands of the potter to determine whether it shall be fashioned into the fair beauty and symmetry of the shapely vase, or flung away a marred and useless thing to dishonour and ruin? Prayer for divine help indeed is possible, but prayer itself to be effectual presupposes, must be preceded and prompted by, the spiritual power it seeks; and prayer is therefore a moral solecism, a thing as powerless to determine the result, as the longing of the husbandman for favourable showers or of the becalmed sailor for a fair wind.

It would seem, therefore, that religion introduces us into an order of things utterly foreign to that of our knowledge and experience. In the world in which our ordinary life lies we seem to see how one thing leads to another; we speak of the uniformity of nature, of the invariable relations of causes and effects, of the action of good or bad motives, of the influence of education and the gradual formation of habits. But here, in the sphere of religion, all these principles of thought and action seem to be upset, intelligible causes and motives become of no account, and what we are accustomed to trace to these is ascribed to an unknown, inscrutable, and wholly incalculable agency. May it not be said then, that with the very advance of our knowledge of nature and man, with the deepening sense of law and order, and the recoil from what is anomalous or arbitrary in the system of the universe, the acceptance of any such doctrine as that of the text becomes still more difficult for the modern mind than for the age in which it was propounded; so that in this point of view, still more natural and irrepressible in our case than in that of our Lord's incredulous auditor is the feeling which found expression in the exclamation, "How can these things be?"

Such, then, are some of the obstacles to an acceptance of the Scripture doctrine of the work of the Spirit which beset many thoughtful minds. Believing, as I do, that that doctrine is not a mere speculative dogma, but one which lies at the very root of the religious life, and the reception of which is of infinite importance for every human soul, I shall endeavour in this, and possibly in some future discourses, to show that, rightly conceived, it is not open to such objections as those which I have adduced. To-day, I shall take up that which I have stated last, as not only in itself the most formidable, but as that the removal of which will enable us more easily to deal with those which remain.

"Except a man be born from above, he cannot enter into the kingdom of God." All spiritual life is of God; all spiritual knowledge and activity are due to the operation of an infinite, omnipotent agent on the human spirit, and without that operation it must remain sunk in moral inertness and impotency. How shall we reconcile such a doctrine with human responsibility, freedom, individuality, with the call to repentance and moral effort, with the ineradicable conviction that we are the authors of our own actions, responsible for the making or marring of our own character and destiny? Does not the assertion that every faintest effort after goodness is to be traced to a power and presence above us, tamper with or suppress that which we are wont to regard as the essential prerogative of our nature, moral freedom and independence? Is not the gift of spiritual individuality that which makes man capable of a kind of excellence, a perfection wrought out by free self-development, that vanishes when his actions are determined by any external force or power. In the face of all human power or authority, it is possible for a man to say, You may constrain my outward actions, fetter or imprison my body, but there is that within me which sets your power at defiance, you cannot make yourself master of my thoughts or force my will. Suppress this right of each soul to be itself and rule itself, and would you not deprive it of its very birthright? Nay, may we not say with reverence, that this is a prerogative which not even Omnipotence can invade? It is because I can offer to God a free obedience and love that He is glorified in my service and devotion. And if we could conceive even a Divine Being encroaching on this inner sanctuary of moral independence, breaking down the barrier which divides my thought and will from his, would not this be to destroy that very element which makes my homage of more value than the movements of unconscious nature or the instinctive actions of the brutes that perish?

I do not think that in the doctrine before us there is implied any such repression of our individuality and freedom, any interference with that law which makes strenuous endeavour and individual effort the condition of all high and noble attainment. On the contrary, I believe that the recognition of the absolute dominion and control of the human spirit by the divine is not paralysis but the intensest stimulus to spiritual activity. I believe that if we could reach a spiritual state in which the divine mastery of the mind, heart, will of man were so absolute that we should no longer think our own thoughts or desire our own ends or do our own will, but have our whole spiritual being suffused, permeated, inseparably blended with the spirit and life of the Eternal,—that then, instead of the levelling down of our spiritual life to nature, there would be reached the highest conceivable pitch of spiritual elevation, that liberation, expansion, perfection which is involved in being sharers of the infinite life of Him in whose image we were made. Let me endeavour briefly to show you that it is so.

How can one mind, one spiritual being act on, command, control another? In the relation of mind to mind, is outward force a possible thing? Can we conceive of a spiritual force or power operating on our minds and hearts before which we are as passive as the wind-swept waves to the force of the storm, or the senseless clay to the hand that shapes it? When we ask such a question, I think we shall see that we are employing words without meaning. To propel a mind by external force is a thing as unintelligible and impossible as to move a stone by argument or melt a metal by affection or love. It would not be to exalt the power of God, but simply to talk absurdly and incoherently, if we spoke of Omnipotence as persuading the planets to revolve, as by overwhelming reasons causing the earth to turn on its axis, or the magnet to point true to the north; or again, as lulling by soft appeals the stormy winds and waves to rest, or tempting by motives of love and gratitude the summer fields to yield up their wealth of fertility and beauty. Nor, in like manner, would it be any exaltation of the power of God, or aught but a thing simply unthinkable and inherently absurd, to conceive of him as, by any mysterious application of power propelling a soul into goodness, injecting rational convictions into a thinking mind, pouring in pure and holy thoughts and dispositions into a moral and spiritual intelligence.

Yet there is a power, none more potent, subtle, commanding, by which the Infinite Mind can and does act on the finite, and yet the exerting of which is in fullest harmony with our own spiritual freedom and activity, and is, indeed, the very means whereby that freedom is manifested and realized. If there is one thing more than another to which our deepest experience as spiritual beings witnesses, it is that we are not our own masters. It is so, for instance, in our intellectual life. Not merely what we call religious knowledge but, in one sense, all knowledge witnesses to a presence and power which exerts over our minds an absolute and unbounded dominion.

What is the mental attitude of the scientific or philosophic thinker when ideas, conceptions, logical and systematic relations of thought flow in upon his mind? Is he simply master of his own mind, creator, originator, determiner of the whole process that is passing within him? When, for example, you are engaged in the study of the truths with which the mathematician deals, can you will what the action of your mind shall be? In every step of the process is not your mind moving at the beck of a power which is not your own, which discloses to your thought laws, relations, sequences, which you can neither make nor unmake nor in the faintest measure modify, an infinite and absolute reason which quells and suppresses all individual fancies, notions, opinions? Is it not as if the thoughts you think, as you advance in knowledge, were descending upon your mind from a boundless, inexhaustible realm of reality, and that only as you open your mind to receive them, dismiss all self-assertion, become the pure, passionless organ, so to speak, of an intelligence that infinitely transcends your own,—only, in one word, as you are intellectually born from above, can you enter into the kingdom of truth?

So again, what is the attitude of the mind in what, with an instinctive recognition of the principle on which I am insisting, men have agreed to call the 'inspiration of genius'? When the imagination glows with the ecstasy of creative intuition, when the splendour of the vision of beauty descends upon the soul of the poet or artist, quelling all personal thoughts and aims, kindling a divine fire within it till it breaks out in the music of rhythmical speech or in the language of colour and form, is this a thing born from the shallow material of his own individual feeling or fancy, or will not the highest and noblest of the sons of genius be ready to acknowledge that in their best and loftiest moments they seemed to themselves to be but catching glimpses of a realm of infinite beauty, of an ideal yet most real world, that stretched far, illimitably beyond them? What indeed is the dissatisfaction which the greatest of them feel with all that in their rarest utterances or most successful works they have accomplished? What but the tacit acknowledgment that they are but the inadequate interpreters and organs of a larger, diviner life, into a transient contact and communion with which, in moments few and far between, they have been permitted to rise?

So, finally, look to the moral life of man, the life whose experiences we express by the words righteousness, goodness, purity, and is there not here a still more emphatic witness to the principle before us? When the imperative of duty utters itself in a human spirit, can you explain or account for it simply as the self-originated movement of your own mind, or in obeying it are you merely following the current of your own thoughts, giving expression to your own private and personal feelings and volitions? **Try it by your own** experience. Is there any one here who, in the midst of a life of self-indulgence, or perhaps sinking into the slough of sensuality, has been awakened to a sense of moral degradation and wretchedness, has heard sounding on the inner ear an accusing, condemning voice, speaking with an authority he dared not question of his guilt and vileness, calling him to shake off this ignoble bondage, and at all costs, as for his very life, to struggle to escape from it,—if any one here has passed through such an experience, I ask him, in that hour of moral awakenment, was that his own or any mortal voice to which he listened? No, the instinctive conviction of the soul, as it trembles like a guilty thing surprised before the tribunal of moral judgment, is, that the power that thus arrests him is one that comes before him clothed with the majesty of eternal truth and righteousness, and speaking with an authority which no earthly power can claim. As I listen to it, I am irresistibly impelled to think of it as an authority before whose revelations the things of time shrink away, which lies beyond all finite limitations, remaining unchanged amidst all my fitful frames and feelings, which will follow me through all the changes of my earthly life, yea, wherever my destiny may lie in regions and worlds unknown, and which, not only over me but over all finite spirits in

God's universe, must for ever assert its absolute supremacy.

Here then, apart even from what we technically term the religious life, in all spheres of human attainment, we can discern the evidence of a presence and power above us, infinitely greater than our own, acting on us, and controlling all our thought and life. And now I ask, Is this a power whose influence when it is most absolute arrests or is incompatible with our own activity and freedom? And the answer, paradoxical as in form it is, I unhesitatingly pronounce will be, No! Subjection to this unseen power is not the paralysis of thought and effort, the slavery of the human spirit, but its emancipation, its freedom, the secret of its highest power and perfection. When the presence that speaks to him in the eternal laws and relations of thought constrains irresistibly the mind of the mathematician or philosopher or man of science, is his own intelligence suppressed, his mind degraded by this intellectual submission? Is his surrender to it the extinction of any intellectual life of his own? Nay, in this surrender, in the abnegation of all notions and opinions save those which the eternal voice announces, in becoming its pure and passive organ, is he not laying hold of his own intellectual birthright? Does he not find in yielding to it an escape from his own individual narrowness and poverty, entrance into a larger inexhaustible life, the liberation, quickening, ever advancing expansion and elevation of his spirit?

Is, again, the imagination of the poet or artist prostrated and paralyzed when it is enthralled and captivated by the vision of ideal beauty descending upon his spirit? Nay, rather, does he not feel that it is when he is left to his own poor devices, when no flash of a genuine inspiration vivifies his soul, that he is at his weakest, that all he can produce is stale, flat, and unprofitable; and that only then when he seems to himself as if possessed for the moment by a spirit and power above him, swept along by the visitation of a loftier impulse,—that it is then and only then that his work becomes ennobled, that his thoughts flow, his lips move, his touch grows vivid with the free play and subtle activity of imaginative power?

And now, waiving for the moment the illustration of that higher freedom which is gained through submission to the absolute imperative of duty, let us turn to what we specially term the religious or spiritual life, and ask whether the same principle does not hold good there also, whether we do not find there also absolute control, yet perfect freedom. "Except a man be born from above, he cannot see the kingdom of God." Religion is from beginning to end the work of the Spirit of God. As surely as the tiniest plant peeping above the vernal earth witnesses to the action of a mighty germinating force in nature, as surely as the tremulous motion of the needle witnesses to the operation of that resistless magnetic force that pervades and sways the universe, so surely do the faintest signs of spiritual life, the first sigh of godly sorrow that heaves the breast, the first accents of contrition that tremble on the lips of the penitent, the faintest movement of faith and love in the heart, bear witness to the presence and operation of an omnipotent life-giving power, of that invisible electric force that draws by a divine attraction the finite spirit to the infinite.

Yet, though viewed from the one side religion is all of God—the expression of the absolute control and constraint of the human spirit by the divine—viewed from the other it is a control which emancipates while it binds, a constraint which elevates while it humbles the soul that yields to it. And if we ask what is the explanation of this paradox—God's absolute control man's highest freedom—I will ask this other question, How from their very nature can spirit rule spirit, one mind master and dominate another? Think of what you mean by the power of mind over mind. How is it that even in our earthly experience one greater, loftier mind can sway and influence other and lesser minds? When we recall the names of the few master minds whose works have survived the lapse of ages, and have exerted an almost unbounded influence over the thoughts and hearts of men of all climes and classes, all individual and national diversities, and who still in our day, as we say, 'rule us from their urns,' what is the secret of their nameless, measureless power? What but this, that these men, while they rule us, make us free; that there are in us hidden springs of thought which they unseal, dumb inarticulate instincts for which in their words we find a voice; slumbering aspirations, longings, gropings after light, which at their magic touch leap to life. If age cannot wither nor custom stale the undying products of their genius, it is because they appeal to what is highest and best in man—not to his lower desires or ephemeral interests, but to that eternal yearning after what is true and fair and good which lies latent in every human breast—to

"those first affections,
Those shadowy recollections,
Which, be they what they may,
Are yet the fountain-light of all our day,
Are yet the master-light of all our seeing."

And in like manner, if we may compare things earthly to things heavenly, the power of the Infinite Spirit of truth over the human spirit is a power which is due to this, that it appeals to, elicits, quickens into new life and activity the hidden springs of thought, the dormant spiritual intelligence within us, and that at its illuminating touch the light within—obscured it may be and darkened, but inextinguishable—flashes back in response to the eternal light without. What, for instance, is meant by religious awakenment? What is the experience of the soul in repentance and conviction? Could the revelation of the righteous judgment of God against evil touch the human spirit, if there were nothing in that spirit which responded to it? Is repentance nothing more and deeper than selfish craven fear of the heart that quails at the authoritative announcement of future punishment, the cowering of the terror-smitten soul before the awful threatenings of an arbitrary judge? No, it means that the soul within is roused to respond to the revelation of eternal righteousness from without, that there has begun to dawn upon it, within it, the vision of an infinite purity and holiness, in the light of which it sees its own misery and degradation and feels in the moral taint that clings to it a worse penalty than any material torture.

What, again, is the meaning of the sense of forgiveness and of the peace and joy which the Spirit of God breathes into the renewed, converted soul? Is the revelation of God's redeeming love and mercy in Christ a mere arbitrary announcement received on some infallible external authority? Does the doctrine of the Fatherhood of God in Christ—of a love to us as His children which no ingratitude can alienate, no disobedience exhaust, no degree of infamy render hopeless of its object—awaken no new and hitherto dormant susceptibility within the heart? Nay, I make answer, what is the experience of every believing soul that has ever turned to God? Is it not that the child-instinct, the long latent filial longing and aspiration springs up within the soul to verify and welcome the revelation of the Fatherhood of God, that the spirit of adoption arises in our hearts whereby we know that we, too, are sons of God, "heirs of God, and joint heirs with Christ"?

What, finally, is meant by the spiritual life, the life of love and purity and holiness which the Spirit of God impels us to lead? Is obedience to God simply obedience to an omnipotent will, blind submission to a law imposed upon us by an external power? Nay, if that were all, there would be some reason for saying that the religious life is one in which the freedom of man is repressed and overborne. Nor is the answer simply that the revelation of God's holy law appeals to the conscience, awakens a moral sense within us. That indeed is true. It is no little thing to respond to the call of duty, even when our human inclinations and passions war against its dictates. There is a certain dignity and nobleness in the life of duty and self-discipline, of repressed impulses and restrained passions and actions persistently regulated by reason and conscience. But the ideal of the Christian life, the life human yet divine which broke upon the world in all the glory of its perfection in him who is our pattern and example, is something far beyond this. It is that of a life in which not merely our reason, our conscience, our spiritual intelligence recognizes and responds to the law and will that is above us, but in which, with reverence be it said, there is enkindled in our hearts a love, a sympathy, a passionate aspiration after goodness akin to that which burns in the very heart of God. "Be ye therefore perfect, even as your Father which is in heaven is perfect."

The perfection to which this sublime command bids us aspire is that of a spirit in which obedience to God has ceased to be a thing of self-denial, and has become the sweetness and joy of our life, a frame and temper of mind in such harmony with the mind and will of God that duty passes into spontaneity and becomes the manifestation of an inward impulse, the gratification of the deepest passion of the soul. The man who rises to this spiritual elevation of nature may still be a creature of appetites, desires, sensuous impulses; but there will be no longer any painful or protracted struggle with these. Under the dominating force of a new and boundless affection, a love which is not merely love *to* God, but God's own very love glowing in our hearts—a love that binds us to Him by an imperious, yet sweet and joyous enthralment—the soul attains an unfelt supremacy over all other desires, and "the law of the Spirit of life in Christ Jesus" makes it for ever "free from the law of sin and death." Alas!

as we depict this exalted ideal of Christian goodness, how far short of it must we confess is the life which even the best of us are living. Nevertheless it is this and nothing short of this to which as Christian men and women we are bound to aspire, and the command to aspire to it is the pledge and assurance that we may hope to attain to it. And then when it is attained, when we reach that perfect unison of our spirit with the Spirit of God, then will come, not the suppression, but the full and glorious realization of our own deepest nature, the last shred of our moral bondage will be swept away, and we shall know in our blessed experience the truth of that profound saying of Holy Writ, "Where the Spirit of the Lord is, there is liberty."

THE CHRISTIAN WAY OF RECONCILING MAN WITH HIMSELF.

"I see another law in my members, warring against the law of my mind, and bringing me into captivity to the law of sin which is in my members. O wretched man that I am! who shall deliver me from the body of this death? I thank God through Jesus Christ our Lord." ROMANS vii. 23-25.

THE words of St. Paul bring before us that too common stage in the spiritual experience in which duty and inclination are at war with each other, in which the soul has been awakened to the sense of guilt, the conviction of the bondage and degradation of sin, and yet is powerless to break away from it; or in which it has become alive to the call of duty, the demand for a better life, yet, under the overmastering power of temptation and evil habit, has no power to fulfil and respond to it. So long as we are living a life of mere natural impulse, or of thoughtless contented worldliness, unbroken by any consciousness of higher demands and aspirations, the feeling of unrest, of spiritual bondage and incapacity which these words express, is altogether foreign to our experience. For in our inward as in our outward life it is the baffled struggle that brings home to us the sense of our impotence. Swim with the current, drive before the wind, and the force and impetuosity of either will be comparatively unfelt; but breast the stream or beat against the storm that is bearing you to destruction, and you discern your incapacity to cope with them. When a nation's spirit has been so quelled by despotism that it has long ceased to resist, it is in no condition to discover the hopelessness of its bondage; but when the spirit of freedom rises and the attempt is made, and made in vain, to throw off the hateful yoke, it is then that, in the mortifying sense of abortive effort, it finds in its bitter experience a measure of the power that enthrals it. So, let your life drift with the stream of impulsive desires and inclinations, or be swept away by the fiercer force of passion; or let all higher aspirations be repressed by the tyranny of worldly interest or ambition, and you are in no condition to measure the imperious silent strength of the lower nature.

On the other hand, it is when the imperative of duty, the voice of conscience, begins to make itself heard, when the degradation and misery, the shame and guilt of a life of sensuality or self-indulgence begin to be felt, and the moral will is roused to assert itself—it is then, in the effort to be free, to escape from spiritual bondage, that we become aware of the fatal strength of the power that masters us. For it is to be remarked that at the stage indicated in the text the conflict is always an unequal one. Whether it take the form of a struggle with sensuality and the grosser desires of the flesh, or with the love of ease and pleasure, or with worldly interest, the love of money, honour, applause, social distinction and preferment, on the one side there is the force of passion and inclination, on the other the cold, stern, unimpassioned sense of duty; here the meretricious charms of sense and sin, there the loveless law of right with, as yet, no smile upon its face.

Moreover, it is another fatal condition of the conflict that it is waged with a foe who has, so to speak, the advantage of long and undisturbed possession; and every one who has ever tried to conquer an evil and inveterate habit knows how great that advantage is, how feeble the voice of reason and the sense of obligation to loosen the iron grip of long unresisted appetite or passion. If the will were simply an unbiassed umpire between contending claimants, between the right and the pleasant, between the lower or carnal and the higher or spiritual nature, the conflict would be waged on equal terms, and the issue at worst uncertain. But it is not so. The life of impulse long precedes the other and claims, so to speak, a prescriptive right to rule. When the struggle comes, the will is no impartial arbiter. A thousand acts of selfish indulgence have woven themselves into its very essence and given it an evil bias against the unfamiliar demands of duty. No wonder then, in such circumstances,—with emotion, passion, inclination, and the ingrained force of habit on the one side, and only the authoritative voice of a law we respect and fear but have not learnt to love on the other,—that the endeavour after a better life should issue only in a profound and painful sense of impotence and baffled effort.

Finally, it is to be considered that the one thing that would equalize the strife, or lend victorious power to the side of duty, is a thing that will not come at our command. Love, a larger, deeper love, reinforcing reason and conscience, would make them more than conquerors. But alas! as many an awakened, sin-burdened soul in the endeavour after a better life has felt, the love that would disarm law of its sternness and make duty easy, is a thing which no act of will can compass. It is possible, indeed, to yield a hollow and painful outward obedience to a law we hate or to an omnipotent will we dread. Compunction and remorse, slavish fear and selfish interest, have often made men outwardly moral. To propitiate the power in whose hands they believe their eternal fate to lie, it has been possible for them to conform to the requirements of morality, to submit even to penances, sacrifices, painful and protracted austerities, to drag through life a lengthened chain of galling, self-imposed moral servility. But love, the love that would turn duty into delight, comes not at our command. If there be nothing in the law of right, or in the power that ordains and enforces it, to call forth my sympathy, kindle my admiration, touch my heart; if this emotion which would more than redress the unequal strife, spring not up unprompted and unbidden in my heart, by no effort of will, though it were to save my soul from perdition, can I force it to come.

Such, then, is the nature of the inward conflict here depicted. How in any individual case it shall terminate is, if we understand its meaning, a question of enormous importance; for it is a conflict on the issue of which, it is no exaggeration to say, depends our whole destiny as spiritual beings. Put it in other words and this is what it means—Shall I let my life go, and all that is noblest and best in me succumb to what is lowest and meanest? Shall that side of human nature in which it is allied to what is infinite and eternal, its boundless possibilities of knowledge, goodness, happiness, become in me the prey of what is transient and corruptible? Shall I suffer the fascinations of the world and the things of time and sense to kill out the immortal part in me? Is the fair ideal of moral and spiritual perfection, that ever and anon rises before me, only a dream and a phantasm, an unsubstantial vision seen for a moment afar off through a rift in the clouds of sense, and must I regard the effort to realize it as quixotic and vain? Conscious at least of the capacity to conceive of a destiny so sublime, with the heaven of purity and blessedness in sight, shall the deadweight of selfish desires and passions baffle every effort to reach it? Is there no power in heaven or earth that can reinforce my better nature and quell the fatal dominion of that which wars against it? It is this sense of the painfulness and seeming hopelessness of the moral struggle, this yearning after spiritual emancipation, which is expressed in St. Paul's pathetic words, "O wretched man that I am, who shall deliver me from the body of this death?"

And now let us turn for a moment to the answer—confident, unhesitating, almost exulting—which St. Paul gives to his own enquiry: "I thank God through Jesus Christ our Lord." What do these words mean? What help, in other words, does Christianity give us in the endeavour after a better life, in the seemingly unequal strife between the higher and the lower self, the law in the members and the law in the mind?

I answer, for one thing, that Christianity supplies just that new motive force which makes the strife between duty and inclination no longer an unequal one. Love—a larger, fuller, deeper love—this is the new commanding force which it summons to the help of the weak and wavering will. It transforms, if I may briefly express it, the sense of duty into love to Christ. Christianity does not supersede the conception of right, the moral ideal, as a principle of rational intelligence; on the contrary, it incalculably expands and elevates that ideal, and so, in one way, renders it more difficult of realization. But, on the other hand, in all who will yield themselves to its influence, it lends to moral effort the wonderful accession of power, the ardour and intensity, the sweetness and joy, which belong to the personal affections. In the person and life of Jesus Christ, the moral idea, so to speak, takes visible form and embodiment; truth, goodness, purity, righteousness, present themselves to us, not as abstract ideas or qualities, but as living, breathing elements of the character of One for whom we can feel, what law can never create, the admiration, reverence, love of a personal devotion.

And who does not know, in our earthly relations, the power, transcending all the maxims of reason, of an intense personal affection, to deprive toil and self-denial of their irksomeness, and to transform even suffering and self-sacrifice into sweetness? Who does not know the added charm of work that is performed, not from prudential calculation or even a rational sense of obligation, but of work in which these and other motives are suffused with a new inspiration from the inexhaustible springs of love? There are many whose daily life would be one of hard, dreary toil and drudgery, were it not that the secret motive of love to those for whom they labour deprives it of all irksomeness. When sickness and distress threaten the life of one who is dear to us, what is it that supports and strengthens the wife or mother through many a long and watchful hour, through days and nights of anxiety and ceaseless ministration to the sufferer's wants? It is that the hands are strengthened by the secret fire of unselfish love that glows within the breast. Or what is it that in the hour of their country's danger has often nerved men to a thousand sacrifices, yea, to the offering up of life itself for the sake of home and country? It is that love in the patriot's breast made that country's disaster and ruin felt with a keener pang than all personal suffering, and the thought of that country's deliverance a joy sweeter and deeper than all personal happiness. And so, whilst in Christian morality the eternal law of right has lost nothing of its imperativeness, it has gained the new attractiveness, the influence over the deepest springs of action which arises from the possibility of a personal self-devotion. Christianity, indeed, does not substitute obedience to an arbitrary authority or will for deference to the inherent authority of the moral law, but it adds to that authority the subtler, but more constraining power that belongs to the behests of a Being who has touched our hearts, captivated our affections, and bound us to himself by this tie of a profound yet passionate self-surrender.

Moreover, there is this further to be said, that Christianity not only identifies law with a Being we can love, but with a Being who loves us. Even if we could love an abstract law, it cannot love us back. Its very nature is to be impersonal, unbending, inexorable, remorseless. It knows neither pity nor anger. It has no sorrow for the transgressor, no throb of sympathetic approbation for the obedient. We may personify law or duty, but it is only a poetic or personifying imagination that can say of it

> "Thou dost wear
> The Godhead's most benignant grace;
> Nor know we anything so fair
> As is the smile upon thy face."

We may philosophize on the imperative of duty, and construct from it a speculative argument for the existence of a personal God; but law itself has no personality, no face to smile on us, no heart to feel for us, no ear into which our sorrow and contrition can be poured, no tender voice of forgiveness to bring back peace to the penitent. But what law cannot do, Christ does. The one thing that lends surpassing power to the Christ-life over human hearts and lives is that in him eternal truth and righteousness clothe themselves in a living, breathing form, and come to us with an aspect and a voice of personal love and forgiveness. From the impersonal uniformity and unbending rigidity of law, we turn away to find the absolute purity of heaven embodied in One who is aware of all our moral aberrations and weaknesses, who condemns our guilt and imperfection, and yet, even while he condemns, can love and pity and forgive.

And think what a power of moral quickening and regeneration lies in this aspect of our Christian faith. In the love of eternal purity for guilty and sin-burdened souls lies the profoundest appeal to our better nature, the all-potent secret of moral and spiritual restoration. Does not all experience tell us, —in our relations to each other, in dealing with the morally degraded and abandoned,—of the wonderful recuperative power of pure and pitying love? Often and often when nothing else could re-awaken hope and resuscitate moral endeavour, often the consciousness of love and forgiveness has achieved it. Even when to human eye the problem of moral recovery seems insoluble, if the faintest spark of moral vitality be left in the human spirit, here is an agent that will fan it into a flame. There have been men and women, not a few, whose moral nature has been paralyzed and all but suppressed by the ban of society on their lapses from virtue, who have become lost to their own respect because lost to the respect of others—men and women who could never be reached by moral teaching, still less by denunciations and threatenings and penal terrors, yet in whose breasts the spring of moral revival has been touched by the sympathy of some pure and gentle human spirit, and by the thought that, if such an one did not despair of them, they need not despair of themselves. And so, the marvellous power, whether over self-abandoned guilt, or struggling, conscience-smitten, half-despairing virtue, which Christ exercised in his earthly life, and which through a hundred generations his gospel has exerted over human breasts and lives, is due above all to this, that through him eternal law and rectitude speaks to us, not with a voice of condemnation, but with a voice of forgiveness and love. As we listen to that voice, the paralyzing sense of guilt loses its hold over us, and the whole moral forces of our nature spring forth into new vitality at the touch of the Lord of life and love. All the miserable past, with its record of moral failure and disaster, passes away as a hideous dream. We cease to doubt, we dare to hope of the possibilities of a nature which he, the All-pure, All-holy One, has never ceased to love. We no longer, in the consciousness of our moral frailty and impotence, shrink beneath the shadow of an awful unalterable law, but we cast ourselves into the embrace of One in whom law and love, the righteousness we reverence and the tender compassion we need, are blended in perfect unity. Instead of baffled energies and broken resolutions, a new, yet ever growing, deepening consciousness of power steals into our souls as we yield ourselves up to that subduing, controlling, commanding impulse of which St. Paul elsewhere writes: "The love of Christ constraineth us," to live no longer to ourselves, but to him that loved us and gave himself for us, and the consciousness of which drew from him that exclamation of exuberant gratitude, "I thank God through Jesus Christ our Lord."

II. But, let me now add very briefly, we have not exhausted the meaning of these words in saying that Christianity furnishes to us the new motive of love to Christ. There is another idea which runs through the context of this passage and re-appears often in St. Paul's other epistles—the idea, namely, that in our moral struggles and in the endeavour after a purer and nobler life, there is a sense in which we have the actual presence of Christ to help us. As our Lord when about to vanish in visible form from the world declared, "Lo, I am with you alway, even unto the end of the world," so St. Paul writes, "If Christ be in you, the body is dead because of sin; but the spirit is life because of righteousness"; "If the spirit of him that raised up Jesus from the dead dwell in you, he that raised up Christ from the dead shall also quicken your mortal bodies by his spirit that dwelleth in you." And the same idea constantly recurs in his writings, as in the words, "I live; yet not I, but Christ liveth in me," "To me to live is Christ," "That Christ may dwell in your hearts," "Christ in you, the hope of glory." We need not, St. Paul seems to say, in the sense of our own weakness, flinch from the strife with evil, or be discouraged in our endeavours after the better life; for the Lord whom we love and trust is ever with us, ready to support, to succour, to control, to blend his infinite energy with our own.

What then is meant by this thought of an abiding presence of Christ co-operating with us in our moral struggles and endeavours, reinforcing our better nature in the conflict with worldly and selfish desires and passions? Shall we explain it away as a mere metaphor? Shall we interpret the expressions I have quoted simply in the sense in which we say that the spirit of a good man's life becomes an undying legacy to the world, that there is that in the career of a noble and exalted personality which never dies, but constitutes a permanent contribution to the spiritual life of the race? The largest factor in the social life of mankind consists, not of the work of living, contemporary agents, but of that abiding, ever accumulating influence which, by the books they have written, or the noble, heroic, saintly lives they have led, the great and good of the past exert over us. And in the narrower sphere of individual experience there are some of us, I doubt not, who know something of the sacred, hallowing, ennobling immortality which may belong to a personality that in visible form is no longer with us. Of one who was very dear to us we can sometimes say, We loved, we revered him while he was with us, we leant on his counsel, we treasured his friendship and affection as our most precious possession; and death has not diminished but added new strength and sacredness to his influence over us. More vivid may be the image, more powerful the influences of a vanished life even than we were conscious of in its outward presence. It comes back upon us idealized and elevated, with a rounded completeness for imagination which it had not for sense, and with a subtle charm for feeling in which memory is more potent than sight. The idea of such a life has "crept into our study of imagination," and all that was gentle and holy and beautiful in it, doth

> "come apparell'd in more precious habit,
> More moving-delicate and full of life,
> Into the eye and prospect of his soul,
> Than when she lived indeed."

It comes back upon us, it is with us perpetually, hallowed, elevated, consecrated by the touch of death and by all those memories which death has rendered sacred—a restraining, purifying, exalting presence that never while life lasts can lose its power over us.

And no doubt in this sense it is pre-eminently true of Christ that he is ever with us. Measured merely by its traditional influence, no such life as his has ever been lived on earth. No other life has so triumphed over death, has gone on as his has done re-living itself through the ages, penetrating, pervading by its undying power the individual and social life, the whole moral and spiritual existence of humanity. From no other life has ever emanated so potent an influence against the power of the world, the seductions of passion, the falser, meaner motives that war in our breasts with our better, nobler selves. And no wonder! For the ideal which the life of Christ holds before us is that of a life of absolute unworldliness and unselfishness, of transparent simplicity and purity, of superiority to the attractions of wealth, ease, honour, ambition, of unflinching devotion, at all cost and hazards, to God and truth and the service of mankind. To be in sympathy with it is to be in sympathy with a life to the outward eye poor and mean and obscure and joyless, yet at the same time, measured by its inward essence, a life of unparalleled grandeur and affluence, radiant with spiritual beauty, rich in that ineffable blessedness that flows from the eternal springs of thought and joy.

But the abiding presence of Christ is something more, as St. Paul conceives of it, than simply the undying memory and influence of his earthly life and of the sacred traditions of his gospel. So to interpret it would be to thin down to a mere metaphor the notion of a real, living, personal contact and communion of Christ with every individual soul in all time which is expressed by such words as I have quoted. Such language would be exaggerated and overstrained, if it did not point to a more than figurative perpetuity of Christ's presence, to a presence which we can realize here and now, as truly and more profoundly than when men looked upon his face and listened to his living voice. Men sometimes speak as if our Christian faith and hope—our belief in Christ —were a thing that stands and falls with the sifting of historic evidence, with the proof of the authenticity, credibility, and consistency of ancient documents, and the demonstrated accuracy of every incident in the records of Christ's life on earth. I believe that these records have in their substance stood the test of criticism, but I believe also that our faith in the Christ they reveal rests on a basis more impregnable than historic evidence, even on the inward witness to the perpetual presence and operation of the ever-living spirit of Christ, that spirit of redeeming, purifying, hallowing love that was incarnate in him, and that is still and for ever, if we will but open our hearts to receive it, living and breathing within us.

How do we know that the principle of life, the germinating, animating force and energy of nature, has not departed from the world? We know it because every successive spring we witness the annual miracle of nature's revival, every summer and autumn the waving corn clothing the fields with fertility, and the leafy woods waving with foliage and ringing with the sounds of multitudinous life. How do we know, as we read the works or contemplate the productions of the master minds, the great poets and artists of the past, that the spirit from which they drew their inspiration is not a thing that pertained to a dim and distant age, and that has long vanished from the world? Partly we know it because in communion with them we feel it. By the inner response, the sympathetic thrill, which the undying products of their genius awaken in our own minds, by the thoughts, emotions, aspirations, which at their touch leap to life within us —by these experiences we have the assurance that the spirit that was in them, and without which their works would be a meaningless blank to us, in some measure lives and moves within our breasts, and is not therefore a transient visitant, but a perennial presence and power in the thought and life of man. In like manner, but in a far higher sphere, we may know that the spirit that was in Christ, and that made all his human life resplendent with the glory and beauty of the eternal light and love, has not passed away, and will never pass away from the world. We need not go up to heaven to bring Christ down from above, nor back in thought to a dim and vanished age to revive a fading image and memory of the past. He is near us here and now, the light of all our seeing, the ever-present, inexhaustible fountain of spiritual life and strength. If we do not realize his presence the hindrance is not in him but in ourselves. The eye of the soul may be darkened to the heavenly light, the ear dulled or deadened by the tumult of earthly passions to the heavenly voice. But he is never far from any one of us, the divine element of his presence surrounds us, even when in our hardness and coldness we know and think not of it, like light rippling round blind eyes, or sweet music seeking entrance into deaf ears; and nothing but our own moral opacity and dulness hinders it from penetrating and suffusing our souls.

And, if you ask me where I find the evidence of this abiding contact of the human spirit with the Spirit of Christ, of this invisible, divine, restorative energy that is ever near us, ever ready to lift the soul above itself and the world, and to impart to it the strength, the purity, the peace of that life that is hid with Christ in God, I answer that I find it in the experience of every soul that has ever loved and lived for Christ. As I know when I witness the ever-returning revival of nature that the spirit of organic life is not a thing of the past, a tradition of a distant forgotten spring or summer; as I know when I feel the responsive thrill that awakens within me in the products of human art and genius, that the spirit of beauty is not dead and gone with the vanished years, but lives and breathes around and within the spirit of man; so, in the living experience of every Christian heart, I find the irrefragable witness to the abiding, life-giving presence, the proof that that redeeming, forgiving, hallowing, saving spirit, that once in human form visited the world, is not a thing of the past, but a living, operating spirit and power in the present life and experience of men. When the truth, the reality, the beauty of that glorious ideal of infinite love and goodness that was in Christ discloses itself to the intuitive apprehension of the believing soul, touching and captivating the spiritual imagination with its loveliness, elevating and quickening the whole moral being with its soul-subduing power,—then we need no historic proof of its existence; we know, we feel that it is not a thing of time, that now and here it is living and breathing within us. When again, as we listen to the revelation of God's redeeming love in Christ, when on the softened, contrite spirit there dawns the sweet sense of forgiveness and reconciliation with God; when the fetters of sin, of evil desires and passions, which no human strength can break, fall from us at the touch of a divine liberating energy, and we are free; when the call to a nobler, better life appeals to its inmost nature, raises its dormant aspirations and energies; when in the conflict with temptation it is upheld, strengthened, borne onwards by the sense of an invisible sympathy; when the sweetest joy of which the heart of man is susceptible, the joy of self-conquest, of self-renunciation, of sacrifice and suffering for the good of others, penetrates and suffuses the heart; or when in those moments of elevated feeling of which we hear in the recorded experience of devout and saintly spirits, in the hour of prayer and communion with God, heaven seems nearer, earthly interests and ambitions are forgotten, and every ignoble desire and passion is silenced, and in the ineffable bliss of divine fellowship the spirit catches a glimpse of the glory yet to be revealed;—in these and such experiences there is the witness to the presence, behind the veil of visible things, of a loving, gracious, ever-living spirit of goodness raising us above ourselves into participation in its own eternal life—to that presence and inspiration of the indwelling, ever-living Christ, which drew from St. Paul's lips that rapt ascription of adoring gratitude, "I thank God through Jesus Christ our Lord."

CAN RIGHTEOUSNESS BE IMPUTED?

"Knowing that a man is not justified by the works of the law, but by the faith of Jesus Christ, even we have believed in Jesus Christ, that we might be justified by the faith of Christ, and not by the works of the law: for by the works of the law shall no flesh be justified." GALATIANS ii. 16.

MODERN thought, we are often told, has drifted away from the point of view of the creeds and confessions of the sixteenth and seventeenth centuries, and, amongst others, from such doctrines as that of justification by faith, the imputation of Christ's righteousness, and the immediate salvation of the soul by the act of faith in Christ. These doctrines were no doubt accepted by many simply on the supposed authority of Scripture, and the submission of human reason to them may even have been regarded as part of that self-renunciation which is of the very essence of religion. But it is no longer possible to keep our reason and our religion, our theological and our rational and scientific beliefs, in separate compartments of our minds, accepting in one mental attitude what in another we are constrained to doubt or reject. Our religious beliefs, if they are to have any real influence on our lives, must be in harmony, or at least not in glaring contradiction, with our ideas and the principles which determine them in science, in morals, in philosophy, in the whole content and substance of our ordinary intelligence. A revelation from heaven, it is felt, must authenticate itself by throwing light on intellectual and moral enigmas, not by adding to them; it must be a help to faith, not a burden to it.

Now, it will be asked, if we try to apprehend the doctrines to which I have referred, do they not seem to be in direct conflict with what we must regard as elementary principles of morality? Can we, for instance, bring ourselves to accept or even attach any real meaning to a doctrine which turns on the transference of moral qualities and of moral desert from one human being to another? Does not the conviction of our individuality as spiritual beings, of our inalienable responsibility for our actions, lie at the root of our whole moral life? However close our relations to others, is there not given to each of us a career of duty which no other can fulfil for him, and which in time and eternity he, and he alone, must accomplish? You may be enriched by another man's possessions, but can you conceive yourself made good by another man's goodness? Is not counting or imputing one man's righteousness to another a notion as self-contradictory as counting or imputing to a square the qualities of a circle? At a human bar one man may personate another, but even though the attempt should succeed, would not the verdict turn on an illusion and imposture? And can we conceive a divine, omniscient Judge practising on himself the illusion of seeing any man to be what he is not, of forming his judgment of us, not by our own character and conduct, but by what another and better than we, has been and has done? Whatever faith in Christ may mean, it must still leave the two, Christ and ourselves, different beings; it can never annul our separate identity or suppress the distinction between one human soul and another.

If we say that Christ is the highest, the perfect ideal of all human excellence, the only way in which our belief in that ideal can benefit us is by our setting it before us as the example to which, though we can never hope to equal it, we may strive more and more nearly to approximate. But can our faith in any ideal of purity and nobleness ever supersede by any short-hand or summary process the slow and gradual way in which all moral improvement is attained, the course of continuous persevering effort and self-discipline by which evil inclinations and habits are conquered, and the moral character is matured and consolidated? Can we become good, any more than we can become wise and learned, at a single stroke? Imagination may picture an infantile or ignorant mind by a magical act becoming possessed in a moment of all human knowledge and culture, and so it may picture to itself an imperfect or sinful nature instantaneously endowed with ideal purity and perfection; but we know, in point of fact, that the greatest natural ability or precocity does not supersede the discipline of education and culture. And is not moral attainment subject to the same conditions? Is there any royal road to goodness any more than to learning? Can we conceive of a single initial act anticipating and forestalling the long course of moral progress, condensing into itself the innumerable acts and experiences of that practically interminable career of gradual improvement of which a good and holy life must consist? In one word, can a man be *counted* righteous on any other condition than by *being* righteous, or can he become perfectly righteous in a moment simply by believing in the righteousness of another?

Such then are some of the objections which obviously present themselves to the doctrine of justification by faith and of that imputation of the merits of Christ to the believer on which it is based. But though they are, as I think, fatal to any intelligent acceptance of that doctrine in the hard, crude, unspiritual form in which theological systems have presented it, they have no force against what I believe to be its real significance. Justification by faith and not by works is, rightly apprehended, no mere theological dogma to which, however unintelligible or repulsive, however foreign to our human sympathies and moral experience, as divinely revealed, human reason must bow. It is, on the contrary, a doctrine which is in profound adaptation to our spiritual nature and needs, and into which with deepest moral and spiritual sympathy every devout soul may enter. Let me endeavour briefly to show you that it is so.

The springs of human character lie beyond the reach of outward observation. External action is but an inadequate and often deceptive measure of inward spiritual capacity. What a man does or has done, or within the limits of our brief and bounded life can ever accomplish, is but an imperfect and often blurred and confused expression of the hidden potentialities of the spirit. Of that which constitutes the essence and reality of a human soul an outward observer may easily form a mistaken, *can* only form a partial and inadequate estimate. Only to an eye which penetrates to the root of character, which can embrace in its judgment the unrealized and boundless possibilities of the future as well as truly interpret the meaning of the past, only to an eye which measures life, not by action merely, but by the principles from which action springs and the inexhaustible productive force that is in them—only to such an eye does the true complexion and character of a human soul lie open. It is perhaps on this principle, translating the technical language of theology into our ordinary forms of expression, that we may represent to ourselves what is meant by being justified not by works but by faith. Stated generally the principle is this, that the true criterion of a human spirit is not outward performances but the ideal to which it is devoted; and, in its application to religion, it is the principle that the divine measure of a Christian life is not outward works or doings but devotion to Christ as its ideal.

Now the truth of this general principle we may easily bring home to ourselves. It is no doubt true that conduct is the test of character, that we form our opinion of what a man is by what he does. Not by the creed he professes or the fine moral sentiments he utters, nor even by his good and virtuous impulses or his devout and pious emotions, is our estimate of his real character determined. These may easily prove deceptive. Your orthodox creed may be but a cant, your high-flown sentiments, your tender susceptibilities, your gushing emotions, are no genuine signs of sincerity or depth of character. The only real, infallible test is the practical one. By the habitual tenor of a man's actions, by deeds, not frames and feelings, by the life—pure, gentle, generous, earnest, self-sacrificing, or selfish, sensual, frivolous, ignoble—we form our estimate of the spirit, beautiful or base, mean or exalted, from which such actions proceed. In the judgment of reason, at the bar of public opinion, it is by moral action, by the deeds of the law, that a man is justified or condemned.

Yet, on the other hand, it needs but little reflection to see how inadequate in many respects such a criterion is. Action is the form in which thought or spirit embodies itself. But, in the first place, it is by its very nature an imperfect form. The medium of expression, from its own inherent poverty, often lags behind the inward wealth it would express. In the intellectual sphere we see at once the truth of this contrast between thought and action, principle and performance. Why is it, for instance, that in literature, in art, in every line of intellectual achievement, it is ever the highest minds that are least satisfied with their own performances—that the poet, painter, author, orator, is often his own severest critic? A dream of beauty has visited the imagination of the artist, and through the medium of form and colour, or of oral or written speech, he has tried to embody it. But when he contemplates the result, looks on the finished picture, reads over the poem, comes away from the great oratorical effort, even though he may have succeeded in gaining the plaudits of the multitude, it is often with a feeling of profound dissatisfaction. And the reason is, that the conception far transcends the expression, that the ideal that floats before the mind is something immeasurably loftier and grander than the actual form in which he has tried to realize it. Conceit, self-satisfaction, is possible for commonplace minds, but never for minds of the loftiest order. A certain divine discontent is ever the characteristic of genius.

In like manner, in a nobler art, the art of goodness, of embodying in action the ideal of what is fair and holy and pure, is it not precisely, and for the same reason, the very best and holiest of men who are most dissatisfied with their own doings, who feel that when they have done all, they are but unprofitable servants? The man who has no moral ideal, or but a low and poor one, is easily satisfied with himself. There are thousands whose life, if not positively vicious, is destitute of all moral elevation, never rising above the level of decent conventional proprieties and common-place respectability, who are perfectly self-contented. They are visited by no compunctions of conscience, no humiliating sense of short-coming and failure, the even surface of their placidity from day to day is undisturbed by a single ripple of spiritual disquietude. But can we explain what may be termed the moral paradox which meets us in the history of the holiest and saintliest spirits, that their recorded language is often that of profoundest humiliation and self-disparagement? When St. Paul speaks of himself as the "chief of sinners," when we hear him giving utterance to such language as we have read to-day, "When I would do good, evil is present with me,"—language which would seem more appropriate on the lips of a remorseful criminal than of a Christian hero and apostle—are we to set down such expressions simply as the language of hyperbole and exaggeration? No! the explanation of this seemingly exaggerated self-depreciation lies mainly in this, that measured by the infinitely higher standard or ideal of goodness which has dawned on the mind, actions that seem flawless to others have become full of blemishes and imperfections. In the knowledge and love of Jesus Christ, a vision of what is supremely holy and fair, a radiant image of moral loveliness, had taken possession of St. Paul's spirit; with intense spiritual conviction he had embraced it, with all the devotion of his ardent nature he yearned after it, and sought in his own life to realize it; but his highest attainments fell ever far short of the mark, and in the light of that celestial purity his best actions seemed stamped with poverty and failure. Not by anything he did, or could do, could he regard himself justified in the sight of God.

Again, as another proof of the inadequacy of works, actions, outward performances, as a criterion of character, it is to be considered that the measure in which the spirit and character reveals itself in action depends greatly on the circumstances and opportunities of a man's outward life. Moral and spiritual power may be undeveloped for lack of opportunity, or may be repressed by the force of untoward circumstances. In the spiritual as in the natural world there is such a thing as latent or potential energy, force that is locked up and unapparent because the conditions necessary for its manifestation have not yet arrived. You cannot judge even of physical strength, of the energy that is deposited in the human frame, by what meets the eye in our ordinary activities. Popularly, though not with strict scientific propriety, we may represent this to ourselves by saying that there may be in our physical nature a latent stock of unexpended energy of which its possessor as well as others may be unconscious, if the fitting occasion or opportunity for its development have not come. On a great or sudden emergency, under the stimulus of danger or duty, there has often come upon a man what seems an access of hitherto undeveloped power. The weak woman, for instance, delicately reared and seemingly incapable of exertion, at the cry of her helpless offspring will rush into the burning house, and amidst suffocating smoke and crumbling beams, and over calcined floor, with tread firm and fleet, bear forth her loved one to safety. The fugitive in battle, the escaped captive with the pursuer on his track, will face dangers, put forth a speed, perform feats of strength of which, had the occasion never come, he would have seemed utterly incapable. So, in like manner, moral power depends greatly for its eliciting and manifestation on the accidents of our outward life. The life of most of us is uneventful—moves on in the placid routine of common-place duties and trials, and there is no room for the display either of heroic virtues or of tragic crimes or failures. Our Christian fortitude is not tested by the risk of the martyr's fate, our devotion to Christ by the call to sacrifice wealth, ease, honour, every other earthly hope and ambition, and even life itself, for the Master's sake. Judging of us merely by our present actions, by anything we do or have had the chance of doing, who could tell whether, if such tests of principle occurred, we should rise to meet them? The strength, or, alas! the weakness of our character may thus remain concealed from others, and even from ourselves. Sometimes indeed, it may be unexpectedly, an occasion does arise that goes to the root of character, that presents a demand for some high act of moral courage or of the resistance to the temptations of money, or brilliant preferment, or of some great sacrifice, for the sake of others, or the terrible necessity to choose between worldly ruin and disaster, and the preservation of integrity and honour. And then there have come strange and unexpected revelations of character.

A modern writer on this subject, refers,—to take a

single instance,—to some of the incidents in the story of the Indian mutiny. "I recollect reading," says he, "the experience of one shut up in that beleaguered city for which our anxieties were then so strained, who tells of having then first discovered the true character of persons supposed to have been familiarly known before. Some gave way under the test, and men who had passed without reproach in the ordinary intercourse of life, exhibited craven fear, pitiable vacillation, or miserable selfishness. But with others the occasion called forth traits of calm endurance, generous self-devotion, unselfish heroism, which the world would never have known but for the fiery trial which elicited them." So, again, if we compare our own with other times in the history of the Christian Church. Many of those who nobly met the trial, seemed perhaps in the ordinary course of life men and women in nowise remarkable. Had life passed away for them without any exceptive call for the manifestation of Christian principle, how incommensurate would its outward form have been to its inward force and intensity! But the hour came and with it the dread alternative—dark death, torture, the cross, the fangs of the wild beast, or, by one word of treachery to their Christian faith, instant escape and safety. And who knows not how often the answer was that of St. Paul, "I count all things but loss for the excellency of the knowledge of Christ Jesus my Lord."

And so in many a lowly Christian heart there is a latent heroism that, if the demand came, would do and dare all for the sake of the Master they love; but their love finds no other field for its display than the quiet round of domestic and social duties, no other expression than acts of gentleness and kindness and unselfishness, which court no observation and call for no exceptive power. Only he who seeth in secret knows what is in them.

Finally, it is to be considered that outward action is no measure of the endless progressiveness of the Christian life. Action, deeds, external performances are definite and limited, but intellectual and, still more, moral and spiritual capacity is inherently boundless and inexhaustible. The mind of the author or artist is immeasurably greater than the works he has produced, and after the production of many books, pictures, poems, the intellectual fount of genius from which they spring is still there, the immortal source of other and greater results that are still hidden in the unknown future. Of that which even within the brief limits of human life, a great mind can accomplish or has accomplished, could you have formed a true estimate if your judgment had been limited to its first immature productions, or to the actual results it achieved in the earlier stages of its career? And more obviously of moral and spiritual progress does the same principle hold good. In one sense it is true of most of us that the range of our intellectual attainment is a narrow and limited one. Labour and industry combined with fair ability may accomplish much; but, whatever our intellectual ambition, we soon discover that there is a point beyond which our utmost efforts cannot carry us. There are intellectual tasks with which we can never cope, investigations, problems, subtle ratiocinations, which baffle our powers of intelligence, regions of lofty and recondite thought which it is not given to us to enter. At most we must be content with the second-rate ability which can apprehend the ideas and discoveries of the masters of thought, but to the great poet's, artist's, scholar's, philosopher's fame, we feel and know, it would be folly in us to aspire.

But herein lies the distinction between the two spheres of attainment—that there is no region of moral and spiritual excellence that is not open to us, no limit to spiritual aspiration, no height of attainment in the life divine that is beyond the reach and range of the lowliest alike with the highest spirit on which God's image has been stamped. From its very nature the law of moral and spiritual attainment is this, "He that hath, to him shall be given." And no bounds can you ever set to the future of moral advancement. Every moral effort we make, every victory over self and the world we achieve, is the means and the impulse to further conquests. The goal of spiritual perfection recedes as we advance. As to one climbing some Alpine height, often the nearer eminence seems the summit, yet when reached becomes only the point of view for another, as that when reached for another and yet unscaled height beyond; so is it here. With every step in the spiritual life our vision widens, our aspirations become more elevated, and as we ascend to each new moral height, still peak beyond peak, Alp beyond Alp, the yet unscaled summit, the infinite ideal of goodness, rises afar beyond and above us, bathed in ineffable light and glory. Hence it is that our present or past performances, the very best that the best of men accomplish, are no adequate measure of the inherent, inexhaustible wealth of the spirit.

And now let us turn to what I can only indicate in a few words—the principle on which, in contrast with works or external performances, St. Paul finds the ground of justification. What we are in God's sight, he teaches us, is determined not by what we do or have done, but by the presence in the soul of that inward spirit, principle, characteristic motive and aim—in one word, by that self-surrender, that identification with a divine ideal, which constitutes the Christian faith. Poor, imperfect, fluctuating, inadequate may be our attempts to realize that ideal in action, the very best which the best of men do can be only a gradual approximation to it; but all they fain would be, all the splendour of the spirit's future career is already and virtually contained in it. In the soul in which that divine principle dwells, in the soul in which devotion to Christ has become the one supreme, all-dominating motive and aim, it is *that*, and not the dim imperfect life, the blurred, confused medium through which it struggles into expression,—it is *that* which determines God's judgment of us, makes us what in his sight we are. Underneath the poverty and meanness of the present life, its manifold imperfections and shortcomings, its feeble virtues, its often abortive aspirations and ever imperfect attainments,—all that is but as the beggar's raiment disguising an inward nobility,—underneath all that, what the omniscient eye beholds is the radiant image of a son of God, the hidden splendour of a Christlike purity, the transfigured glory of a soul that has already washed its robes and made them white in the blood of the Lamb.

I can well believe that the idea I have thus feebly expressed may to some of my auditors have an air of extravagance and unreality. But the extravagance is not mine, but that which pertains essentially to St. Paul's doctrine. And that the words I have used are not those of exaggeration, but of truth and soberness, two simple reflections may serve to show.

The first is the obvious thought that it is the principle or motive which constitutes character. It is a common-place of morality that we judge a man, not simply by his actions, but by the motive and intention from which they spring. Action, as we have seen, may be hindered or modified by circumstances, or in other ways may be only a partial expression of what is in the mind and heart, and we may often be led into a rash, superficial or mistaken interpretation of what action means. The only real criterion is the spirit, the temper, disposition, motive from which action proceeds. And if through a man's actions there runs one leading motive or aim, one dominant principle that in the main controls his conduct and gives its prevailing tone, its characteristic aspect and complexion to his life, furnishes the explanation of his past life, the prophetic source from which we foreshadow or divine what his future career will be,—*that*, could we penetrate to it, is the moral essence of the man, the heart of his mystery the thing that determines our moral estimate of him.

Now, I have said that in St. Paul's view there is one principle or motive which, when it effects a lodgment in a human spirit, becomes the mainspring of all its activities, the key to its whole life and history, namely, the principle which he designates as "the faith of Christ." And by this does he mean belief in the historic person and life of Christ, or belief in any theological dogma concerning the work of Christ, or even the recognition of Christ as a perfect example, a faultless specimen of humanity, the highest type and exemplar of human excellence? Nay, if that were all, there are deep and ineradicable instincts in human nature to which the Christ-life had never appealed, dumb hopes and longings for which it had never found a voice, infinite aspirations which at its touch would never have waked to life. The secret of the regenerating, transforming power of that life, that through which it has appealed to man's deepest nature and exerted its wonderful revolutionary influence over human souls, is that it is the revelation in man of divine possibilities, of a more than mortal elevation and grandeur which he may claim as man,—that it discloses in the human spirit an affinity with the Spirit of all truth and beauty and goodness, and that it calls each human soul to no meaner destiny than to be a sharer in the very life and blessedness of God. In the midst of our sins and sorrows, to souls burdened with the consciousness of guilt and cramped by the heavy yoke of evil passions and desires, by the haunting memories of the past and the fears and forebodings of the future, the Christ-life comes with a voice of hope and consolation that penetrates and thrills through every awakened spirit—a voice that proclaims, 'Not this is your true life: awake from the torpor of selfishness that benumbs you, from the dreams and shadows of the life of sense that hide from you your true and glorious destiny. Lay hold of your immortal birthright, ye sons of God and heirs of a heavenly inheritance. The arms of everlasting love are stretched forth to receive you: now and for ever in the bosom of the Father is your true rest and home.' And so as men looked, and through a hundred generations have looked, with the eye of faith on the face of Christ, a strange new life has taken possession of them, a spirit not born of earth has passed into them, and the Spirit within them has borne witness with Christ's Spirit that they too were sons of God.

And then, lastly, comes the thought that in this principle of faith all the future progress and perfection of the soul is involved. It is no arbitrary promise of perfection and blessedness which the religion of Christ conveys to us. The heaven of Christian hope is no visionary future of pious imagination, nor is our aspiration after it the vague longing for the unknown and the unattainable,

> "The desire of the moth for the star,
>   Of the night for the morrow,
> The devotion to something afar
>   From the sphere of our sorrow."

The gospel not only reveals to the quickened eye of the mind a far off ideal of celestial purity and blessedness, but it declares to every human soul, 'Seek it, aspire after it, lay hold on the hope set before you, and on that height of heavenly perfection you one day will stand—nay, in God's idea, you are already standing.' Apart from this, the gospel would be no message of gladness to us. Sing the song of freedom to the slave, and you only mock his misery. Let a dream of health and happiness visit by night the imagination of the incurable, and you only make the sad awakening all the sadder. So, tell of a heaven of moral perfection to men cramped by the heavy weight of earthly desires and passions, paralyzed by selfish inclinations and habits, and you only deepen the depressing sense of moral incapacity. But herein lies the encouragement, the divine impulse and strength of the Christian life, its conquering power over evil, its ever growing aspiration and endeavour, that the glorious future will be but the realization of God's ideal for us. Already, here and now, the prophecy, the potentiality of it lies hidden in us, and if we be true to God and ourselves nothing can ever baulk us of our hope. It is no arbitrary imputation that sees in the first faint ray of light gilding the horizon the sure pledge and prophecy of the perfect day, or in the first stirrings of nature awakening from its winter slumbers the anticipation of the summer glory and loveliness of the golden harvest that is yet to be. In every great work of human art, again, the beginning is instinct with the end, the ideal in its completeness lies in the earliest and faintest initial strokes; and it is no arbitrary imputation that discerns in the first touches of colour on the canvas that which has in it, and is determined by, the finished masterpiece of art. So, it is no arbitrary imputation by which, in the eye of Him to whom all hearts are open, the first motions of the life of the Spirit, the first throb of genuine self-devotion, self-surrender to Christ, is the anticipation of the unborn spiritual perfection and beauty of the life that is hid with Christ in God. "It doth not yet appear what we shall be." "Eye hath not seen, nor ear heard, neither have entered into the heart of man, the things which God hath prepared for them that love him." In moments of spiritual elevation devout and saintly minds may catch a glimpse of that glory that is yet to be revealed. They may think of a future from which all sin and sorrow, of a world from which all imperfection and evil shall for ever have passed away; they may conceive of a love that shall burn with a deeper, intenser fervour, of a purity on which no shadow or taint of evil shall rest, of a peace from which all restlessness of earthly passion shall have vanished, of a fulness of joy over which no satiety shall ever steal. But all such anticipations, it is no extravagance to say, will fall far short of the reality. There is only one thought that implies all that they contain, and that thought is, we shall one day be like to him who is the object of our adoration, clothed with his righteousness, transformed into his image. We know not what we shall be, but this we know, that "when he shall appear we shall be like him, for we shall see him as he is."

IS REPENTANCE EVER IMPOSSIBLE?

"Lest there be any . . . profane person, as Esau, who for one morsel of meat sold his birthright. For ye know how that afterward, when he would have inherited the blessing, he was rejected: for he found no place of repentance, though he sought it carefully with tears." HEBREWS xii. 16, 17.

IT is very difficult, with the Old Testament narrative before us, to recognize the justice of this terrible sentence, which seems here to be pronounced on Esau. For as we read that narrative, I daresay there are few who do not feel their sympathies attracted much more to him than to his more fortunate and prosperous brother. There are many redeeming features in his character, and it is on the whole one of a type whose faults lean to virtue's side, and which, when it is presented to us in real life, despite of much in it to condemn, we often cannot help liking. He was, no doubt, a creature of impulse, reckless, hot-blooded, headstrong, swept along by the passion of the moment, heedless of ulterior consequences; and he did many things which the sacred writers justly censure. But, on the other hand, he was obviously a man of no little tenderness of feeling, of some generous instincts, and not incapable, on occasion, of really magnanimous actions. His sins, as we read the story, were not the sins of deliberate malice, but of sudden passion and impetuous impulse; and he was utterly incapable of the steady, calculating selfishness, the occasional knavery and undeviating eye to self-interest, by which his more successful brother made his way in the world.

In the few incidents in which the story brings them together, to ordinary judgment Esau seems, to say the least, to be as much sinned against as sinning, the victim not more of his own passions than of the cool, designing selfishness of others. In the transaction of the bartered birthright, for instance, we see, indeed, in Esau one whom the ungovernable rage of appetite rendered blind as an animal to everything but immediate gratification; but, on the other side, there is the surely deeper baseness in one who could coolly calculate and play on a brother's weakness to extract from him in a moment of passion a sacrifice enormously disproportionate to the paltry boon given in exchange for it. In the somewhat inexplicable affair of the patriarchal blessing the two brothers are again presented to us. But when we contemplate the characters of the story: the astute, designing woman and her no less crafty son —the one contriving and the other lending himself to a miserable plot to impose on the weakness of old age —the unsuspecting simplicity of the elder brother, returning from the chase to find that the blessing which he had wrought for and which was his by right had been surreptitiously diverted to another,—to which of the personages do our sympathies turn, to the perpetrators or the victim of the trick, to the intriguing mother and her accomplice, or to the simple, thoughtless, open-hearted son and the unhappy father mingling their ineffectual tears and regrets for an act that could never be recalled? Lastly, when, after the long exile of the younger, the two brothers are brought face to face once more, the contrast seems still the same. In the one we have the prudent, persevering man of the world returning with the wealth and consequence which were the results of long labour and much dexterity, and seeking by timid precautions, by presents and pleasing professions of deference, to avert the consequences of a life-long grudge which he knew so little of Esau as to suppose him still cherishing for the wrongs of the past: and in the other, the same impulsive character as long years before, incapable of brooding over injuries or nursing a revengeful purpose; or, at least, in the joy of rekindled affection and the fresh touching of the springs of old memories of love and home, forgetting all but that this is the brother he has long lost and found again.

Whatever, then, we are to make of the preference for Jacob which the sacred writers record, there is in these incidents, and in what else of his career we can gather from the narrative, something at least to abate our condemnation of Esau or even to win for him a qualified approval. He was obviously a man of strong animal passions which he never learned to control; he was of an excitable temperament, played upon by every passing wind of impulse, averse to thought and reflection, and steady self-denying labour; he was what is here called 'a profane person,' meaning by that, a man without spiritual insight or depth of feeling, seeing no deeper than the surface of things, bounded in his thoughts and aims by the narrow limits of the world of sense and sight, for whom the grandeur and mystery of human life were things unknown, and in whose eyes privileges and blessings, which it requires a measure of intellectual breadth or spiritual susceptibility to appreciate, had absolutely no value. Yet with all these defects, as I have said, his nature, if not a very elevated one, is not one of the worst. It is not unrelieved by indications of native tenderness and generosity. If it exhibit not a little of the savage, lawless, untamed ferocity of the feudal chief or the border freebooter, it combines with this some of those more chivalrous elements which we are accustomed to ascribe to such personages—courage, manliness, scorn of mean and sordid ways, a certain free-handed generosity and rough magnanimity, forbearance with the weak and helpless, and a susceptibility to sudden fits of passionate tenderness and self-forgetfulness. Altogether it is not the character of a very bad man. It is not by any means what we should ordinarily regard as that of a man of unredeemable depravity, but rather one containing the stuff, out of which, under favourable conditions, much might be made. So that when we read the New Testament commentary on it, there are perhaps few of us who have not felt it somewhat strange that it should be pronounced of this man, that he was a reprobate who had sinned beyond the reach of mercy—that "he found no place of repentance, though he sought it carefully with tears."

It will be interesting and not unprofitable to reflect for a little longer on this text, and especially on the light which it throws on the question of the connexion between repentance and the forgiveness of sin. "He was rejected"; "he found no place of repentance, though he sought it carefully with tears." Does this mean that, in the case of Esau, or of any other man, it is possible to repent and yet remain unforgiven, or that there are sins for which no repentance will avail us? There are some expressions in the context and in other parts of this Epistle which, at first sight, might seem to favour such a construction of the words. The case of Esau is adduced to enforce a warning of the danger of 'failing of,' or falling away from, the grace of God. And in a former chapter the writer speaks of certain flagrant and hardened sinners, apostates from the faith, of whom he pronounces that "it is impossible for those" who thus "fall away, to renew them again unto repentance," and that their fate can be only that of barren ground from which no tillage has been able to extract anything but thorns and briars,—to be consumed as noxious things by fire.

But that this can hardly be the meaning of the text—that it does not point to any such doom of exclusion from God's mercy—a moment's consideration may serve to convince us. For one thing, as to the particular case here referred to, the sin of Esau does not seem, as I have already pointed out, to have been one of very special enormity. If the birthright were a sort of right of primogeniture entitling him to the inheritance of the family estate, it was doubtless a very foolish thing, an act bordering on insanity, to barter it away in order to appease a momentary appetite. But, at the worst, there was really nothing more culpable here than reckless improvidence and disregard of his own interest, a fault which every man commits who makes a very foolish or unthrifty bargain. If, in addition to this, there were some mystic privileges, some dream of a reversionary glory in the far future of the race, connected with the line of patriarchal succession, the conception which could be formed of them at this early period must have been very vague,—little better, in the most far-sighted minds, than a dim, undefined prognostication, constituting a motive to human conduct about as powerful as an augury of England's future greatness at the time of the Heptarchy, or a prevision of the destinies of the American continent at the time of the Pilgrim Fathers. What impression could such a notion be expected to leave on the mind of a half-savage Bedouin, or is it possible to think that he could be blamed at all, not to say banished from God's mercy for ever, for insensibility to this as a motive of action?

But, turning from this particular case, let us enquire for a moment whether it is possible on general grounds to attach to **any of** the passages I have quoted the construction that, in **any case, it is** possible to repent and yet remain unforgiven. Can repentance and forgiveness or restoration to God's **favour** ever be dissociated? Is there any other condition of forgiveness than repentance? Is there any arbitrary will or sovereignty in God that can interpose to prevent it; or any forensic or other kind of justice whose demands must first be satisfied before forgiveness is possible, any scheme or plan by which in the court of heaven justice is to be compensated? That this is not so will be obvious if you reflect for a moment on what the words repentance and forgiveness mean. Whatever may be the case in the relations of man to man, in our relations to God you cannot separate these two. Nay, when you examine closely what you mean by the words, you will see that the idea of repentance is only another aspect of the idea of forgiveness, that repentance is just forgiveness with a different name; so that to say of any soul that is filled with sorrow for its sins that it can remain unforgiven, or that its forgiveness may be delayed for some other reason, is to utter what is really a contradiction in terms—a contradiction as great as to speak of the vanishing of darkness without the approach of light, or of the earth becoming nearer to the sun without the sun becoming nearer to the earth.

The reason why this does not at first sight appear self-evident is, that in the relations of man to man repentance and forgiveness are not only distinguishable in thought, but are in point of fact often dissociated from each other, and that in our conceptions of divine justice we naturally but erroneously apply to divine relations notions that are true only of human relations. In the relations of man to man it is possible to repent and yet remain unforgiven. The sorrow and regret of a human offender, however intense, do not necessarily effect any change of sentiment in the mind of the man he has offended. The exasperation and resentment of the latter and his desire and determination to avenge his injuries may quite possibly, despite the former's penitence, remain without the slightest abatement. And the same is true of public offences or crimes. Not only is a felon's repentance for a criminal act quite distinguishable from the remission of its penalty, but we know that human laws take absolutely no cognizance of the emotions of a convict. However bitterly and sincerely he may grieve for his evil deeds, his penitence, his grief, his tears avail him nothing; the law must take its course. The penitent thief goes to the hulks, the remorseful murderer to the gallows, all the same. He finds no place of repentance though he seek it carefully with tears. But this distinction between penitence and forgiveness does not apply to the divine jurisprudence; and the reason is that in human law, crime and punishment are arbitrarily connected, but under the divine law they are absolutely indivisible; so that wherever the crime, or the criminal or sinful state of mind, exists, there the punishment necessarily follows; and conversely, wherever or whenever the sinful state of mind begins to cease, there and then the punishment begins to cease too. Punishments for offences against human laws are such things as fines, imprisonment, banishment, or, in extreme cases, death; and these, obviously, are penalties which may continue to be inflicted whether the criminal be in a repentant state of mind or remain hardened to the last. If God's punishments were of this kind, if the punishment of sin consisted of stripes, or incarceration, or banishment to some dismal penal settlement of the universe, or in the application of material fire or other means of torture to the person, then it would be possible for such penalties to run their course altogether irrespective of the mental condition of the offender. As by a freak of good nature or an arbitrary act of mercy they might be remitted to the most hardened, so, by an unrelenting determination or decree, they might continue to be exacted from the most contrite soul. The sinner's breast might be filled with godly sorrow at the very moment when the lash of retribution was unsparingly falling upon him; and the sincerest sorrow softening his spirit might avail as little to mitigate his doom as the agony of the sick and dying man to arrest the ravages of disease or to stay the approach of death.

But in the system of divine justice there is no such separation between offence and punishment, and therefore no such divorce between penitence and pardon. In God's dealings with men there is no arbitrary punishment and no arbitrary mercy. With God, to forgive an impenitent man and to continue to punish a penitent are equally impossible. For the very essence of sin's punishment is not any outward infliction, but the moral state to which it reduces the culprit. No fines and exactions reduce the wealthy profligate or sensualist to poverty; no! but the punishment of sensuality—worse than any outward impoverishment—is this, that the soul by its own act is beggared and pauperized, bereft of that which is man's true wealth, subjected to the unspeakable loss of pure feelings and gentle and tender affections, stript and shorn of that which constitutes the worth, the dignity, the true blessedness of man. There is no dark and distant corner of the universe to which a selfish, godless spirit can be locally banished from the omnipresence of God; but a selfish nature is self-banished from love, from goodness—segregated from the life and liberty of the soul, shut up in a more terrible than material isolation from the Father of Spirits. There is no lash of torture or blazing fire of wrath that can affect a spiritual nature; but evil desires and debased inclinations and unrestrained passions, a soul lost to self-respect, and filled with "envy, hatred, malice, and all uncharitableness"—these are internal elements of moral self-destruction which, only give them time to work, must make a hell of every heart that was born for better things.

And so, when we reverse our point of view, and ask what are the conditions of pardon, of remission of penalty, and reconciliation to God, is not the answer this—The way of reconciliation is open, ever open; no outward conditions bar the door of return; let the heart but begin to turn to God, in sorrow and self-abasement let the soul begin to respond to that infinite love which Jesus Christ revealed to the world, and instantly and inevitably the penalty begins to pass away? It is not that, on condition of repentance, the sinner's Judge may possibly remit his stripes; repentance is itself the arresting of the hand that wields the lash, the exchange of a remorseful, self-accusing, self-tormenting spirit, for the inward satisfaction and peace of a spirit whose very sorrow shows that already it has begun to be on the side of righteousness. It is not that, possibly, if we have not incensed our Judge too deeply for re-admission to his presence, the sentence of banishment may on our repentance be reversed. Nay, but the first throb of true spiritual feeling, the first sigh of a contrite heart, is itself the sign that its fetters are falling, that the bonds of its moral imprisonment are being broken. It was inward hardness and estrangement, not spatial distance, that kept it away from God; and the melting of the hardness, the hatred and horror of sin and yearning after goodness of which the penitent soul is conscious, is the proof that already, as by an inward moral gravitation, it is returning back to the bosom of Eternal Love. Thus we conclude on this point, that repentance is not a condition that may or may not, according to an arbitrary act of mercy, be followed by forgiveness. It is already forgiveness, reconciliation to God begun. It is altogether inconceivable, therefore, that there should be any absolute sentence of exclusion, that any soul should ever desire to go back from sin and find the door of mercy shut against it, or, in the words before us, should find no place of repentance, though it seek it carefully with tears.

But though in this wider and more general sense the notion of unavailing repentance is irrational and immoral, there are, as I now go on very briefly to point out, other and very numerous cases in which it is undoubtedly true. The blessing, whatever its significance was, which Esau sought, had by his own folly or indifference been irrevocably lost. There was a time when it might have been his; but words had been spoken which could never be recalled, and it was now for ever beyond his reach. And in like manner human life in general is so ordered as to contain the possibility of irretrievable errors, of acts or omissions which carry with them irreversible results, and to which the warning of the text, in the full force of the words, does apply. The briefest experience of life teaches us that it is full of single chances, of opportunities of good which are offered to us but once, and which, if let slip, can never be recalled, and of possibilities of evil which, when they have once become realities, no regret can remedy. Too late! there are few of us who have not felt the pathetic significance of these little words. Each successive stage of life, each day, each passing hour almost, comes to us fraught with its own special gift; and there come ever and anon to most of us critical times, conjunctures, calls for momentous and decisive acts, opportunities of resistance or exertion, when our happiness trembles in the balance, opportunities which, alas! often in our thoughtlessness, our indolence, our foolish pre-occupation with trifles, we let go, to discover what might have been ours only when it is for ever gone. The tide which taken at the flood might have led to fortune has ebbed away, the favourable conjuncture has passed, and the heavens roll not round again to reproduce it; the hour when the healing virtue perturbs the waters is passed, and the angel's visit is never repeated.

The simplest and most obvious illustration of these remarks is that which is derived from the relation which the earlier years of life bear to its future. As one looks back in mature life on the years of our boyhood and early youth, is it not with the deep conviction that they were fraught with opportunities which never recur; and that, be a man's subsequent career what it may, these are the years which, in most cases, make or mar it? Advancing life may bring with it its own peculiar advantages—experience, caution, sobriety of judgment, superiority to impulse, worldly sagacity and prudence; but the ready apprehension, the quick and retentive memory, the buoyant energy, the elasticity that rebounds undepressed from troubles, the wonder and delight of the world of thought bursting on us with the charm of novelty and freshness, the freedom from prejudice, cynicism, scepticism, the liberty of opinion yet untrammelled by worldly interest or cowardly caution or false fear of inconsistency or lethargic contentment with things as they are, the enthusiasm yet unchilled by disappointment, and the confidence to which all things seem possible—these and such as these are the precious gifts of the earlier stage of life, and which, with the narrowing circle of the years, pass rapidly away. In so far as our intellectual life, our opportunities of knowledge and mental culture, are concerned, is it not so that these and similar characteristic advantages of early life never come again? Never again can the free and unencumbered mind, the unanxious spirit of boyhood be yours. Never again in the midst of the cares and responsibilities of life,—your hours absorbed, your energies taxed by the engrossing duties of a trade or profession,—can a time recur, fenced off from every duty but that of self-culture, in which the whole force of your nature may be concentrated on the acquisition of knowledge. And so, when advancing years force upon us the consciousness of our ignorance or imperfect culture, there are not a few who can only look back on that time with the bitter sense of the irretrievable.

And the same principle applies also to our moral and spiritual life. It is never too late to begin to serve God, but for the moral education and development of our nature as well as the intellectual, the earlier years have advantages that are all their own. There is a kind of goodness which is the fruit of early piety, and which by no later penitence can be reproduced. It may indeed sometimes seem as if there were a kind of truth in the saying, 'The greater sinner, the greater saint'; as if the piety of what is called 'conversion' had in it an ardour and intensity unknown to the religion of quiet and continuous growth. There may be a rapture in the sudden sense of relief from the guilty fears and forebodings of a conscience troubled by the haunting sense of evil deeds, which is an impossible experience for one whose life from the beginning has been spent in obedience to duty and to God. The new-born zeal of the converted profligate may glow with a fervour, and manifest itself in an enthusiastic activity, seldom witnessed in those whose spiritual life has admitted of no such convulsive changes. Nevertheless there are blessings peculiar to the religion of quiet growth and development which, with all its emotional elation and high-pressure activity, the piety of conversion cannot know. It can never know or regain the happy ignorance of evil, the sweet stainlessness of a mind innocent of foul experiences and hateful associations. It can never know the blessed exemption from thoughts, imaginations, recollections of acts which, once done, can never be undone, which no waters of absolution can make never to have been. It cannot know the serenity, the strength, the stability, the superiority to sudden relapses, which are the result of long self-discipline and the silent consolidation of habits that have grown with our growth and strengthened with our strength.

In these and similar experiences we have illustrations of the law that repentance and forgiveness, though they may obliterate the guilt, do not and cannot altogether undo the effects of past sins. And besides this, whatever may be the case with the future, the present and outward penalty of former sin may never in this life be remitted. No agony of penitence can bring back health to the intemperate man, or absolve the sensualist from the misery of disordered nerves and a sickly habit, or bring back the hue of health to the cheek and the vital energy to the frame that by a course of vice has wasted it. The man may repent, he may grieve with godly sorrow, he may be forgiven, but these are penalties from which there is no absolution. For him there is no place of repentance though he seek it carefully with tears.

Lastly, the social effects of our actions, the influence they have had on the character and happiness of others, furnish one other, and that the saddest, illustration of the principle of the text. Though it were possible by repentance to obliterate every trace of the past from our own lives, to free ourselves from all the pain and shame and sorrow which our sins have entailed on us, the evil they have done to others it is almost wholly beyond our power to retrieve. We cannot live for ourselves. We cannot stand or fall alone. Our words and deeds are continually helping to make or mar the happiness and to mould for good or evil the characters of our fellow-men. And the thing to be noticed is, that if a man has long led a selfish and sinful life, the evil it has done to others he may never be able to undo. Though he himself may repent and turn to God, he cannot arrest the action of that malignant force which has gone forth from his former life. Many of its effects he cannot trace, and those which he can trace he may have no power to counteract. Some to whom he has done harm have been drifted far away from him by the exigencies of life; others have gone where no earthly influence can ever reach them. If in the days of his folly he has done irremediable injury to the bodies or souls of others, what avails it to them that he has now repented and begun to lead a better life? Can his sorrow give back peace to those whom his sin has rendered wretched? Can his penitence restore a lost virtue to her whom he led astray from purity? Can it give her back the smile of girlish innocence, take away the brand from her name, or the shame and sorrow from the hearts of those to whom she was dear? Or, if in the past you have done injury to those who are gone, if you have been a bad son, or a false friend, or an unkind husband; if you have neglected or abused the almost creative influence of a parent over the characters of his children; if you have encouraged others in vice, or seen them fall into evil ways without exerting your influence to save them, —what matters it that now, when they are far and beyond your reach, late repentance has visited your soul? It may avail for you, for them it availeth nothing. And oh, surely all the more that your sin has been repented of and forgiven,—all the more keen and poignant must be the anguish with which you recall the irretrievable wrong you have done to others. Surely till memory sleeps, till human hearts are steeled in selfish indifference, or lost to any other consideration than that of personal security, there must be something to trouble the bliss of forgiveness, to overshadow the joy even of souls redeemed from sin, in the thought that they have done irreparable wrong to the souls of others—a wrong for which there is no place of repentance, though we should seek it carefully with tears.

May we never know the bitterness of that vain regret of which I have said so much. If life yet lie before us, may it be our endeavour so to live that it shall never be ours hereafter to mourn over wasted opportunities and irretrievable errors. Are you in the early critical period of life, when your path is still to choose, your career yet to be, when your habits are unformed, your powers fresh and vigorous, and golden opportunities of goodness, usefulness, happiness, of a fair and noble life are crowding upon you, and you have but to reach forth the hand to grasp them? Then may it be given you to know their preciousness, and eagerly to appropriate them. That voice of counsel or warning from the lips of those who love you dearly, listen to it now, for the day is coming when it will be silent, and the time for profiting by it will be gone. That affection that perhaps you are lightly prizing, that is now watching and waiting for a response, let it not pass away unrequited, to awaken hereafter in your heart the bitter pang of remorse when it is far and for ever beyond the reach of your penitence. That appetite or passion that is only beginning to steal over you, stifle it with determined resolution now, for the day may come when it shall become tyrannous, and you will in vain struggle against it. That sin you feel tempted to commit, that degrading connection you are drifting into, break off from it ere it become a haunting memory, staining your soul, embittering your peace, and cramping your energies through life. Oh, blessed time of vernal freshness; oh, happy period when the blurred page of life is yet unwritten; oh, days of hope and opportunity, may it never be yours to recall them only to long in vain that the wheel of time could roll backwards, and those golden opportunities again be yours which can come no more!

But if that may not be: if the past has already been to you one of wasted opportunities and neglected responsibilities, though *that* it is too late to undo, let us feel that it is not too late to do with redoubled energy what yet remains to be done. To shake off the lethargy of spiritual indifference, to renounce all unmanly and ignoble selfishness, to respond to the call of duty, to begin a life of earnest, active beneficence, to crowd our days with deeds, and, God helping us, in what remains of life to be as good and to do as much good as we can—for this at least it is not too late. The harvest indeed is past, the summer is over and gone! Gone are the sweet days of innocence, gone the vernal time of youthful ardour, gone the sunny harvest hours of manhood's effort and activity. But oh, still happy you if, when the sands of life are running out, in that supreme moment when earth and earthly things shall be passing for ever from your sight, you can look back on this last period of your earthly probation with the blessed consciousness that *that* at least has not been given in vain! And may God forbid that when the last comes to the last, as we lie waiting the inevitable summons, it should be with the terrible conviction that for all the higher purposes of existence, for all the ends for which God has given us our life, our life has been a failure—a failure for which there is now no place of repentance, though we seek it carefully with tears.

THE REVERSAL OF NATURE'S LAW OF COMPETITION.

"We then that are strong ought to bear the infirmities of the weak, and not to please ourselves. Let every one of us please his neighbour for his good to edification. For even Christ pleased not himself; but, as it is written, The reproaches of them that reproached thee fell on me." ROMANS xv. 1-3.

IN this text, St. Paul, as his manner is, passes by an abrupt transition from a special and somewhat limited case of conscience, arising out of the particular circumstances of the primitive converts, to a comprehensive expression of the general principle of Christian morality which it involved. The particular question was as to the duty of abstaining from certain kinds of food in deference to the prejudices of some weak, or rather weak-minded brethren; and the solution which St. Paul gives is, in substance, this, that the stronger-minded ought not to disdain or harshly trample on the conscientious scruples of the weak, however exaggerated or futile, from their own point of view, these scruples might appear to be; and that, if a small sacrifice of Christian liberty in matters of indifference would prevent needless offence even to the foolish prejudices of others, that sacrifice should be cheerfully made. No doubt, conscientious weakness and narrowness are often a grievous source of trouble in the Church as well as in the world. When great questions of Christian faith and duty are occupying the minds of thoughtful men, when the fundamental principles of religion are imperilled by sceptical assaults, when the combined wisdom and energy of Christian men are all too little to cope with the moral plagues that are preying on the very vitals of society, it is a sore trial to the larger-minded to see the fuss that is made about some matter of Church order or etiquette, the time that is wasted, the heat that is called forth by discussions about questions of ritual and ceremonial, in themselves absolutely unimportant and having no necessary relation to Christian principle. To St. Paul's great and magnanimous spirit, glowing with zeal for the highest welfare of humanity, the settlement of such disputes either way seemed a thing not worth a breach of charity, and he might naturally have treated them with contemptuous indifference. But, as is generally the case with minds of the largest and noblest order, he could enter into the feelings, and look at things from the point of view of smaller and weaker minds. He could be tender to prejudices and considerate towards scruples which he himself could never feel. Firm as a rock where Christian principle was involved, he could be pliant and yielding where only matters of indifference were concerned. And so, in the first place, he advises those who sympathized with him to subdue their impatience with the scrupulosity of the feeble-minded, and to put a tax on their own Christian liberty, if by such harmless concessions the peace and welfare of the Church could be promoted. And then, brushing aside all minor considerations, he passes by a leap to the great, fundamental principle of Christian ethics, that all Christians, as members of a common body, ought to share each other's burdens; the stronger and more advanced, like Christ himself, taking upon themselves the perplexities and troubles, the sorrows and sins of the feeble and imperfect. "We then that are strong ought to bear the infirmities of the weak."

From the context it appears that this precept forms one of a series of practical admonitions which are all alike based on the general principle with which the writer started, namely, that Christians, "being many, are one body in Christ, and every one members one of another." In other words, to be indifferent to the weaknesses, the difficulties and trials of others is to be faithless to the very ideal or essential principle of the spiritual life. Selfishness, in a being endowed with a spiritual nature, is not simply a sin, but an anomaly and self-contradiction. To attempt to go our own way, to live for the satisfaction of our individual desires, to secure for ourselves in the general scramble as much enjoyment or happiness as we can get, irrespective of what befalls our less fortunate brethren, is, rightly viewed, to aim at the impossible. It is like the eye saying to the hand, I have no need of thee, or the head to the feet, I have no need of you. Inhumanity, according to St. Paul's conception, is what the word expresses, an outrage on the very idea or essence of human nature, for that idea is what we express by the phrase, 'the organic unity of mankind,' the idea, that is, of a connexion with others as intimate and inseparable as that of the members of an organism with each other. To live for ourselves, to make our own individual welfare or happiness our sole or chief end, is the endeavour of a mutilated limb to live and grow, of a severed fragment of the body to retain in isolation that functional health and activity, that symmetry, order, proportion, perfection, which is attainable only in living action and reaction with the whole organism. Self-absorption is equivalent to moral paralysis. Neglect of the weak, hardness and indifference to the sorrows and sins of others, is a vice which surely avenges itself on those who fall into it, for the same reason that carelessness or insensibility to the disorder or weakness of any one organ of the body interrupts the health and happiness of the rest. On the other hand, the ideal of the spiritual life is that of a community in which every man's welfare is an object to every other, and the pain or weakness or dishonour of one is the pain, weakness, dishonour of all. It is that of a community in which it is impossible for any one individual to gain or grow rich at another's expense; but, on the contrary, in which the loss, infirmity, limitation of any one soul is a distinct diminution of the welfare and happiness of every other; in which, therefore, there is not only no temptation to neglect or crush the weak, but every man is impelled by the very law of his being to remove the spiritual disabilities of others, to increase and multiply the number of those who participate in the common good.

Now, in reflecting for a little on this as one of the main principles or laws of the spiritual life, that the strong are to care for, support, cherish the weak, it may strike us as a singular fact that we live in the very midst of a world where the very reverse of this seems to hold good. We are confronted every day by the spectacle of a life in which, so far from the strong bearing the infirmities of the weak, it is the condition of their very existence that they should crush and destroy the weak. Interesting analogies have often been drawn between the natural and the spiritual life, and attempts have been even made to show that the same laws hold good in both. But here at least we have a case in which the law of the spiritual world is the very reverse of that which obtains in the natural. The law of nature, we are told, in regard to all the lower forms of life, is success to the strong, failure and extermination to the weak. Everywhere around us, it is said, on the surface of the earth there is going on a struggle for existence, in which, as there is not room for all, the weak must inevitably succumb, while the strong survive and multiply. The order of physical nature constitutes a stern and unchangeable environment which favours, at the expense of all others, those natures which have any special fitness to combat with its hostile, or avail themselves of its favourable, conditions. To all others nature is absolutely merciless. If we can trace advancement or progress in this sphere, it is an advancement every step of which is marked by the crushing out of the feeble, and the survival only of the strongest and fittest. To care for or try to prolong the existence of the weak, if we could conceive such a thing possible, would be suicidal on the part of the strong. It is their interest, the condition of their very life, that the weak should be left unhelped and unimproved till they are swept away by nature's ruthless hand. We have here a system in which the well-being and ultimate perfection and happiness of the few is the end and result, and in which that end is attained and can only be attained by the merciless extinction of the many.

Now if we turn from the natural to the spiritual order, it is no doubt true that there have been interpretations of the latter which would represent it as in this respect precisely analogous to the former. Theological systems in their merciless dogmatism have found in the sphere of intelligence and moral life a principle of supernatural selection as absolute as that of nature, and only differing from it for the worse in being purely arbitrary and capricious. The heaven of the theologian, like that of nature, has been a heaven only for the few, and as for the vast myriads of human beings besides, the analogy has failed only in this, that the hell which nature assigns to its victims is the hell not of endless conscious misery, but simply of annihilation.

But, happily for those who cannot reconcile any such ruthless dogmas with even the most primitive conceptions of justice and beneficence, when we turn to the spiritual world as interpreted by St. Paul's conception of it, we find it to be a world the conditions and laws of which are not only not analogous, but in diametrical opposition, to those which obtain in the natural world. And this law is not an arbitrary one, but is based on the very nature and essence of spiritual life. It is of the very essence of a world of moral and spiritual intelligences to be absolutely exclusive of any such laws as that of natural selection and survival of the fittest and strongest,—to be, on the contrary, a world in which the strong shall find scope for their strength, the fittest shall manifest their fitness, in the preservation, the restoration, the salvation of the weak. Let me briefly attempt to show that it is so.

I may remark, in the first place, that even in the sphere of man's physical or animal life, civilization, and still more religion, is in conflict with, and tends to modify and supersede, that law of natural selection which is fatal to the weak. The physically weak, as society advances, are no longer necessarily at a disadvantage in the struggle for existence. Mind asserts its superiority over the forces of nature and the accidents of outward environment, and in the competition for wealth, power, greatness, a grain of thought goes often further than the utmost that can be achieved by rude and undisciplined animal strength. But it is when intelligence unites itself with the spirit of religion that it tends most palpably to subvert and counteract that law which is merciless to the weak. As Christians, we are followers of One whose chief care was not for the strong, the wealthy, the happy; but for the poor, the down-trodden, the diseased, the feeble and blighted specimens of humanity, who taught men to identify reverence for God with pity and tenderness towards the meanest thing that lives. And in so far as the spirit of Christ has leavened society, it has led to a new care for the feeble and forlorn. Instead of leaving them to the ruthless exterminating force of natural law, it has kindled in men's breasts a new impulse of philanthropy, which makes the sickly, the maimed, the deaf and dumb and blind, even the insane—the imperfect and enfeebled forms of human life—the objects of its especial care. Instead of letting these dwindle and die out, it has quickened ingenuity to prolong their existence and make it tolerable; it has given a new language to the dumb, a second sight to the blind, even a gleam of intelligence and human fellowship to the insane. It repudiates, as altogether foreign to the genius and spirit of Christianity, the cynical selfishness which tells us that it would be well to perpetuate only the finer strains of physical strength and beauty, and let the marred and imperfect die out as only serving to spoil the breed.

But passing from this, I remark that whilst Christianity modifies the law of success to the strongest even in the sphere of man's natural life, it wholly subverts it in the sphere of man's spiritual life. And one reason for this is that spiritual good, unlike physical or material, is not diminished but increased by the multiplicity of participants. Wherever life multiplies faster than the means of living, wherever the demand for a thing tends to outrun the supply, there competition and the struggle for existence arise, there grasping cupidity, rivalry, envy, jealousy, cruelty, oppression, and all the tribe of the selfish passions come into play, there it becomes the interest of the stronger to quell and crush the weak. But a moment's reflection teaches us that there is this essential difference between natural and spiritual possessions, that in the case of the latter, however numerous the competitors, the demand can never exceed the supply. To care for our own souls without caring for the souls of others, still more to do so at the expense of the souls of others, is an absolute impossibility. For that which constitutes the wealth and blessedness of the spiritual life is of such sort that it cannot become mine without becoming yours, nay, becomes more truly mine just in proportion as it becomes yours. Sensuous enjoyment and the means of gratifying it are purely individual things. My pleasant sensation is not yours. Food, drink, soft raiment and personal adornment, fine houses and lands, and even the money that buys them, cannot become yours without ceasing to be mine. I may give them away, but in giving I cease to have them. And when these things are the objects on which men's hearts are set, it is possible for one to gain by another's loss, to grudge what others get, and in the wild scramble and competition for success, that multitudes may be impoverished to promote the wealth and enjoyment of a few.

But with the things of the mind it is not so. Even apart from religion, in the world of thought, of science, art, literature, we see at once that what one possesses does not diminish, but increases, the common property of all. A new idea or discovery in the realm of knowledge is not exhausted by him who first apprehends it, an original thought is not lost to one mind when it passes to another or to a thousand other minds. As knowledge spreads, the ideas, discoveries, intellectual wealth of the world become the possession of an ever-widening circle of participants; while the treasure which is enshrined in the literature of the past, by which myriads of minds have been enriched and ennobled, remains for us still fresh and unexhausted, the unbroken, undiminished inheritance of every mind that has the desire and the capacity to appropriate it. Nay, more than that, it is of the very nature of the wealth of the world of thought to be not only undiminished, but actually increased by sharing it with others; so that with the possession of truth, instead of the tendency to secrete and monopolize, comes the impulse to communicate. With every new discovery in science, every vision of truth or beauty that dawns on the mind of the individual thinker, there is instantly awakened the desire for intellectual sympathy, the impulse to get other minds to recognize the truth we see or to reciprocate the emotion we feel. And in the very process of giving, what we give, instead of being lessened, grows and gains new value for ourselves. In the very endeavour to communicate ideas to others we gain a firmer grasp of them, see them in new lights reflected from other minds, acquire new confirmation and force of conviction from the consent of kindred intelligences.

In the very act of getting others to share in our emotion for what is noble or beautiful, that emotion glows with a richer fervour in our own breasts, comes back upon us intensified from the very consciousness that other hearts are thrilling with the pathos or the passion that stirs our own.

And still more emphatically does this hold good in the religious life. Here, beyond all other spheres, each man's getting is not the loss but the gain of those who already possess. Goodness is of all things that which does not lose but gains by diffusion. Let another mind be kindled from yours by the light of divine love, and the flame of your own piety, instead of being extinguished, will be intensified and brightened by reflexion. If this congregation were composed of men who are one and all imbued with the spirit of Jesus Christ, then by their spiritual contiguity and fellowship, and the electric force of a common element of faith and love passing from heart to heart, the share of each would be redoubled and the common life become ineffably richer than the sum of the individual lives that partake of it.

There is a yet further development of the same thought. In the spiritual world the paradox holds true that what you have is not only not lost by giving it to others, but cannot truly become yours until you have given it away. It is the property of spiritual wealth that loss is gain, that he that saveth his life shall lose it, he that loseth his life shall win it unto life eternal. Selfishness is here not **only a vice** but an absurdity and irrationality, because our true self is never to be realized till we ignore and forget self, **our** highest happiness never to be attained till the very desire for and endeavour after happiness becomes lost and extinguished in our hearts. No doubt it is possible to exaggerate this doctrine of Christian self-sacrifice till it becomes not only fantastic, but self-contradictory. No doubt, in religion as elsewhere, there is a sense in which self-satisfaction, self-realization, is what all men seek and cannot but seek. To desire anything, **to** endeavour **after** any end however noble, is to find my pleasure, happiness, delight therein. The most disinterested beneficence cannot go beyond identifying my **own** satisfaction and enjoyment with the good of others. The most heroic deed that was ever done on earth must still be described as a deed in which the doer sought and found his own joy and bliss. Mystical devotion has sometimes dreamt **of a** suppression of **self, a** losing or absorption of self in God which is simply spiritual suicide; and in so dreaming, the mystic unconsciously contradicts himself, for the very rapture of self-extinction is a rapture of which he conceives himself as being **conscious, and** in the ecstasy of self-extinction he re-creates the self he annihilates.

Nevertheless it is not the less true that in the **spiritual** life it is by losing ourselves that our true self is **won.** It is a moral truism that we mar or prostrate our own happiness by thinking about it and of set purpose pursuing it. To make self our end is the sure way to impoverish the self, to narrow and contract our nature and to dry up the deeper springs of happiness within it. It is when some worthy object or end draws us out of ourselves, bears away thought, feeling, will, energy, with an absorption that leaves no room for the thought of self, that we gain,—unsought, unbidden,— the joy and strength with which that work is fraught. There is exquisite pleasure in the life of thought, in literature, in scientific investigation; but it is not the man who studies for some ulterior end, for money, reputation, success in life, who is haunted by the desire to create an impression, to strike or dazzle the world by his achievements, that knows the full sweetness and gains the reflex ennoblement of which intellectual work is capable. There is a lofty pleasure that pertains to the work of persuasive speech, but the orator who is pursued by the thought of self, under whose seeming fervour runs the restless desire for applause, cramps his powers and falls short of the very oratorical triumph at which he aims. There is elevated enjoyment in art, but that enjoyment reaches its highest pitch only when artistic production has the spontaneity and abandonment of inspiration, when the poet, painter, sculptor, works, not from any calculation as to the pleasure, honour, emolument, his work will bring, but simply because the creative impulse is upon him, because his subject has taken possession of him, because a dream of beauty haunts his imagination, and he cannot choose but seek to realize it.

And the same principle holds good in the moral and spiritual life. Here, above all, it is true that to gain ourselves we must lose ourselves, that we must die to self in order truly to live. What is the sweetest ingredient in the cup of happiness? What, constituted as human nature is, is the kind of life that will bring out and develop the latent wealth and nobleness of the individual nature? To such questions it must, I think, not as a piece of sentimental rhetoric, but as a simple and sober truth, be answered, that the mere pleasure-lover, the man who makes the satisfaction of his individual desires his end, frustrates his own aim, loses his own happiness in the search for it; and that the richest wealth of the human spirit, all its best and highest qualities spring to life, only in merging our individual life in the life and happiness of others. Rare indeed is that love which is absolutely self-forgetting; but of what its blessedness may be you can form some conception, if it has ever chanced to you to know or come across one of those beautiful natures whose existence is heaven's richest blessing to the home or circle in which they live. You can recall, perhaps, the image of such a life—the life of one who seemed to live only to make others happy, who, by a certain sympathetic tact, possessed an intuitive insight into the character and feelings of others, whose thoughtful love anticipated your wants, on whose ready interest in all your perplexities and troubles you could infallibly count, whose own comfort and enjoyment were ever willingly deferred to that of others, who seemed never to be thinking of self, whose gentle presence smoothed the roughnesses and sweetened the harshnesses of domestic life, whose very existence was a sunshine to her home; and yet who was and did all this with a certain sweet grace of spontaneity that half disguised from others the life of daily sacrifice she was leading. Who can doubt of such natures that though they never sought their own happiness, the happiness they sought not came in richest, fullest measure unbidden to their hearts?

And if we turn to life on a larger scale and think of those rare and exceptive cases in which, by the universal verdict, human nature has touched the supreme height of excellence—of those heroic spirits who for the sake of friend or country, for the cause of freedom, for the redress of human wrongs, the alleviation of human sorrows, the salvation of human souls, have counted not their very lives dear to them; and if we ask concerning these whether this sacrifice of individual interest, this suppression and quelling of self, this seemingly reckless squandering of personal enjoyment, was all loss to them; will not the answer be that, as to all that constitutes human greatness and happiness—expansion of thought, deepening of feeling, elevation of the moral nature, the pure unbidden joy and blessedness that crown a life devoted to a great benignant purpose,—to such men loss has been gain, and death to self the portal to a nobler, diviner life?

There is yet one other consideration, which I can only mention, in support of the principle that caring for the welfare, the salvation of others is the law of the spiritual life, and it is this: We must seek the salvation of others because we ourselves cannot be saved without them. For good or ill, according to St. Paul's conception, our spiritual destiny is bound up with that of others. There is a point of view from which we may say that the salvation of each individual is conditioned by the salvation of all. If we think of the salvation of the soul simply as admission to a heaven of safety and happiness beyond the grave, there is nothing in such a conception inconsistent with the possibility of an isolated or exclusive salvation. Our relation to others would be that, at most, of fellow travellers towards a place which it is possible for some to reach irrespective of the general advance. As the caravan moves on under the scorching sun, over the arid waste, the protracted conflict with nature may prove too trying for many, at each successive stage one and another of the weaker sort may give in, fall aside and be left to their fate. It is, at least, a possible thing that only the exceptionally strong and vigorous may ever reach the goal. **When** in the sinking ship the fierce struggle **for** life that brings out the brute element in man arises, the strong may force their way to safety and leave the weak to perish. But St. Paul's conception of human life and its relations is one which **renders** any such separation impossible. It makes an **isolated** salvation as little conceivable as the general health and happiness of the **body can** be thought of as compatible with the pain, weakness, paralysis **of one or more of** its **members** or organs. And indeed, a moment's reflection teaches us that in the spiritual life, so far from the **more** advanced leaving others to their fate, it is just in proportion as they advance in Christian principle that they become more **and more** implicated with the fortunes of the weak, more and more incapable of any salvation in which the latter **have no** share. It may be **even said** that the spiritually strong feel the infirmities of the weak more keenly than the weak themselves, that the burden of the feeble falls on the strong with a heavy and intolerable weight of which the feeble themselves are all unconscious. It is not the ignorant who are most alive to their own ignorance. It is not the erring, the faltering, the morally infirm **and** impotent who are most keenly sensitive to their own shame and degradation; but it is they whose moral perceptions are clearest and who know and love them better than they know and love themselves. **It is** the latter, the good, the holy, the loving, the pure, who see, as they who are living godless lives cannot see, the wealth they are squandering, the hopes they are blighting, the love from which they are shutting themselves out, the infinite possibilities of goodness and blessedness they are blindly foregoing.

What does religion, what does spiritual growth and advancement mean? It means a fuller and richer sympathy with God's boundless love; the nearer a human soul comes to God so much the more does it yearn,—with a compassion which reflects the infinite pity and tenderness,—over the spiritually forlorn and wretched. And if it be so, so much the more does a happiness which is consistent with their ruin become a thing impossible. Can the heart or lungs attain perfect rest when the limbs are racked with pain or the nervous system is disordered? Can a parent, brother, sister, whose heart is the seat of a deep and devoted affection, be in unalloyed enjoyment of individual happiness, aware all the while that those who are dear to them are lying in intolerable pain and wretchedness, or that they have fallen into infamy and guilt? Or could they be content to be wafted away to some far-off region of unbroken felicity where all thought and care for the piteous fate of those who are bone of their bone, flesh of their flesh, shall be drowned in the raptures of personal enjoyment? And can anything analogous to this be the picture of a happiness possible for perfect souls? Does it find its nearest parallel on earth in those whose natures are of noblest, divinest mould, and not rather in those whose better nature has become ossified by selfish indulgence, the basest, meanest, most despicable of our kind? No! it is of the very nature of religion and the religious life to be incapable of an isolated perfection and blessedness. Heaven would be an incomplete and troubled heaven to those who knew that by an irrevocable fiat there were others who could never share in their happiness, never escape from their doom of misery and despair. The cry of one solitary soul in its agony would suffice to mar the eternal harmony. Here or elsewhere in this world, or in regions and worlds unknown, the strong in God shall never be able to tear from their hearts God's own infinite pity and compassion for the infirmities of the weak.

I must here arrest the discussion of the subject, but to avoid misconception, there is one word which I must add in conclusion. I have spoken much of the spiritual life as a life which we share with others, which is destructive of selfish individualism. It is not inconsistent with what I have said to add that there is a sense in which religion deepens human isolation, brings home to us the profound conviction that every man must bear his own burden, and bear it alone. Whether our life be hard and selfish, or open as the day to all the sweet charities and sympathies that unite us to our kind, the responsibility for that life we can never share with others. In the deepest essence of our being, in our moral character and destiny, we are each of us alone before God. To each of us as spiritual, self-conscious beings has been given an incommunicable life, to each of us has been assigned a career of duty which no other can fulfil for him, which in time and eternity he only can accomplish; and the guilt of failure or the glory and blessedness of success will be his and his alone. We are indeed so bound to each other by the ties of home and kindred, by the bonds of love and affection, that it is possible for each of us to mar the lives of others, to disappoint the hopes and blight the happiness of those who have linked their lives with ours. There are perhaps amongst those whom I address not a few who have come to this place of study from homes where, through the years of their past life, they have been the objects of fondest care and affection, for whom perhaps their present opportunities have been gained at the cost of ungrudging self-denial. If your life here be one of manly and conscientious effort, there may be hearts that will beat high at the tidings of your success; if your life here be one of idleness and self-indulgence, of opportunities wasted and talents misemployed, there may be those whom your misconduct will cost many a bitter pang. But, in either case, the result—the growing intelligence, the character strengthened by self-conquest, or, on the other hand, the ignorance and shallowness, the undisciplined mind and enfeebled character—is one which no other can share with you, which, with all the future consequences it involves, is inalienably your own. And the same is true of life as a whole. Whatever our relations to others, we tread each of us a solitary path; of each human soul it is the awful prerogative to be master of its own actions, shaper of its own moral life, creator of its own destiny, whether to make or mar it. We may not feel it to be so now. Amidst the manifold distractions of social and public life, the rush of business, the pleasures of society, we may escape from ourselves and the thought of our individuality and isolation. But whether we realize or evade it, there is coming surely and stealthily to each of us an hour when every earthly association will fall off from us, every social tie be snapt asunder, when the affection that clings to us to the last can follow us no further, and with all the issues of our life for good or evil resting on us, God's ideal of our life fulfilled or frustrated, we must pass onwards on the spirit's solitary path into a world unknown.

CORPORATE IMMORTALITY.

"These all, having obtained a good report through faith, received not the promise: God having provided some better thing for us, that they without us should not be made perfect." HEBREWS xi. 39, 40.

THERE is something at once of exultation and of sadness in the words with which the writer of this book closes his recapitulation of the glorious roll of the saints and martyrs and heroes of ancient times. They were men "of whom the world was not worthy." They were inspired with a noble enthusiasm for great ends, with dauntless fortitude and self-devotion, with an unquenchable faith in things spiritual, with high hopes for the future of humanity. But, judged by the outward eye, their life was a failure: they never attained to the end of their aspirations; one after another, like breaking waves on the strand of time, they were compelled to succumb to the universal limits of human endeavour. In the midst of their noble struggles they were constrained in succession to yield to the inevitable summons, their work unaccomplished, their hopes unfulfilled, the dearest object of their lives nothing better than a far-off goal. "These all died in faith," it is written, "not having received the promises, but having seen them afar off." And again, "These all, having obtained a good report through faith, received not the promise."

At first sight, therefore, the language of the text is simply a repetition of the old refrain, "Vanity of vanities," with which writers, inspired and uninspired, have summed up their trite moralizings over the evanescence and incompleteness of human life. The saddest aspect of human existence, this writer seems to say, is, not simply that it is full of care and sorrow and trouble, but that it suggests the impression of frustration, abortiveness, incompleteness. We never receive the promise. We never are the thing we seem designed to be. There are in our nature the beginnings and materials of great things, but they are never realized. The foundation is ever grander than the superstructure, the outline than the picture, the promise than the fulfilment. We can form soaring ideals of individual and social perfection, but they only serve to throw contempt on the poverty and meanness of our actual life. Human nature seems to be a thing of boundless possibilities but of miserable performances, of capacities which are never, or only feebly and partially, developed, of desires, hopes, aspirations, to which, even when the will to realize them is present, the poor result which our brief life permits us to reach is ludicrously disproportionate.

Moreover, it is precisely in the case of the best and greatest of men that this incompleteness is most marked. If all men were, what so many seem to be, creatures of mere animal and selfish desires, finding all the satisfaction they care for in eating, drinking, money-making, in dress and gossip and foolish display and petty social rivalries and triumphs, there would be no sense of incongruity in the brevity of human life. There would be nothing to startle or surprise us in the fact that an existence of such mean and shallow aims should cease for ever when its brief earthly career had run out. Far less, indeed, than threescore years and ten suffices often to play out that poor plot, to exhaust its whole interest and significance.

But it is when we turn to contemplate human life in its nobler representatives that the sense of unfulfilled promise forces itself on our notice. Its minds of rare and piercing intelligence, filled with the ever-growing thirst of knowledge, catching glimpses on all sides of unexplored regions of thought, into which it would be their delight to penetrate, and who seem to themselves, after the labours of a lifetime, to be only standing on the very outskirts of the realm of truth; its great originative intellects, capable of striking out new discoveries, of penetrating into the secrets of nature, of discerning the wants of society, and of framing comprehensive plans for its amelioration and progress; or, finally, its beautiful, heroic, saintly spirits, refined and purified by the discipline of years, exalted above all that is selfish and sensual, and sometimes doing deeds at the mere recounting of which our hearts thrill with involuntary admiration, and which are the silent prophecy of an unrevealed splendour in the spiritual nature of man,—it is in the case of such natures as these that the cruel limits of life strike us most palpably. The whole being of such men seems moulded on a scale that is pure waste and extravagance, measured by the few and rapid years of our individual life. The infinite hunger for truth and goodness, the thoughts that wander through eternity, the feelings of love and adoration which point to an object nothing less than infinite,—it seems strange and monstrous that these inexhaustible capacities have no longer time for satisfaction than the lust or appetite which an hour will cloy. Of what use the vision of infinite perfection, if the same fell stroke is to shatter it alike with the poorest dream of worldly success? What meaning is there in the capacity of conceiving and living for objects the very least of which it would require many lives to accomplish—in a mind filled with great designs, the results of which it needs generations to develop, or fired with enthusiasm for the progress of the race in civilization and goodness,—when soon and for ever it shall cease to have any more a part in all that is done beneath the sun?

Now it is this view of human life which in the latter clause of our text the sacred writer seems to meet. Is our life indeed an incomplete and broken thing? Is human existence but at the best a splendid failure? Is the promise which our nature contains never fulfilled? The common answer, as we all know, to such questions is that which finds in the notion of the 'immortality of the soul' the solution of the difficulty. The life that seems so incomplete is only a part of man's duration. It will receive its complement in a future world. But whatever truth there is in the notion of individual immortality, it was obviously not this, but another and different idea, which was before the mind of the writer of our text, as that in which he found consolation for the fragmentariness and imperfection of the life of man. "These all died in faith," he writes, "not having received the promises." "These all, having obtained a good report through faith, received not the promise." Their life, replete with immortal hopes, instinct with the spirit and promise of a splendid future, was abruptly terminated. But it was not really so. The promise was not left unfulfilled, the continuity was not broken. Their story has not been left without a sequel. The life they lived is one that is never broken, that never dies, that is ever deepening, developing, ever through the ages advancing to its consummation. Every one of these ancient saints and martyrs, he seems to say, has had a share in the growing life of humanity, and in the Christian Church of his own day he sees only the flower and fruit of the same plant of which they were the seed or germ, the maturity of the same organic life of which the Church of a former day was the childhood or youth. These passed away, he exclaims, and life in them was one of unfulfilled promise. But of that promise *we* are the fulfilment: "God having provided some better thing for us, that they without us should not be made perfect."

Let us for a moment consider what is involved in this view of the spiritual life of man, and try to gather from it the lessons with which it is fraught.

The imperfection which this writer ascribes to the individual lives of a past time arises necessarily from this; that it constitutes the very grandeur and nobleness of human life to be incapable of a purely individual perfection, and that each successive generation can say of the men and the ages that are past, 'They without us could not be made perfect.'

And to see this you have only to consider how all existences rise in the scale of nobleness just in proportion as they are incapable of individual perfection. The stones which are intended to form part of a building lose their separate unity and any independence which might be attributed to them as stones. Taken apart, they might seem unmeaning or even grotesque and unshapely in form and outline. But it would be a foolish and vain thing to try to give them a kind of individual completeness by rounding off a ragged edge here or filling up an unsightly gap there. It is just that which makes them individually imperfect that lends to them the capacity of contributing to a higher perfection. When the stone is built into the shaft or column, or when around and above the unsightly structural fragment rise the other portions which form its complement in the unity of some fair and stately edifice, we perceive how, lacking or losing individual completeness, it has become a sharer in a greater and higher completeness, a necessary contributor to and participant in the perfection and beauty of the whole.

That incapacity of individual perfection is the measure of inherent dignity and excellence is still more clearly seen when we take the example of the living organism. Here, too, as in the previous illustration, we have a multiplicity of individual parts or members, each of which, taken apart by itself, has no worth or significance. Here, too, that which would be a mere imperfect fragment, a maimed or mutilated thing, if disunited from the other members, receives, in its union with them, a share in that larger life, in that symmetry, order, proportion, that excellence and beauty of diversity in unity, which belongs to the organic whole. It is in the absolute surrender of any isolated existence, in the fulfilment of its function, as existing for and contributing to the welfare and growth of the other parts of the organism, that the individual member or organ receives back into itself the fulness of a richer and ampler existence. Its own perfection is impossible without them. So long as in the living organism any one part or member is undeveloped, there is something lacking to the perfection and happiness of the rest. They without it cannot be made perfect.

Lastly, there is this peculiarity in the final perfection of the organism, that it is reached, not, as in the former example, by accretion, but by the perpetual change and renewal of its elements,—by absorption and development. As it rises through its successive stages, the materials of which it is composed do not remain, like the stones of a building, fixed and permanent, one stone or series of stones superimposed on another, each, from foundation to copestone, continuing to the last what it was at the beginning. On the contrary, wherever there is life, its earliest beginnings are present indeed, but in a far more intimate and subtle way, in the beauty and perfection of its latest and highest form. Seed or germ, rising stem, leaf and blossom, fruit and flower, do not continue side by side; the last is the perfection of the first, but it is a perfection attained by unresting mutation, by the seeming extinction and absorption of all that went before.

When you have reached the rich profusion of summer, the tender grace of the vernal woods is a thing that is gone; when you gather the fruit, the gay blossom has passed away. And each successive phase of the living organism, as it passes from the embryo to the full-grown frame of manhood, is the vital result of all that it has been. The past lives in it—it could not be what it now is but for the past,—but nothing of that past remains as it was; it does remain, but it remains as absorbed, transformed, worked up into the very essence of a new and nobler being. The unity of the fully developed life gathers up into it, not by juxtaposition or accumulation, but in a far deeper way, the concentrated results of its whole bygone history. Thus the nobleness of the imperfect life lies in its very imperfection. It is greater than even the most complete and finished of material things, because it is full of yet unfulfilled promise, because the possibilities of an ever-advancing progress are concealed in it, because it contains in it the promise and prophecy of a future without which it cannot be made perfect.

Now it is in this idea, rather than in that of a merely individual immortality, that the writer of the passage before us finds the explanation of the seeming incompleteness and evanescence of human life. It is here that he seeks the solution of that contrast of greatness and littleness, of nobleness and meanness, of beginnings so full of promise and results so poor and insignificant, on which moralists in all ages have been fain to dwell. Regarded from the individual point of view, human life *is* the paradoxical thing which such reflections make it to be. Individual happiness, individual perfection, are never attained; but it is, he declares, the very greatness and glory of man's nature to be incapable of it. The key to the riddle of human life, the explanation of the scale on which our nature is constructed, of the boundlessness of its hopes, the inexhaustibleness of its desires, of its eager longing for a larger, fuller, more lasting life, of the splendour of its ideals, and the dissatisfaction with their best attainments which the noblest spirits feel, is this: that he who lives nobly and wisely, who rises above the narrow life of sense to identify himself with that which is universal and infinite, is sharer in a life of humanity that is never arrested, and shall never die.

It needs little reflection to perceive that the order of things in which we live is not constructed on the principle that we are sent into this world merely to prepare for another, or that the paramount aim and effort of every man should be to make ready for death and an unknown existence beyond the grave. On the contrary, in our own nature and in the system of things to which we belong, everything seems to be devised on the principle that our interest in the world and human affairs is not to terminate at death. It is not, as false moralists would have us believe, a mere illusion, a proof only of the folly and vanity of man, that we do not, and cannot, feel and act as if we were to have no concern with this world the moment we quit it. It is not a mere irrational impulse that moves us when, in the acquisition of knowledge, in the labours of the statesman and legislator, in the houses we build, the trees we plant, the books we write, the works of art we create, the schemes of social amelioration we devise, the educational institutions we organize and improve, we act otherwise than we should do if our interest in all earthly affairs were in a few brief years to come to an end. It is not due to a universal mistake that we work for a thousand ends the accomplishment of which we shall not live to see; that the passions we feel are more intense, the efforts we put forth immeasurably greater, than if we were soon and for ever to have done with it all. Even the desire of posthumous fame, which has been the theme of a thousand sarcasms and satirical moralizings, the passion that impels us to do deeds and create works which men will be thinking of and honouring when we are gone, does not rest on a mere trick of false association which your clever psychologist can explain so deftly, but is the silent ineradicable testimony of our nature to the share we have in the undying life of humanity.

So, again, it is no mere logical abstraction which rises before the mind when we talk of a national life, which embraces and **transcends that** of the individuals who pertain to it, and which, while *they* seem to come and go like shadows, goes on broadening, deepening, developing in knowledge and power and freedom. It **is no imaginative** fiction, for example, but a sober fact to which we refer, when we speak of the silent, steady growth of that organic unity, that system of ordered freedom, which we designate the Constitution of England; or when we say that that constitution is the collective result of all that was valuable in the intellectual and moral and religious life of the myriads who, from the first pioneers of England's civilization downwards, have contributed to her progress; **that all that her** poets have sung, and philosophers taught, **and** statesmen, legislators, warriors, patriots, have achieved —**nay, all that** has been accomplished by thousands **of nameless and** unhonoured **lives** which have been poured out like water in the cause of her civil and religious freedom,—all this, assimilated and transmuted into the very bone and fibre of her social existence, lives yet in that great and still growing personality, the national life of our country.

And when we take a wider range **it is no** mere figure of speech when we say that there is another and still grander personality, which comprehends within it the life of nations as well as of individuals, and which, when the **place** of nations knows them no more, when their function in the providential order of the world has long been finished, and their glory and splendour is a thing of the past, retains in it the elements of spiritual good which it was their vocation to work out, gathered up and transfused into that undying life of humanity without which they could not be made perfect. The perfection of man is not the perfection of the Jew, nor of the Greek, nor of the Roman; but there is a richer, fuller, more complex life, into which the Hebrew consciousness of holiness and sin, the ideal beauty of the Greek, the sense of law and order which Rome left as her legacy to mankind, flow together and are blended in the unity of the Christian civilization of the modern world.

And that too, in its turn, is still far short of that ideal perfection which our Christian faith reveals, and for the realization of which it calls us to live and labour. Eighteen centuries ago a vision of human perfection, a revelation of the hidden possibilities of our nature, broke upon the world in the person and life of Jesus Christ; and as we contrast with this the highest attainments which the best of men or communities have yet reached, it seems an ideal towards which as a yet far distant goal, with slow and stumbling steps, humanity is tending. Yet for *this* at least the belief in it suffices in the hearts that have become penetrated with the sense of its sublime reality and beauty—to assure them that whatever of greatness or goodness in the long course of ages humanity has attained, is but an augury of that splendid future which is yet in store for it. For no ideal of a perfect state, no dream of a golden age or paradise restored which has ever visited the imagination of genius, or risen before the rapt gaze of inspired seer or prophet, can surpass that future of universal light and love which Christianity encourages us to expect as the destiny of our race—that time when human society shall be permeated through and through with the spirit of Jesus Christ, and the whole race, and every individual member of it, shall rise to the point of moral and spiritual elevation which that life represents, when we shall "all come in the unity of the faith, and of the knowledge of the Son of God, unto a perfect man, unto the measure of the stature of the fulness of Christ."

It is then in this idea that we find, as I have said, the true solution of that contrast between the largeness of human desires and hopes and the brevity of human life, between our far-reaching aims and aspirations and the contempt which death seems to pour on them. Death does *not* pour contempt on them. You can think and desire and work for more than the petty interests of your brief individual life, because you *are* more and greater than the individual, because it is possible for you to share in a universal and undying life, with the future of which your most boundless aspirations are not incompatible. It is little indeed that each of us can accomplish within the narrow limits of his own little day. Small is the contribution which the best of us can make to the advancement of the world in knowledge and goodness. But slight though it be, if the work we do is real and noble work, it is never lost; it is taken up into and becomes an integral moment of that immortal life to which all the good and great of the past, every wise thinker, every true and tender heart, every fair and saintly spirit, have contributed, and which, never hasting, never resting, onward through the ages is advancing to its consummation. Live for your own petty interests and satisfactions, waste the treasure of an immortal nature on the lust of the eye and the lust of the flesh and the pride of life, and death will indeed be the destroyer of all your hopes and ambitions. But live for the good of others, live to make your fellow-men wiser and happier and better, take part with those nobler spirits of all time who have striven for the rectification of human wrongs, the healing of human wretchedness, the redemption of human souls from evil, the advancement of the world in knowledge and wisdom and goodness,—live for these ends, and the whole order and history of the world, and that Gospel of Heaven's grace in which we believe as the revelation of God's purpose and plan for our race, must prove a fable, if your hopes and aspirations be doomed to disappointment.

But what, after all, avails for me, does any one ask, this idea of a future perfection of humanity, these hopes and endeavours for a world in whose good or ill I shall soon have no place or part? It is not the immortality of the race, but my own, that is the great and all-important question for me—not whether the progress of mankind shall go on in a world I am so soon to quit, but whether there is another world beyond the grave, and whether death shall find me prepared for it. Even if it be true that this dream of a perfect social state is in some far distant day to be realized in this world, what personal interest can I have in a perfection and happiness I shall never know and in which I shall never participate?

I answer, that the idea of the text, far from destroying, only lends new significance and reality to, the hope of a personal immortality. It leaves the arguments for immortality which reason and Christian faith suggest precisely what they were; only it bids us think of that immortality, not as a vague and shadowy state of blessedness in some unknown existence beyond the grave, but as the realization of those possibilities of perfection which our nature contains, and which are present here and now, ready to be elicited in the earthly life of man. "These all died in faith, not having received the promises." That for which these ancient heroes and martyrs lived and laboured, that which would be to them the crown and consummation of their dearest hopes and the reward of their sacrifice and self-devotion, was not a heaven of dreamy isolated happiness, to which at the hour of death they should withdraw, no longer to be affected by the struggles and sorrows of humanity. They toiled and suffered and died for the good of mankind; their dearest, deepest desires were not for selfish happiness here or hereafter, but for the redemption of the world from evil; this was the heaven they longed for, and the bliss of any other heaven would be incomplete without it.

And we too, if we inherit their spirit, shall feel that for the heaven we seek we need not fly away on the wings of imagination to some unknown region of celestial enjoyment where we shall summer high in bliss heedless of mankind—where, lost in seraphic contemplation, steeped in voluptuous spiritual enjoyment, we shall forget or be unaffected by the good or evil of the world we have left. The materials of our heaven, the elements of that glorious future in which we hope one day to share, are present here, within us and around us, in our very hands and in our mouths. The Divine and Eternal are ever near us. God does not dwell in some far-off point of space; he is not more present anywhere else than on this earth of ours, nor could any local transition or physical transformation bring him nearer. God is here, above, beneath, around us; and the only change that is needed to bring us to the beatific vision of his presence is the quickening and clarifying of human souls. **Purify and ennoble these,** let pure light fill the minds and pure love the hearts of men, and heaven would be here; the common air and skies would become resplendent with a divine glory. The eternal world is not a world beyond time and the grave. It embraces time; it is ready to realize itself under all the forms of temporal things. Its light and power are latent everywhere, waiting for human souls to welcome it, ready to break through the transparent veil of earthly things, and to suffuse with its ineffable radiance the common life of man. And so, the supreme aim of Christian endeavour is not to look away to an inconceivable heaven beyond the skies, and to spend our life in preparing for it, but it is to realize that latent heaven, those possibilities of spiritual good, that undeveloped kingdom of righteousness and love and truth, which human nature and human society contain.

Does any one press on me the thought that, say what we will of the future, death to each of us is near, and no ulterior hope can quell the nearer anxiety as to what is to become of us, and how we are to prepare for that fast approaching, inevitable hour? Then I answer, finally, that to whatever world death introduce you, the best conceivable preparation for it is to labour for the highest good of the world in which you live. Be the change which death brings what it may, he who has spent his life in trying to make this world better can never be unprepared for another. If heaven is for the pure and holy, if that which makes men good is that which best qualifies for heaven, what better discipline in goodness can we conceive for a human spirit, what more calculated to elicit and develop its highest affections and energies, than to live and labour for a brother's welfare? To find our deepest joy, not in the delights of sense, nor in the gratification of personal ambition, nor even in the serene pursuits of culture and science,—nay, not even in seeking the safety of our own souls, but in striving for the highest good of those who are dear to our Father in heaven, and the moral and spiritual redemption of that world for which the Son of God lived and died,—say, can a nobler school of goodness be discovered than this? Where shall love and sympathy and beneficence find ampler training, or patience, courage, dauntless devotion, nobler opportunities of exercise—than in the war with evil? Where shall faith find richer culture, or hope a more entrancing aim, than in that victory over sin and sorrow and death, which, if Christianity be true, is one day to crown the strife of ages? Live for this, find your dearest work here, let love to God and man be the animating principle of your being; and then, let death come when it may, and carry you where it will, you will not be unprepared for it. The rending of the veil which hides the secrets of the unseen world, the summons that calls you into regions unknown, need awaken in your breast no perturbation or dismay; for you cannot in God's universe go where love and truth and self-devotion are things of naught, or where a soul, filled with undying faith in the progress and identifying its own happiness with the final triumph of goodness, shall find itself forsaken.

TRUTH AND FREEDOM.

"Ye shall know the truth, and the truth shall make you free. Henceforth I call you not servants (slaves); for the servant knoweth not what his lord doeth: but I have called you friends; for all things that I have heard of my Father I have made known unto you." JOHN viii. 32; xv. 15.

THE astonishment with which these Jews received our Lord's implied accusation of servitude proceeded, as we see by the narrative, from two causes. In the first place, they were, they alleged, unconscious of being in any such condition, and it was impossible they could be slaves without being aware of the fact. In the second place, the only idea they could form of servitude was that of subjection to an outward master, and if that could not be asserted of them, how could they be held to be other than free? As to the former of these points, we can see that our Lord's words were particularly galling to them, because he quietly took for granted, not only a defect of which they were unconscious, but their lack of that very thing on the possession of which they especially prided themselves. To tell them how to become free was like offering alms to a purse-proud man, or elementary instruction to one who thinks himself unusually well informed. And at first sight it might seem as if their unconsciousness was indeed a sufficient disproof of the charge brought against them. For an evil, it may be said, of which I am unconscious, is no evil. A pain I do not feel, a loss I do not know, is no pain or loss. It takes, at any rate, the sting out of any calamity or affliction if I am utterly insensible to it. What mattered it to these Jews that another man looked upon them as slaves? Whether it was so or not they had all the comfort of thinking themselves free. Is a bondage any real bondage which I do not feel? Is not felt bondage, the sense of checked or resisted inclination, the painful consciousness of being hindered from going where I want to go, or doing or getting what I desire to do or get, that wherein consists the very essence of the thing? Were these men not right, therefore, in thinking that there could in their case be no restraint of liberty when they felt none?

Yet when we look more closely into the matter, we see that this unconsciousness of theirs is no sufficient proof that Christ's description did not apply to them. For, in truth, a slave may be only all the more a slave that he is insensible to his bondage. There is no sense of bondage when the instincts of freedom are unrepressed; but neither is there any when despotism has lasted long enough to kill them out. A man's nature may have become so thoroughly habituated to slavery that he has ceased to know or think of anything better. On the other hand, the very consciousness of bondage is a kind of emancipation. He who has begun to know and feel the irksomeness of his limits, is already, in a sense, beyond them. There must at least be in him some measure of, and sympathy with, what transcends the bounds that hem him in, before he can feel them *as* bounds. Pain is the proof that vitality is not extinct. Shame is the witness that the soul is not utterly lost to goodness. And the blush on the slave's cheek and the sense of degradation in his heart, are at least the sign that he is not *all* a slave.

The second ground on which these Jews repelled our Lord's accusation was, as we see, that their only notion of servitude was that of subjection to an *outward* master. "They answered him, We be Abraham's seed, and were never in bondage to any man: how sayest thou, Ye shall be made free?" The assertion, to any person acquainted with the national history, was a monstrous one; but even had it been consistent with fact, exemption from outward bondage might yet, as our Lord proceeds to show, leave their boast of freedom an empty vaunt. "Jesus answered them, Verily, verily, I say unto you, Whosoever committeth sin is the slave of sin." Far deeper and more degrading than any external subjection is the bondage of him who is the thrall of his own baser self; whose hands may be free, yet who has yielded up his soul to the sway of evil passions and desires, or let his mind be mastered by irrational prejudices or superstitious fears. Under the most galling external tyranny, a tyranny which represses civil, social, even individual and personal liberty, following you into your home and laying its hateful restrictions on the most sacred relations and most private actions of your life, there is still a shrine to which freedom may fly, a sanctuary to which no tyrant's emissary can follow you. In the unchecked movement of thought, in the activities of the spirit, despising the oppression to which you are compelled to submit, you may still be free. But what if the master be one whom you have introduced into your very soul; what if the bondage, say of sensuality, or selfishness, or covetousness, is one which has been woven around your affections, your conscience, your will, so that you cannot think your own thoughts nor carry out your own volitions, nor be your own self? If it would be bad to have a tyrant dwelling continually within your home, is it not a worse thraldom to have him dwelling within your heart? What, then, if your burden is such that there is no place sacred from a hateful intrusion, no tranquil hour or moment when you are safe from the inroad of foul thoughts and evil recollections, and the degrading eruption of licentious impulses to which, though in the very act of gratification you despise yourself for yielding to them, your enfeebled and enervated will cannot choose but yield? Surely, if to be given up to the **mastery of** a power **that never** quits us, whose rule we know to be base, **from whom in our** better moments we would fain be free, yet **with whom we** feel it vain to struggle,—if this be bondage, and **there** be one being in all the world to whom the name is applicable, of him of whom this can be said **it may** emphatically be pronounced that he is a *slave.*

But the kind of slavery which our Lord had here in view is not simply or mainly that to which I have just referred—subjection or servitude to our lower appetites and **passions;** for besides the slave of sin, **he proceeds to speak** of one who is a slave in God's house, **side by** side with his own child: "The slave abideth not in the house for ever: but the Son abideth ever." It is the master's house in which both slave and son **are,** but they bear a very different relation to him. We may carry the degradation of a slavish spirit into the service of God. Our very religion may have in it the baseness of servitude. In order to be a religious man it is not enough to profess belief in God and his word, to obey God's command, to abstain from vices and sins, to lead a decorous and respectable outward life. That is well, and when you have got so far, you may, in a **sense,** be said to be in God's house; but you may be **there only** as a hireling or slave is in the house of the master. Now it is this kind of slavery more specially than open subjection of the soul to sin, to which the words of the text, "Ye shall know the truth, and the truth shall make you free," are applicable.

And if we proceed to ask what this kind of bondage is, and how knowledge of the truth gives us spiritual emancipation from it, on this point our Lord instructs us still further in the second text which I have quoted from the same Gospel: "Henceforth I call you not servants (or slaves); for the servant knoweth not what his lord doeth: but I have called you friends; for all things that I have heard of my Father I have made known unto you." Your condition of servitude passes away, is the idea, when you do God's will intelligently as friends and not blindly as slaves, when you come to know and sympathize with the spirit or principle of the commands you have hitherto blindly obeyed. The mind and will of God has been to you an outward and arbitrary law; now that the spiritual significance and grounds of it have been made known to you, you do it, not merely because you are ordered to do it, but because you know and take delight in it; you obey it henceforth, not as slaves, but as intelligent agents, as sympathizing friends. "Ye shall know the truth, and the truth shall make you free." Let us dwell on this thought for a moment.

A servant may obey his master's will without any intelligent apprehension of its meaning, or sympathy with his intentions and aims. If he be sent on an errand, he may carry correctly the words of a message which he does not understand. He may go on a mission the nature of which is quite above his apprehension, simply following out certain precise directions without any discretionary power of action. He may construct, if he have mechanical skill, an elaborate piece of mechanism, simply working, bit by bit, according to the detailed plan or drawing placed before him. But suppose that by diligent study the workman's mind has become developed and his knowledge increased, so as to enable him to understand the *principle* and enter with intelligent appreciation into the idea of the thing; or even more than that, suppose advancing knowledge and culture have raised him generally into a capacity of sympathy and fellowship with the master's mind—then, in that case, though he might continue to obey the master's behests, there would be a complete change in the character of the work. Even though he might continue outwardly to do the same work, or to be employed in executing the same commissions as before, they would be no longer really the same. *Formerly* he could do nothing without book, he could not move a single step without specific directions. *Now*, all that would be necessary would be to explain to him generally the object or end aimed at, leaving him to carry it out at his own discretion and from the resources of his own intelligence. *Formerly*, if new and unforeseen emergencies arose and there was nothing in the plan or instruction directly applicable to them, he would be at his wits' end. There would be nothing for him but to give it up, or wait for further explicit directions. *Now*, knowing the principle of the thing, he would have no difficulty in applying it to the new exigency. His own originative intelligence would be an inner directory, a revelation of the absent master's mind, better than any fresh verbal or written communication, of the authenticity of which he might not be sure, and the meaning of which might be misinterpreted. Finally, the spirit in which the work would now be done would be immeasurably improved. He would do it no longer as a hireling for the sake of the wages, but from love to the work itself, finding an immediate interest and delight in accomplishing it, realizing his own mind in doing it. And as all work is done best that is done lovingly, so in all he did there would be a new grace and freedom of touch, a spirited vivacity and originality, a lavish, ungrudging fulness and finish, as of a hand that lingered lovingly over its work and spared nothing to make it perfect. Of a man thus emancipated by sympathetic intelligence from the slavery of work done by rote, might we not say, 'He now knows the truth, and the truth has made him free'?

Now, it is by this analogy that our Lord explains the secret of that freedom to which it is the design of

Christianity to raise us. Consider for a moment what it implies, both as to our knowledge of God's will and as to the manner in which we fulfil it.

First, as to the former: we are free, our Lord teaches us, in the reception of a revelation of God's mind and will, only when we have insight into its truth, when we enter with spiritual apprehension into its meaning and essence. There are two quite different attitudes of mind in which we may accept the contents of a book—say Euclid's *Elements* or Butler's *Analogy*. We may assent to their truth because a man to whose superior intelligence we defer assures us that they are true; or we might possibly accept them if somebody wrought a miracle to accredit them; or we might profess to believe them, and even think we believed them, if preferment and our prospects in life turned upon our assenting to them, or if we should be ruined or burnt at the stake if we rejected them. On the other hand, our belief in the book may be due to this, that we have ourselves gone over every step in each demonstration, or carefully examined and convinced ourselves of the cogency of the arguments on which each successive doctrine is based, and seen into the coherence and systematic consistency of the whole work. So there are two different attitudes of mind in which we may accept a book purporting to contain divine truths. We may receive it merely because we are told that it is true, in blind submission to some external authority, or because we are overawed by the signs of a physical omnipotence which are alleged to be its credentials, or because we have been persuaded that we shall be saved if we assent to it, and damned if we doubt or reject it;—and then the attitude of our minds toward it is a servile or slavish one. Our spiritual intelligence is not quickened and developed by communion with the infinite wisdom, but arrested and quelled. Only then, on the other hand, are we spiritually enfranchised when we receive a revelation as from God, not because we are awed or terrified or allured by our selfish interests into the reception of it, but because our own minds and hearts respond to it, because we see and know it to be true.

There are many good people to whom it seems to be the most pious and reverential attitude towards divine revelation to say, 'Here is a book the divine authority of which has been proved by miraculous credentials, and every word that is contained in it I will, therefore, implicitly accept and believe; here are certain doctrines which prophets, apostles, inspired and infallible teachers have communicated to the world; it is only for me with unquestioning faith to receive their teaching, and without presuming to judge of the reasonableness of what they say, to take it on trust as the very mind and will of God.'

But, however humble and reverent such language may sound, it is, I make bold to say, the language, not of faith but of unbelief; at any rate, it indicates a state of mind which is yet far short of that depth of conviction of the truth of God's Word which Christianity demands. For that faith for which Christ calls, and which it is our high privilege to be capable of rendering, is not the faith which says, 'I believe this to be God's Word because wonderful physical miracles and prodigies have been wrought in support of it'; but that rather which can say, 'This is the truth of God; I see it, I believe it, I know it, and though heaven and earth should come together to disprove it, my faith in it would not be shaken.' So again, it is but a shallow and superficial belief which says, 'I accept this as a revelation of God's mind, because inspired and infallible men have taught it.' On the contrary, only *then* have I reached the deepest conviction, only then does faith stand on the impregnable rock of certitude when I can say, 'I know this to be the truth of God; its teaching has touched the deepest springs of thought and feeling within my breast, it has awakened my conscience, moved my heart, kindled my aspirations after a purer, better life, brought peace and rest to my spirit, and though a thousand authorities should contradict it, though Paul or an angel from heaven should teach another doctrine, I will not, cannot receive it.'

Nor is there any lack of humility in taking up this attitude of mind. It expresses the truest humility, because the humility of knowledge is ever deeper than the humility of ignorance. There is, no doubt, a kind of humility in rendering blind and unintelligent submission to the arbitrary will of a being whose character I do not understand and whose mind I cannot comprehend. The savage who cowers in abject wonder and awe before the unknown and irresistible powers of nature is the very type and embodiment of such humility. But is *his* humility less real who has learned to look on the world with the eye of intelligent admiration, to discern therein the all-pervading presence and the mighty movements of law, of ordered sequence, of exquisite adaptation of means and ends? In like manner there may be humility of a sort in the blind acceptance of an oracular book. But if, instead of demanding dumb and passive submission, the book is one in whose contents I find that which appeals to all that is highest and purest in my nature, which at once elicits and responds to those infinite aspirations that are the stamp of a nature made in God's image, which discloses to me eternal truths that shed a flood of light on the deepest problems of human existence, and which, while they give new scope and satisfaction to thought, yet the longer I study them, leave me with the sense of an inexhaustible and unfathomed wealth of thought beyond—say, if in the faith which such a book calls forth, in the recognition of its depth and grandeur, in the free intelligent homage I render to its spiritual persuasiveness and power, there be not a profounder reverence and humility than in abject submission to the oracular and the infallible.

And now consider, lastly, how the knowledge of the truth gives us freedom, not only in thought, but in action, not merely in discerning, but also in doing God's will. An act is free when it is the expression of your own thought and will, when your own nature and your whole nature goes with it. If in what you do you are merely doing blindly another's bidding, following mechanically the directions laid down for you, you may be a useful tool, a convenient instrument of a master's purposes, but your work is not your own, but his; you are not free. To make you free, the work itself must constitute or contain the motive of your activity. The satisfaction or delight of doing it, and not any ulterior end or object, must be all in all to you. In the measure in which any other motive,—hope or fear, desire of honour or reward, dread of punishment or disgrace, nay, even a sense of duty or obligation,—interferes or intermingles with your activity, in that measure you are not free.

This does not mean, indeed, that the agent must necessarily have himself originated the design or plan of the work he executes, that his work is not free if there is higher and more comprehensive mind under which he is content to work. But it means that if it be so, if you do follow or endeavour to realize the conceptions of another, your own soul must have caught, in some measure, the inspiration of his genius, and become fired with an enthusiasm akin to his own. For all noble work is work that is done with delight, that has in it something of the spirit of originality and freedom. There is ever a nameless charm, a subtle grace and excellence in work that witnesses to the spontaneity of the hand that did it. In the erecting of a noble building, for instance, all who are employed must follow the architect's design; but a great art critic has told us that ever in the noblest edifice of mediæval and of modern times, it can be observed that free play has been given to the artistic skill and originality of the workman. In the free handling, for instance, of the floral ornamentation of capitals, in the elasticity, grace, and variety of the forms of leafage, in the delicacy of feeling and freshness of spirit that can be infused into the moulding of arch and column and traceried window, it is possible to discern the labour of hands that wrought, not by mere prescribed plan and rule, but under the inspiration of a mind in sympathy with the spirit and genius of the work. An accomplished musician, again, is not necessarily the composer of what he sings or plays; but in the rendering of the works of the great masters of this art, a competent ear can at once detect the difference between the soulless, wooden exactitude which by long drill and practice any school-girl may compass, and the life and power and pathos, the freedom of touch and flow of expression which characterize the performance of one who has caught something of the spirit that inspired the work, and reproduces it with a kindred intensity of feeling.

And so, too, must it be with that highest of all arts, the art of goodness, of working out God's design for our existence, of making music of our lives, of building up the being that we are. Here, too, the original idea is not our own. A higher thought and will has conceived for each human spirit the ideal perfection, the noble harmony of virtues which rounds into the perfect whole of a pure and beautiful and Christian life. But here, too, in order to realize it, the conception is one which must not only reveal itself to our intelligence, our reason, our conscience, but must also enkindle our affections and flow into our will. We must not merely recognize the law of duty as an obligation laid upon us by a Divine Lawgiver. We must become inspired with that passion for perfection, that spontaneous love of goodness and of God which turns service into freedom. The demand that Christ makes upon us, "Be ye therefore perfect, even as your Father which is in heaven is perfect," can never be fulfilled till we rise above even the position of law and morality, of conscientious obedience to duty, and a life ordered in conformity to the will of God. It is no doubt a great thing to be a conscientious man. We cannot help respecting and honouring the man who methodically and deliberately orders his life, not by regard to public opinion, not from the desire of safety and happiness present or future, but simply from a sense of right and in obedience to the supreme conviction of duty enthroned within his breast. There is ever a certain dignity and nobleness in self-command, in a life of repressed inclinations and restrained passions and actions uniformly regulated by the dictates of reason and conscience; and our sense of the stern dignity of such a life is, from one point of view, enhanced by the amount of struggle and self-discipline which it costs to maintain it. When, for instance, a man of intense sensuous susceptibilities puts a bridle on his passions, checks with iron resolve the waywardness of thought, turns away from tempting scenes and objects, or in the midst of their allurements deviates not one hair's-breadth from the self-determined path of purity and temperance; or, again, when a man of a naturally cold, self-absorbed, unsympathetic temperament lays down for himself rules of practical beneficence, and submits to great sacrifices of time and money and labour for philanthropic objects,—in all such cases of rational self-discipline, the persistent subjugation of impulse by reason and conscience, creates a character of no ignoble order, and one which calls forth just respect.

And yet, dignified and praiseworthy though it be, it

is still a character which falls far short of Christ's ideal. For the state of mind which our Lord contemplates as the realization of perfect spiritual freedom is reached only when duty has ceased to be a thing of deliberate self-denial, and has become itself the sweetness and the joy of life. Christ declares that it is possible for a man to attain to such a temper and frame of spirit, that doing the will of God shall be to him a kind of self-indulgence, the expression of an irresistible inward impulse, the gratification of the deepest passion of his soul. His moral life will no longer have the character of obedience, even to a Master whose authority his reason recognizes, but that of the unconscious service rendered to One who has touched our hearts and captivated our affections, and awakened in us a devotion that binds us to his service by an imperious yet sweet and joyous enthralment. The man who rises to this spiritual elevation of nature may still be a creature of appetites and passions, of sensuous impulses and desires; but, according to Christ's conception, under the all-dominating force of a new and more potent affection, there will be no longer any painful or protracted struggle with these. Do not we know how work loses its irksomeness when a strong passion urges us to do it? We know that even an intense earthly passion or desire taking possession of our nature will give us an easy and almost unfelt supremacy over other desires, which otherwise it would be hard to conquer—that ambition, or love of fame or honour, for instance, will quell sensuality, indolence, the love of money, or pleasure and personal indulgence; or again, that ardent love or patriotism, taking deep hold of a human spirit, will bear down before it, without the sense of effort, all other and meaner impulses, and make it no hardship to sacrifice self, to undergo pain and toil and danger and disaster, for its object. And so, what Christ contemplates is the awakening of a new and commanding principle within the breast—a love to him who is the supreme ideal of all that is divinely fair and holy and good, more entrancing, conferring a superiority to self more magnanimous, more ennobling, more sustaining, more capable of rousing those who are swayed by it to labour and sacrifice and endurance, that have lost all their severity and become transmuted into sweetness, than any earthly principle or passion by which the spirit of man can be impelled.

Alas! as we depict this exalted ideal of human goodness, how far, how very far short of it, are we not constrained to confess, is the life which most of us are living. To very many of us religion is a thing which has its source in our fears, our interests, our hereditary traditions, our social conventions, at best our intellectual convictions. How seldom has it gone deeper than all that, to entrench itself in our affections, to become that for which such expressions as these are no longer exaggerations—"I delight to do thy will,

O my God: yea, thy law is within my heart"; "I count all things but loss for the excellency of the knowledge of Christ Jesus my Lord."

Nevertheless, as Christian men and women, it is this we should aim at; with nothing short of this should we be content. For as all things are a bondage to us till our hearts be in them, as our work in life, our profession, our calling, our social duties and relations, the very ties of home and kindred are a drag upon us, if our heart be not in them; so our religion can then only cease to be a yoke upon our necks, a heavy servile task work, when our whole nature—mind, heart, soul, the convictions of our reason, the witness of our conscience, the constraining force of our affections—go with it. For then only in us shall our Lord's saying be fulfilled, "Ye shall know the truth, and the truth shall make you free."

THE GUILT AND GUILTLESSNESS OF UNBELIEF.

"If we believe not, yet he abideth faithful: he cannot deny himself." 2 TIMOTHY ii. 13.

Is unbelief a sin? Are doubts, difficulties, aberrations in matters of religion, of the nature of moral delinquency? Can the attaining of correct opinions be the condition on which a man's fate, either in this world or the next, is made to turn? If he has the misfortune to entertain doubts as to the credibility of certain facts or the authority and interpretation of certain documents, or the logical accuracy of the deductions by which certain doctrines are established, are we right in excluding him from all Christian fellowship, and, if he die in his unbelief, in regarding him as finally rejected of God? There can be no question that there is much in the language of Scripture which may be made, and has been made, to sanction the affirmative answer to these questions, that is, which seems to sanction the assertion that belief in certain objective facts and doctrines is essential to salvation, and that he who rejects, or doubts, or hesitates to accept them, does so at the peril of his soul's salvation. It is this doctrine which seems to be taught in such familiar passages as these: "Without faith it is impossible to please him"; "That whosoever believeth in him should not perish, but have eternal life"; "He that believeth on the Son hath everlasting life: and he that believeth not the Son shall not see life; but the wrath of God abideth on him"; "He that believeth and is baptized shall be saved; but he that believeth not shall be damned." And to adduce no other passage, that which I have taken as the text of this sermon seems not merely to maintain the same proposition, that faith is the condition of salvation, but to go further, and point out the reason or principle on which it is based, namely, that the penal consequences of unbelief are not arbitrary but involved in the very nature of the unchangeable God. To suppose it possible for an unbeliever to escape from the penalty of his religious errors would be to ascribe self-negation, self-contradiction to the Immutable, or, which is the same thing, inconstancy to that absolute and unalterable moral order by which the universe is governed. Into whatsoever regions and worlds unknown the doubter or disbeliever may go, unless he can go where eternal truth can become falsehood, infinite righteousness change into iniquity or wrong, and God give the lie to himself, his unhappy fate is sealed: "If we believe not, yet he abideth faithful: he cannot deny himself."

There are, however, certain obvious considerations which lead us to question whether inspired authority can really sanction the notion that unbelief is penal, that honest doubt or conscientious error can bring down upon man the irrevocable wrath of the Almighty. To many minds it is almost a truism that mistaken opinions may be absolutely blameless; and the grounds on which this is maintained are so familiar as scarcely to bear recapitulation. Belief or unbelief, it is said, are acts to which neither merit nor blame can be attached, simply because, in the last resort, they are purely involuntary. Produce satisfactory evidence to a man of sound mind, and however reluctant he may be to admit the thing proved, his understanding yields its assent by a law as necessary as that by which a physical or chemical result follows under given conditions. In matters of demonstrative certainty every one sees this to be beyond question. When you work out a sum in arithmetic, or an algebraic equation, or a problem in geometry, the conclusion follows entirely independently of the will, it forces your assent whether you will or no; and if, after having done your best, you do not see it, no demerit can be ascribed to you except that of being dull or puzzle-headed. And even in matters that are not demonstrative but probable, where the conclusion depends on a careful weighing of conflicting proof, or on generalization from a multiplicity of scattered and diversified facts and instances, though here of course the risk of error is much greater, the moral merit or demerit of the result is just the same. In a question of historic criticism, in a civil or criminal investigation in a court of law, in a medical diagnosis, in the examination and verification of a scientific hypothesis, the result turns purely on our competence to observe and compass the facts, and to deduce correctly their significance. And if, in any such case, a man does his best, the conclusion to which he comes, whether it take the form of assent, or dissent, or suspended judgment, may indeed be a test of intellectual vigour, but evinces no moral qualities whatsoever. Whether the characters and events of the early period of Roman history are mythical and fictitious, or Romulus and Remus, Numa and Egeria, are as real historic personages as Cato and Cæsar; whether Mary Queen of Scots was cognizant of Darnley's murder or altogether innocent of it; or, again, whether the atomic theory of matter, or the theory of natural selection, or that of spontaneous generation has been satisfactorily or with great probability established,—are questions on which different investigators may and do reach very different convictions. The conclusion *you* have reached may be the right one, and it is possible you may be correct in thinking that those who differ from you are of feebler capacity, and their opinion less worthy of respect than your own. But you would never think of ascribing moral guilt to them, of insisting that they should be regarded as suspicious characters, or that they should be condemned and punished for their involuntary and conscientious mistakes.

When we turn to the special province of religious belief, there does not seem to be anything there which renders these considerations inapplicable to it. There is no apparent reason why there should be one canon of historical criticism for events that are said to have happened in Italy and another for events that are said to have happened in Palestine, one way of testing the authenticity, or of construing and developing the ideas of books written by Greek or Roman authors, and another and different one for books written by Jews; nor can the attitude of the mind which applies and honestly works out these principles be considered more or less meritorious or censurable in the one case than in the other.

Is religious belief of the nature of assent to matters of fact? Does it turn on the question whether certain persons lived and acted, and certain extraordinary events occurred, under certain conditions of time and place more or less remote from the enquirer? What course, then, is open to the searcher after truth but to collect and sift the evidence, oral or documentary, for the alleged facts, to reject what is, to the best of his judgment, ambiguous or unreliable, to accept what is trustworthy, and, having carefully weighed and deliberated, to determine as the evidence leads him? If the facts be true, and he come to the conclusion that they are, so much the more credit may be due to his sagacity, his judgment, his powers of patient and persevering investigation. But suppose, after the most careful enquiry, he feels constrained to come to an opposite conclusion; suppose he cannot disabuse himself of the conviction that a more or less fabulous element has insinuated itself into the historical books of the Old Testament, or that the record of Christ's sayings and doings in the fourth Gospel is in many points irreconcilable with that of the synoptic Gospels, and that it is imbued with ideas, allusions, forms of thought and expression that betray a much later origin than the age of the Apostles; or suppose that, as to some of the great events of the life of Christ, the most careful study of the works of apologists, harmonists, critics, leaves on his mind a painful sense of uncertainty—what shall we say or think of the man who has the misfortune thus to doubt or disbelieve facts of which we may be thoroughly convinced? We may deem his judgment weak or inaccurate, we may have a poor opinion of his powers as a critic or historical investigator; but can or ought we to think the worse of his moral and religious character; or can we bring ourselves to believe it possible that his soul shall be finally lost because of his historical blunders and critical inaccuracies?

Or again, is religious belief not simply assent to facts, but also and mainly the acceptance of certain doctrines contained in inspired books? Here again, it is maintained by many, we find it just as difficult to see how faith can be made the condition of salvation, doubt or unbelief a just ground of condemnation. Scripture is not a book of ready-made theological dogmas, nor is its teaching of such a kind as to prevent the widest doctrinal diversities even amongst those who are at one in acknowledging its divine authority. The doctrines which men educe from its informal and unsystematic language depend greatly on the canons of interpretation—literal, allegorical, rhetorical, rational, or other—which they adopt, and these again on the measure of their general enlightenment and comprehensiveness of mind. They depend also on the logical and philosophical method by which men try to determine the significance of its ideas, to analyze, compare, combine, and give systematic unity and coherence to its often verbally contradictory statements. They depend not a little on the power to elicit general principles from historic facts, events, conversations, letters, to throw off what is due merely to local colouring and the conditions of a past age, and to extract and apply the principles underlying them to the ever-changing exigencies of mankind. All this obviously involves an intellectual process, at every step in which, with the best intentions, error is possible. Notoriously, theological doctrines, even those which are deemed of fundamental importance, have been the subject of long and interminable controversies and divisions amongst divines and churches, all alike professing to derive from Scripture their religious belief. If, then, the religious enquirer does fall into doctrinal error more or less grave, if plausible arguments should betray his judgment into Pelagian, or Arminian, or Socinian opinions; or if he cannot come to any satisfactory decision as to whether the Catholic or the Protestant doctrine of grace, sin, justification, is the true one; or if he have the misfortune to come to the conclusion that the Athanasian dogmas concerning the Trinity and the Person of Christ are only meaningless metaphysical subtleties,—does this result, however much you may deplore it, prove anything more than the intellectual difficulty of forming correct theological opinions and the liability of the individual mind to mistakes and errors—mistakes and errors for which neither God nor man can justly condemn us?

From these considerations it is held by many that belief and unbelief are matters absolutely innocent, and that the only conceivable arrangement, under which true theological opinions could be made the condition of salvation, would be the existence of an infallible living authority to whose dictates all might be required to submit. In that case, and in that case alone, could the refusal to renounce honest differences, or persistence in doubt, suspense or unbelief as to any theological dogma, be regarded as criminal, as resistance to the known mind and will of God.

Whilst, however, to some minds these arguments seem to be clear and irrefragable, there are other, and, as it appears to many earnest Christian thinkers, still more cogent considerations which lead to the conclusion that religious unbelief is not innocent, that for our opinions in religious matters we are justly held responsible, and that our doubts, errors, aberrations, expose us to God's anger and will be righteously punished as sins. I shall enquire briefly whether and to what extent this conclusion is true.

Unbelief may, of course, spring from moral causes, and in so far as it does so, we are justly held accountable for it. In many ways, more or less direct or subtle, our ideas, opinions, notions are not the result of a purely intellectual process, but reflect, or are modified by, our moral condition and character. An evil, immoral life may induce scepticism as to ideas which it requires a pure heart to see, and as to doctrines which it would be terrible for the sceptic to believe. Selfishness is colour-blind to the divinity of love and sacrifice; and the wish that there may be no God may be father to the thought that He is not. Even to so poor a motive as intellectual vanity, the pride of mental freedom and independence, the pleasure of self-assertion, the conceit of superiority to universal prejudices and of discovering the fallacy of what all the world believes; or, again, to a carping, questioning, over-critical habit of mind, never at rest but when it is doubting—to these and similar tendencies into which, more or less, a moral element enters, doubt and unbelief may frequently be traced. And though even here, it is not strictly the act of belief or unbelief, but the motive or state of mind which leads to it, that is censurable, yet, in a general way, it may be said that in such cases unbelief is not involuntary, not a mere intellectual mistake, but a sin. In short, wherever, and in so far as, an element of will enters into our religious errors, the same penal character attaches to them as to all other immoral acts.

This, however, is ground so often trodden, that I need not further insist upon it. There is another argument on which the penal character of religious unbelief has been maintained, and which seems to be one which is sanctioned by the text of this sermon. It is, however, an argument which may be, and has been, pressed too far, and can be accepted only under a modification which, after stating what the argument is, I shall point out.

The argument for the penal character of unbelief to which I refer, is that which appeals from theory to fact and experience, and to the necessary sequence of cause and effect. However clear it may seem to you theoretically, that we ought not to be punished for our mistaken or false opinions and beliefs, we live in a world in which we are punished, often severely and mercilessly punished, for our opinions, if they chance to be erroneous or false. Let a man doubt or disbelieve in the existence of any one of the great forces of nature or of the innumerable and invariable conditions by which the material world is governed, and sharp, swift, and severe often is the penalty that follows. Let a man reject sound teaching or hold erroneous opinions as to the laws of health and the sanitary conditions on which human life depends, and nothing will save him—no theory as to the innocence of error —from the chronic debility or sudden and fatal disease which is the penalty of his unbelief. Let the scientific theorist construct his new mechanism, his locomotive or his ironclad ship, on a plan which overlooks or contravenes some one of the physical conditions involved in the experiment, and however elaborate and careful his investigations, however honest his conviction that everything has been done to ensure success, the disastrous result—the terrible railway accident or shipwreck, with the loss and the destruction of human life it involves—will show how inexorably nature punishes unbelief in her laws, and how absolutely disdainful she is of the plea of honest mistake or conscientious error, in the infliction of her penalties.

Calmly, quietly, constantly the great mechanism of the universe moves on its majestic **course**, its sequences never interrupted, its results wrought out with **absolute**, undeviating certainty. Believe in it, and with inexhaustible generosity nature rewards your faith; doubt, mistake, misapprehend it, and with remorseless sternness the sentence falls on you, If **we** believe not, yet *she* abideth faithful; she **cannot** deny herself.

And the same principle which holds good in **nature**, obtains also, it is maintained, in the higher world of spirit. **As** there is a natural or physical, so also there is a moral and spiritual order, so also there are spiritual **facts** and laws which exist and work out their inevitable results independently of our true or false opinions with respect to them. As in the former case so in the latter, we are left free to disbelieve or doubt and reject them, but as surely it is at our peril that we do so. They never are, nor can be, arrested to save us from the consequences of our unbelief. Believe, and you are blessed; believe not, and you are condemned and punished, by a sequence as necessary **as** that by which he who believes in wholesome food is nourished, and he who mistakes **poison for** it is destroyed. It is not an **arbitrary** thing that your whole spiritual happiness **and** well-being depend on your believing in God, in Jesus Christ, in duty, in **immortality.** Say that a man has honestly come to the conclusion that this life is all, that the few brief and hurried years of our earthly career include all of thought and activity, of joy and hope, that are possible for man; and that every hour the lengthening shadow is bringing us nearer to the time when ours shall be the fate of the brutes that perish,—will not this opinion carry with it even here its own retribution—a retribution which no arbitrary power inflicts, and from which no power can save us? The question is not whether the man who so thinks is made a worse man morally by removal of the hope or fear of a world to come; for the morality that is only born of terror is little worth, and the man who would be a liar or profligate if he did not believe in hell, is not a good man because, believing in it, he speaks the truth and lives chastely. But, it is asked, 'Is it not the sad yet irreversible penalty of his unbelief that he passes his life deprived of the consolation, the strength, the patience, the courage, that arise from the inspiring and ennobling hope, amidst all life's struggles and sorrows, that beyond its narrow horizon there is a better life than this?' As he looks around on a world rife with care and crime and sorrow, is it possible for a man to be no less tranquil and happy, that he has persuaded himself that there is no higher destiny for humanity than this; or when he bends over the open grave of one who was dearer to him than life, is it no dire penalty that falls on the heart of the doubter or denier of immortality to think, as he does, that the farewell to love and goodness is a farewell for ever?

Or again, take, as another example, the first great truth of religion, the existence and character of God and his relations to the world. Is it possible, it may be asked, for errors, mistakes, doubts as to this, to be, as respects a man's temporal and spiritual welfare, matters of indifference? There are in the human spirit religious instincts that seem to point to an infinite object; desires, aspirations, inexhaustible longings that press beyond the bounds of the world of sense and sight, that find utterance in prayer, and rest and peace in the divine response that seems to come back to it. Is it nothing as regards the happiness of a human soul that these high instincts should be stifled, that we should come to think of the Hearer of prayer as an anthropomorphic illusion, and the answer that seems to come to us from the world unseen as only the echo of our own vain cry sent back upon the empty winds? If the loss of faith in *human* love and truth would be to any man a terrible calamity, if to cease to believe in *man* would have a hardening, degrading, desolating effect on the mind, can it be that the loss of faith in God should have no like penalty attached to it? Is the world not less bright, the future not darker to him who believes in no Eternal Righteousness enthroned above the tumult of human passions and the changes that make havoc of human happiness;

in no Father on whose arm we can lean our weakness, to whose ear we can confide our sorrows, on whose everlasting bosom at last we shall lay us down to rest? Here surely is a case in which we cannot maintain that belief and unbelief are matters of indifference if we only hold our opinion honestly and sincerely.

Finally, to take but one other example from what are called the peculiar doctrines of the gospel, is there no penalty which necessarily follows the rejection of the doctrine of the incarnation or of the atonement? Can the man who cannot or will not bring his mind to accept these doctrines be left in the same position as to happiness, here or hereafter, with the man who has cordially assented to them? Belief in Christ is no arbitrary condition of salvation. If in the person of Jesus Christ there has been vouchsafed to us a new idea of God, transcending all that the world has otherwise been able to attain to; if humanity has reached in him a point of moral and spiritual excellence, has discovered in itself capacities of goodness and untold possibilities of greatness, has been invested with a grandeur which lends to human aspiration new and unparalleled energy; if in the life and death of Christ a revelation has been made to us of a love in God which embraces even human ingratitude and evil, lifts the heavy burden of remorse from the sin-stained conscience, discloses to despairing souls an escape from themselves and their sins, and opens up amidst their darkness the bright path of eternal purity,—can he who, from whatever cause, remains blind to this glorious truth, be no worse off for his insensibility? From their faith in Christ the best and noblest of the sons of men have derived, in all ages and lands, the secret of their peace and the spring of their purity; from their faith in him has originated a moral power which no other earthly motive has been found to possess—elevating them above themselves, rendering them superior to all base and selfish impulses, inspiring, in innumerable instances, lowly men and weak women to deeds of heroic fortitude and self-sacrifice, at the recounting of which our hearts thrill with involuntary admiration. It is their faith in Christ which has helped men to triumph over temptation; made them truer, braver, purer; filled them with a larger charity and created in them a passionate desire to do good to their fellow-men.

On these grounds, then, may it not be maintained that sincerity in holding our religious opinions does not and cannot exempt us from their disastrous consequences, should they be wrong opinions? The punishment of unbelief, it would thus appear, is the punishment of the infringement of an order which is true and constant, whether we believe in it or no— an order in which moral causes work out their results in human experience as certainly and infallibly as physical causes work out their effects in the material world and in our own bodily nature. We may doubt them, question them, reject them; but though we believe not, that order abideth faithful; it cannot deny itself.

But now, conceding to the utmost the truth which the foregoing view contains, there is yet, I think, nothing in the concession which conflicts with the great principle of the moral innocence of intellectual error, or which forces us to hold that, in all cases, religious doubt or unbelief is penal. Admitting the unspeakable importance of true opinions, whether in things secular or spiritual, granting especially that religious knowledge, right views of himself and of divine and eternal things, is the most precious gift which God can bestow on the human spirit, and that no earthly loss can be attended by consequences so calamitous as ignorance or error on such matters, there is at least one consideration which renders it impossible to think of any such consequences here or hereafter as of the nature of punishment. One is that no calamity however terrible which results from involuntary acts, acts done without intention and will, can ever rightly be called punishment. It is the very simplest principle of justice, that punishment can be inflicted only for acts wilfully and intentionally committed. For that which a man does or omits to do through ignorance or inadvertence, still more for errors into which he falls after honest and painstaking endeavours to find out the right course of action, it would be wanton tyranny to punish him. And though a man may have to suffer for mistakes and errors, the suffering is simply calamity, pain, sorrow; but ever it lacks that which is the essential and most bitter ingredient of punishment, *conscious guilt*. You punish your child for lying; but if you found out that the words which he uttered, though absolutely untrue, were relatively true—that in uttering them he was perfectly ingenuous, sincerely and conscientiously believing them to be true, would you insist in carrying out the threatened penalty? You might, but the suffering you inflicted would be mere pain, it would be attended by no sense of moral degradation; no pang of self-reproach would trouble the sufferer, and add to pain the keener smart of ill-desert. You dismiss or punish your servant for disobedience; but if you discover that he misapprehended your meaning, and in the act of which you disapproved was doing his best to carry out what he supposed to be your will, would it not be outrageous caprice if you refused to acquit and forgive him? And if you did not, he might suffer at your hands; but the sweet sense of innocence would take all the bitterness out of his suffering, if every other feeling were not quelled by the indignant sense of cruel wrong and injury.

And if thus in our dealings with others we distinguish between involuntary mistakes and wilful errors, can we ascribe to God the monstrous injustice of confounding in one indiscriminating sentence of condemnation the self-condemned sinner and the victim of helpless ignorance, or the bewildered and conscientious seeker after truth? We all of us shrink from applying such a principle to the heathen world—to the vast millions in the dim ages past, or in our day, who lie beyond the pale of Christian civilization. We cannot choose but think that their fate is not hopeless, and that, when and where we know not, but in ways known to the Infinite Wisdom and Goodness, God has designs of mercy and grace for them. But precisely the same principle of justice makes it impossible to believe in the final condemnation of multitudes in Christian lands, who have struggled for light and failed to the last to find it. It is sad to think that there should be such, that those truths which are dearer to us than life should be no truth to them; but our hope and consolation is that, sometimes at least, doubt and unbelief are only the covert form of a deeper faith, of loyalty to truth and to the God of truth.

Who that knows anything of the conditions of human knowledge, of the difficulties of the search for truth, and of the innumerable influences that affect human beliefs, can for a moment think that mental unrest and doubt may not in God's sight be free from blame, or that theological errors, even the gravest in our eyes, are sins to be punished **rather** than simply calamities to be pitied? No one acquainted with the theological literature of our day but must be aware how grave, thoughtful, earnest,—how utterly different from the offensive levity or ribald flippancy of a former time,—is **the tone** of many who have been led furthest aside from **the** path of what we deem the orthodox faith, the tone of such thinkers as Carlyle and Sterling and Clough and the brothers Newman. And when we witness or read of the intellectual struggles of such men—of the recoil of their minds when historical, or critical, or other difficulties began to dawn on them, of the pain with which they saw themselves compelled to surrender one after another of their old convictions, and by force of conscience, against which they dared not sin, constrained to break up ties the most sacred, to leave behind dear associations **of** kindred **and** intellectual fellowship, and honourable **hopes** and ambitions, and to set out on a new and solitary path where all was strange and doubtful,—can we apply to such men, or think of God as applying to them, **the** same **anathema** that is **pronounced** on the profligate and **the** vile? When, to make the matter plain, one reads the mental history unfolded in such books as the *Apologia pro Vitâ Suâ* and the *Phases of Faith*—the former the production **of one** of the finest and subtlest intellects and the gentlest and purest natures which England contains, the latter that of a mind of a less refined and delicate texture, but not less honest and true,—and when, following the course of their inner life there delineated, you note, step by step, the process by which the inexorable logic of the head, or the still more inexorable logic of the heart, seemed to urge them on, till both alike, breaking away from old ties and quelling the fairest hopes and aspirations, were led out, one into the embrace of a church that we deem tainted by soul-deluding superstitions, the other into a colder region of unbelief,—shall we, witnessing this spectacle of mistaken yet unflinching loyalty to truth and conscience,—shall we whose cherished beliefs, true though they be, have perhaps never cost us a struggle or a sacrifice, presume to question the spiritual integrity of such men, or think it possible that, for their intellectual errors and perplexities, these high and truth-loving souls shall be condemned and abandoned of God? Is it not, I do not say, more charitable, but more truly reverential to think that these errors and difficulties are but the discipline by which the God of Truth is leading them onwards to himself, and that in his own time and way, here or hereafter, from the labyrinth in which they seem to be lost, his loving hand will guide them out into the light of that eternal truth for which here they have so passionately yet so vainly longed? I believe in God the Father Almighty, Maker of heaven and earth, and in Jesus Christ, his only Son, our Lord; all my hopes for humanity are centred in the gospel of his grace; but it would be a greater denial of that God and Saviour, it would be to ascribe to his nature an incongruity and self-contradiction more monstrous than to deny him altogether, to conceive him casting into irrevocable darkness souls that here in vain have been groping after the light. I do not hesitate to say, that it were better to perish with the unbeliever than to be saved with the believer in such a God as this.

I conclude this discourse with a single remark, namely, that there is nothing in the view I have now suggested which favours latitudinarian indifference to truth—nothing to render us careless in seeking to know the truth for ourselves, or to abate our zeal in bringing others to the knowledge of it. Why should I be zealous for the conversion of the heathen or labour to convince sceptics and unbelievers of their errors? Does not the foregoing line of thought tend to paralyze missionary zeal and withdraw the supreme motive to Christian effort for the salvation of souls? I answer by another question. Why do you teach men secular knowledge? Why do schools and seminaries of learning exist? Why be at so much pains to make men individually and socially wiser and more intelligent? It is because we believe that knowledge, even secular knowledge, is in itself a good and noble thing and the source of unspeakable blessings to mankind, because it elevates and dignifies man's nature, raises him above animal pleasures and impulses, and helps him to realize the true ideal of his being. It is because knowledge is itself his intellectual salvation.

And so, do you ask, why should we send the gospel to the heathen? Take away the monstrous notion that they shall perish everlastingly because of their unbelief in a Saviour of whom they never heard, and that, every day and hour we withhold the gospel from them, unnumbered souls are passing to perdition; and do you not deprive me of the most cogent, nay the only, the all-important, incentive to missionary effort? I answer, No, I do not. Apart from all rash speculation as to the future destiny of the heathen, I know what they are without Christianity, and I know what Christianity can make them. I know that the true salvation of man, now and for ever, is salvation from ignorance and brutality and selfishness, from mean desires and evil passions and ignoble aims, and I am sure that the gospel can give them that. I know that vast nations and peoples exist morally and spiritually in a state of appalling degradation, dominated by base superstitions and irrational fears, given over to low and brutal lusts,—their lives shortened, their whole nature stunted, deformed, destitute of all that gives sweetness and worth and dignity to life; and if I know and am persuaded that I hold in my hands that mighty spiritual force that alone can raise them out of this dismal condition, can introduce them to new ideas, hopes, impulses, restraints, and elevate natures imbruted to the level of the beasts that perish into communion with the God of heaven and participation in the eternal life of his redeemed,—oh, surely, even though I am unmoved by the immoral and blasphemous notion of damnation for ignorance, there is here motive strong and sufficient for obeying the divine command, to preach the gospel to every creature under heaven.

And so finally, though I cannot think, knowing, as I do, the difficulties of the search for truth, that God will banish for ever from his mercy those many perplexed yet earnest minds which have missed the path of truth, or gone blind and stumbling on in the dim and perilous ways of unbelief; yet feeling, as I do, that their ignorance is to them a great calamity; seeing in it a spectacle more pitiful than that of blind and sightless orbs round which in vain heaven's sweet light is rippling, the spectacle of souls blind to the light and cold to the love that streams from the person and life of Jesus Christ; believing, as I do, that there is a peace, rest, satisfaction, joy transcending the dreams of earthly happiness, to which they are strangers; that faith in the name of Christ could give them that, and that there is no other name under heaven given among men that can do it,—is there not here enough, apart from all mean and selfish terrors, to fill the heart of every Christian man with an almost passionate ardour to bring every erring brother to the participation in his own faith and hope?

THE RELATIONS OF LOVE AND KNOWLEDGE.

"And this I pray, that your love may abound yet more and more in knowledge and in all judgment." PHILIPPIANS i. 9.

IT is probably not of religious knowledge in the technical sense of the phrase that the Apostle here speaks, but of every kind of knowledge which will make our love to others more effective. Love to man, he seems to say, is but a blind impulse, unless it be informed by knowledge—knowledge of human nature, its circumstances and wants, of what our fellow-men are and may become, of the hindrances to their welfare and the best means of promoting it. To be of use to the world love must be intelligent. Again, by the word translated 'judgment,' what seems to be meant is the quality we express by such terms as 'discrimination,' 'sagacity,' 'practical wisdom,'—that quality which enables us to bring our resources of knowledge readily to bear on particular occasions and exigencies, which often makes up in a great measure for the lack of *theoretical* knowledge, and without which such knowledge is almost always ineffective and useless. The general import of the Apostle's prayer, therefore, expressed in modern language, is that in those to whom he writes philanthropy may be accompanied by an ever-increasing measure of practical knowledge.

Now the principle here involved is one of the soundness of which there can be no question. In order to attain success in any noble art, we need not merely the intuitions and impulses proper to it, but also the practical knowledge, the technical skill, the training and discipline, without which these intuitions would be unproductive. The inspiration of genius does not supersede study and hard work. It is true indeed that no man can become a genuine artist merely by culture—by the study of theoretical principles or the laborious, mechanical observance of rules. Without the divine afflatus,—the intuition or sense of beauty which comes as an inspiration on the gifted mind,—a man may be a maker of verses, a second-rate painter, a musician laboriously grinding out pieces faultlessly correct according to the technical rules of harmony; but the best achievements of such men will lack the indefinable element of originality, the interpenetrating spirit and life that captivate the soul in the works of the great masters in the realm of art. Yet, on the other hand, grant to a man this heaven-born instinct, endow him in the highest measure with the æsthetic vision, it is not less true that he needs something more, something which patient study and discipline only can give him, before he can command or merit real success. Not only must science come in to furnish technical knowledge, and many an hour of painful labour be spent in acquiring practical skill and dexterity in the use of the materials with which he has to work; but the great artist, above all men, is one who must be possessed of that knowledge of the world, that sympathetic acquaintance with nature, that large discernment of character, that knowledge of man and society and human life, which come only of profound study and observation. A great poem is not the mere frothing up of feeling and fancy—emotion escaping in rhythmical speech. I could name poems into which are distilled the results of the most comprehensive observation and thought, which are the fruit and flower of a mind nurtured by the philosophy, the science, the highest political and social ideas of its time. In short, what success in any great art demands is, that to inward feeling or the ardent creative impulse there should be added a large measure of practical knowledge.

The same principle holds good in the higher sphere of the spiritual life. In the nobler art of goodness, as our text seems to teach, we need, besides the ardour of Christian impulse or the desire to do good, another quality without which we shall not be fully equipped for our work in the world, namely, practical knowledge. Fervent devotion, enthusiastic religious feeling, philanthropic ardour, a spirit glowing with love to God and man—these are precious things in themselves, and a man can scarcely possess them without proving, in some measure, a blessing to his fellow-men. But if we set ourselves to enquire how the individual Christian, still more how the Christian Church, is to fulfil its benign mission in the world; how, for instance, the work of Christian benevolence is to be accomplished with reference to such questions as those which have of late been much occupying the public mind— the remedies for over-population in congested country districts, the improving of the homes and general conditions of the poor in large cities; or again, what Christianity has to say to such questions as the relation of capital and labour, of employer and employed, of the remedy for the terrible social diseases of pauperism and crime,—then, obviously, to meet such questions the Christian Church needs something more than religious zeal and the desire to do good. To do good to men, a Christian must know men. To serve his time, he must understand his time. To take part in the work of helping on the progress of society, the physical, intellectual and moral amelioration of mankind, he must acquire some acquaintance with its existing conditions and relations, its wants and weaknesses, the sources of its corruptions and diseases, and the best means and appliances for alleviating or curing them. If he would not remain a mere religious voluptuary, for ever brooding over his own frames of mind, or let his zeal evaporate in fine feelings and fervid aspirations, he must be, not merely a man of strong faith and sincere piety, but also of sound sense and practical wisdom. He must endeavour that his love shall "abound yet more and more in knowledge and in all judgment."

On the topic thus suggested I shall now take leave to add a few further remarks. In what relation does knowledge, and its application to the purposes and uses of life, stand to religion? Does the religious man derive from religion any motive to make himself, not only a good man, but an intelligent and wise man? Has secular knowledge any ethical or spiritual function to perform, so that the man of culture and intelligence is therefore likely to be a better servant of his heavenly Master? Of all social forces, religion, take it at the very lowest point of view, undoubtedly constitutes one of the greatest. Religious ideas and motives are, of all ideas and motives, those which have taken the deepest hold on the human spirit. Can this divine force be made by knowledge, enlightenment, the cultivation and discipline of the intelligence, more salutary and efficacious, so that a Christian man will be enabled better to fulfil his Christian duties and obligations?

Now, it is possible so to narrow our conception of religion and spiritual life as that neither ignorance can hinder nor knowledge help it. We may, in other words, take such a view of the nature of religion as not only to make fervent piety and goodness possible to the most uncultured minds (which no one for a moment would question), but also to make them gain nothing from the culture of the intelligence and the advancing lights of science and civilization. Religion, according to this view, consists in the belief in a few simple truths or doctrines to which nothing can ever be added, and in the opening of the heart to certain feelings or emotions, which may be experienced by the little child or the unlettered peasant in equal reality and intensity with the profoundest thinker or the master mind that has grasped the whole circle of the sciences. Christian morality, moreover, is as simple as Christian knowledge. To do justice, and love mercy, and walk humbly with God—this is the whole directory of Christian duty, and all that modern thought and investigation have added to human knowledge will not enable us any better to fulfil it. Nay, it may be questioned—some may be disposed to add—whether the unsophisticated Christian does not possess advantages in respect to piety over his more cultured neighbour. His piety may carry with it an unquestioning faith, a freedom from doubt, a quiet simplicity and reality, the fine bloom of which increasing intellectual culture may mar, but never can improve. And in like manner, his virtue and goodness may be characterized by an absence of that self-conciousness or pride of intellect which knowledge and mental accomplishments are but too apt to engender. Science, literature, art, worldly knowledge and erudition—the philosopher's, historian's, politician's lore—are, no doubt, fine things in their way, but they are things of the world; they are foreign to that high and holy region in which we are concerned with the soul and its relation to God and divine things; they have nothing to do with those inner experiences which find their expression in prayer, in the exercises of the sanctuary, and in practical piety and holiness of life.

The line of thought thus indicated is one which it is not surprising that many good and pious people should be disposed to take. But a little reflection will, I think, convince us that it proceeds from an altogether mistaken notion as to the province of religion and its relation to science and civilization. It will not be difficult to show that religion, so far from being independent of the ever advancing lights of secular knowledge, would, as a social agent, be comparatively feeble and ineffective without them; and that only by their aid can it, in the highest measure, fulfil its function as a regenerator of human society. It may with confidence be maintained that the educated man, if not necessarily a more religious man, is certainly qualified to fulfil more thoroughly the duties which religious principle prescribes; and further, that society, as it grows in knowledge, becomes a better organ of the spirit and power of religion.

For the accomplishment of any great social end, such as the physical or intellectual or moral improvement of mankind, two things are necessary—the desire or disposition to achieve it, and the knowledge how to compass it. It is the function of religion to evoke and stimulate the former, to awaken and minister ever new impulse to the spirit of human sympathy and brotherhood. That Christianity can fulfil, and has in a wonderful manner fulfilled, this function, I need scarcely pause here to show. No one can doubt that, regarded merely from the point of view of social ethics, of our duty to our fellow-men, Christianity has introduced into the world a new moral power, in comparison with which all other benignant social influences are feeble and insignificant. It has enkindled in the human breast a new sentiment, an 'enthusiasm of humanity,' as it has been called, of an altogether peculiar and unprecedented character,—a love for and passionate devotion to the good of mankind, which has proved itself more profound, more intense, more potent to quell the selfish impulses, and to rouse those who are swayed by it to efforts and sacrifices for the sake of others, than any other principle by which the spirit of man can be impelled.

Nor is this feeling a mere unaccountable inspiration;

it is one which is directly traceable to the new ideas of human nature and human destiny which Christianity has introduced. For Christianity teaches us to see in every human being a spirit made in the image of God, and capable of rising into a divine and eternal life. It leads us to look on all men in the light of that new ideal of humanity which the life of Christ sets before us, of that love which he bore to them, and of that sacrifice which was not too great to be offered for their redemption. By these conceptions the life of man has been lifted out of its poverty and meanness and become invested with an infinite worth. The pettiness and triviality, the sordid vileness and degradation, that but too often attach to it, become to the eye of Christian observation no longer its essence but its accidents, only the foul accretions that obscure its inherent glory. As we become penetrated by the spirit of our Christian faith selfish indifference is quelled, cynical contempt for any individual or class becomes impossible. On the least, the lowest, the vilest, we learn to look as the possessors of a nature containing in it untold possibilities of greatness and blessedness. We cease to despair of the very worst. The spectacle of human ignorance, vice, and crime, of vast multitudes sunk in almost savage mental and moral degradation, aawkens in us at once a new and profounder compassion and a new hopefulness and energy, when we see in them the brethren of Jesus Christ, and the beings for whom he lived and died. Catching the fire of his divine self-devotion, the Christian philanthropist learns to look on these and such as these with a love to which nothing is too great to be hoped for, and nothing too hard to be endured. Such, or something like this, is that impulse of social beneficence which Christianity has the power to awaken in all who yield themselves up to its ennobling influence. Alas! as we attempt to depict it, we feel how feebly it acts on most of us; how little of this divine fire our languid sensibilities have caught; how incommensurate our feeble philanthropy with the power of self-abnegating love which lies latent in the religion we profess.

But now, when all this has been said—conceding to the utmost the power of Christianity as a new and commanding impulse of love to mankind—it must still be maintained that that impulse, to achieve the highest results with which it is fraught, must call in the aids which knowledge and a disciplined intelligence can lend to it. It is a great thing to be inspired by the impulse of benevolence, but that impulse, however ardent and eager, will of itself carry us but a little way in our efforts to ameliorate society. Christian zeal and love may be the main things for our own souls; but, beyond a very limited range of activity, they are blind and helpless. He who would extirpate the evils that affect the complicated organism of modern society and develop its highest capabilities of good, will soon meet with problems which the instinct of brotherly love is as powerless to solve, as it is to solve problems in mathematics or to perform surgical operations. It is no doubt true that, as instruments of social regeneration, science and secular culture would be but poor substitutes for religion. It is no doubt true also, that a very weak and ignorant man may be a good and pious man, that the feeblest intelligence, the mind devoid of the faintest tincture of letters, or ignorant as a babe's of history, politics, the constitution of human society, the conditions of its progress and development, may yet be full of faith and charity and all manner of good feelings and instincts. But though the state of a man's own soul may be the main thing for him, and, in absence of opportunities of culture, he is not responsible for blunders and failures which only knowledge could have prevented; yet it is not the less true that all his piety and goodness of heart may leave him a very useless and incompetent member of Christian society. If his sphere of life be a very lowly one, religious feeling, supported and guided by the moral traditions and usages that have infused themselves into modern society and become a sort of artificial wisdom to all well-intentioned people, may keep him from going far wrong and doing much harm—may enable him to perform creditably the ordinary social duties. But even in the most unambitious life there ever and anon arise occasions when the uninstructed mind, however pious and conscientious, is at a loss to determine the right course to take, and on which all the pious intentions in the world will not supply the lack of disciplined judgment and practical wisdom. And if we pass beyond such a limited sphere of action, if we are called from our place in life to help in various ways in the work of social amelioration, in systematic attempts to benefit large classes of our fellow-men, or to reform abuses and corruptions that are feeding on the springs of human welfare and happiness,—in such cases we are in a region where religious feeling without knowledge will be utterly at fault, where the most ardent religious zeal and enthusiasm may stand baffled and bewildered.

Nay, I may go further, and say that, just because religious zeal is one of the most potent and resistless principles of action, it may prove and has often proved a source of injury and disaster to society. For religious feeling, though it does not qualify a man to deal with social problems, does not prevent him from dabbling in them; and even intentional malignity has sometimes done less harm to mankind than sincere and well-meaning, but wrong-headed, zeal. Such zeal, for instance, has led men unthinkingly to gratify a benevolent impulse at the cost of the real and permanent welfare of its objects, and to apply sentimental remedies to deep-seated social evils, which they are as powerless to heal as a plaster to cure an **organic disease.** It has often misapplied sacred authorities and precedents, attempted to solve social problems by quoting irrelevant **texts and** examples, or by applying maxims, true in the circumstances of the primitive Christians, to the very different circumstances of our own time, or by trying to **perpetuate in a** changed world the rude institutions and moral **precepts of** a bygone age.

Popular religious feeling, again, has not seldom been raised into baneful action by the importing **of sacred** names and formulas, such as 'the Headship of Christ' and 'Spiritual Independence,' into discussions with which they had no real connexion; or it has raised a **violent** outcry against much-needed reforms, or in defence of abuses which have been accidently associated with hallowed traditions. Mistaking sincerity for truth and strength of conviction for force of reason, Christian men have again and again been betrayed into acts of grossest cruelty and intolerance, or have lent themselves to swell the tide of ignorant but conscientious prejudice and obstructiveness, or have rushed into projects and schemes of a foolish philanthropy, or have **become the** tools of charlatans, whose ill-considered social nostrums a slight tincture of **science would have** sufficed **to** expose. In these and many **other ways,** zeal without **knowledge has** not unfrequently **proved** itself, not only **inefficacious,** but a positive hindrance to the welfare and progress of society.

It is impossible within the limits of a sermon to give detailed illustrations of the principle I have now explained. I will offer you but a single example. The most obvious illustration of the need of knowledge for the guidance and direction of benevolent emotion is that which is derived from the exercise of our charitable feelings in the relief of poverty and suffering. In an earlier and simpler age benevolent feeling might be left very much to its own spontaneous action, and beyond such general precepts as that we ought as Christians to care for the poor and destitute, to succour the needy, feed the hungry, clothe the naked, and give shelter to the homeless, little more might be required. But the work of the Christian philanthropist has been rendered at once a much more elaborate and a much more effective thing than formerly by the conditions of modern society, and by the light which the study of our social relations has thrown on the interaction of material and moral laws. It is as much as ever the acknowledged duty of the Christian benefactor to care for the poor and suffering, and to reform the vicious and criminal. But attention has now been drawn to the fact that very much of the destitution and vice that exists amongst us is due to preventable causes, or to causes which new and improved social arrangements might at least do much to modify. There can be no question, for instance, that a very large proportion of the misery and disease, and also of the vice and sin, which darken the lives of multitudes amongst us, is due to disregard of the laws of health, or to material and physical conditions which render observation of these laws impossible. Cleanliness may not produce godliness, but physical foulness certainly feeds and stimulates vice as well as disease. A man who lives in a fine house *may* be a profligate, but when human beings, as undisciplined as animals, are penned together in unwholesome dens where the rudest instincts of propriety and self-respect are repressed, who can wonder that from brutal conditions brutal excess and licentiousness should be the too common result? Instead, therefore, of waiting till disease, destitution and vice arise, and doing what we can to alleviate or reform them, it becomes the much more elaborate, but also much more efficacious function of the Christian benefactor to examine into the causes and conditions of social misery and degradation, and to set about a systematic attempt to obviate them. It becomes the duty of the individual Christian philanthropist, if he be an educated man, and of the Christian Church as a society of philanthropists, not merely to investigate the more immediate causes and conditions of social misery and vice amongst the poorer classes, to enquire into their employments, their house-accommodation, their sanitary condition, and into the ways in which these can be so improved as to reduce the sources of disease and crime; but the problem to be solved, it is soon found, leads us into deeper and more fundamental enquiries. The question is, not merely, Can we do anything to elevate and socialize the pariah class; but it is the deeper one, Can anything be done to prevent its very existence? Is it possible by a more searching diagnosis to detect and counteract the hidden disease in the social organism to which this abnormal product is due? Is there no conceivable readjustment of the mechanism of society by which we can prevent the accumulation of noxious matter, of decayed and rotten social refuse, which gives birth to this low and hideous form of life? Is there no fundamental cure for this terrible concomitant of modern civilization,—increasing comfort or luxurious affluence on the one hand, and at the same time, on the other, the rise and growth of a class of social outcasts, of masses of human beings sunk to the lowest point at which existence is endurable, who have nothing to lose and nothing to hope for, and whom sometimes, when the brute impulse in them is unkennelled, neither fear of God nor fear of man restrains?

What the remedy is, what or whether any reorganization of the fundamental relations of society—any deeper conception of the rights and duties of property, any modification of the conditions that affect the relations of capital and labour, any ban placed by the State or community on the sale of the greatest provocative to crime—might arrest and prevent the growth of social barbarism, *this* is a question which it is not for me to discuss. But whatever the answer may be, it is obviously a question on which mere pious feeling has no right to be heard, until it allies itself with careful observation and study of social phenomena, with historical, economical, and political science. And yet, if even an approximate answer could be given, it would furnish Christian philanthropy with a means of fulfilling its benignant ends, with a capacity of doing good to mankind, greater, more potent, more comprehensive, than it has hitherto possessed. What Christian charity can do, by sympathy and help to the forlorn and fallen, is but as the withdrawing of a few drops from the sum of human wretchedness; what, if this problem were solved, it would achieve, would be in a great measure to dry up the poisoned springs from which that wretchedness proceeds.

In conclusion, I need scarcely add that nothing that has been said is intended, or save by confusion of thought can be supposed, to throw any doubt on the claim of the gospel to be the supreme regenerator of man's nature. Knowledge may be the handmaid of religion, it can never be its substitute. It may help us to apply the remedy, but can never provide or supersede it. Poor, indeed, would be our aim and worthless our success, if we strove merely to make all men comfortable, healthy, full-fed, easy-minded, and supplied with all manner of earthly satisfactions. It is charity to the soul that is the soul of charity. And if our aim be, not merely to ameliorate the outward life of man, but to renew and transform the spirit, to raise the slaves of vice out of the slough of low desires and animal enjoyments, to make their hearts pure and gentle, their lives sweet and serene with the tranquillity of goodness; if it be our high endeavour to awaken new aspiration in the imbruted mind, and to call forth the possibilities of excellence and blessedness which each human spirit contains—then should we be false to our faith and blind to the experience of ages if we did not maintain that in Christianity, in the gospel of the grace of God lies the secret of this regenerating work, and that now, as ever, it is the power of God unto salvation

And if of those whom we wish to benefit, then also of ourselves is this principle true. The pursuits in which we are here engaged may make and ought to make us more useful to our fellow-men, better and abler agents in all noble and philanthropic enterprises. But the possession of the gifts of intelligence and culture is no security that we possess the highest gift of all. It is possible to be at once accomplished and vicious, keen-witted and cold-hearted, brilliant and sparkling on the surface, hard and selfish at the core. It is well to be possessed of a trained and disciplined intelligence, to have access to the treasures of science and speculation, to know the best thoughts of the wise, and the sweetest fancies and fairest visions that have visited the noblest imaginations of our own and other days—if this were not a thing of inestimable value, eagerly to be sought after, worth all the years of patient toil and self-denial by which we seek to win it, then would our whole vocation here be futile and vain.

But it is no mere pious truism to add, something more than this is needful—something which can lend new preciousness to the gifts of intellect, but without which for the highest end of life they are worthless. There are evils which culture cannot cure, blessings which, in all the storehouse of its affluent gifts, it has not to bestow. It cannot shield us from the sorrows that desolate the home and lie heaviest on the heart. It cannot minister balm to the wounded spirit, or bring peace to the troubled conscience, or lessen the anguish of bereavement, or dispel from our path the awful shadow that is creeping ever nearer and more near. The final standard by which here or hereafter each of us is to be measured is not an intellectual one. We may stand that test well, and yet, weighed in the balance of infinite wisdom and justice, be found wanting. What is the secret moral temper of your spirit? Are you living, not to do your own will, but the will of God; not for selfish ambition or pleasure, but for the good of others? Are you in sympathy with that life which was the manifestation of the eternal love and goodness to mankind? It is this question that is of the last importance for each and all of us; for it is the answer to it that will determine whether in this passing life we are basing our faith and hope upon that which the years are rapidly taking from us, or fixing them, beyond the reach of mortal accident, upon the eternal foundation which was laid in the life and words of Jesus Christ. For "whosoever," saith our Lord, "heareth these sayings of mine, and doeth them, I will liken him unto a wise man, which built his house upon a rock: and the rain descended, and the floods came, and the winds blew, and beat upon that house; and it fell not: for it was founded upon a rock."

THE MEASURE OF GREATNESS.

"Whosoever will be great among you, let him be your minister; and whosoever will be chief among you, let him be your servant: even as the Son of man came not to be ministered unto, but to minister, and to give his life a ransom for many." MATTHEW xx. 26-28.

IN all spheres of human endeavour true greatness is possible only under the condition here indicated. The idea which our Lord's words suggest is not simply that that is the highest sort of greatness which uses its powers and opportunities for the good of mankind, but that from the very nature of the thing it is impossible to become great in any other way. It is of the very essence of greatness to be attainable only by service. The great man in being great is the world's minister, and cannot help being so. His own elevation is possible only by being or doing that which elevates, ennobles, and blesses his fellow-men.

What do we mean by 'greatness'? Without attempting any precise definition of the word, we may say generally that the great man is he who approaches more nearly than others to the ideal of man's nature, who realizes in his own person, beyond common men, that nobleness of being, that fulness of intelligence, feeling, energy, that elevation and intensity of life which are possible to man. And we shall perhaps not go far wrong if we include under the general idea such qualities as these—in the first place, originality of thought, unusual depth and clearness of insight, the presence in greater or lesser measure of that brilliant clearness of soul, that indefinable gift of genius, which enables its possessor to open up new worlds of thought, to solve the problems that baffle the common order of minds, and to exert a controlling, inspiring influence over the thoughts and lives of ordinary men. Again, as another ingredient, may be specified intensity of feeling, the fire of emotional ardour which quickens the pulse of life, the enthusiasm for great ends that constitutes a perpetual inward stimulus to productive and beneficent activity. Once more, I may name as a quality closely allied to this, largeness and quickness of sympathy, the instinct which enables a man to understand men, to enter with an almost personal realization into the thoughts, feelings, wants of many and various classes of minds—that quality, or combination of qualities, which gives to some men a certain magnetic power of attraction over all who come within the range of their influence, a capacity to call forth the love and devotion of human hearts. I might add to these, as another element of human greatness, magnanimity or moral nobleness, the quality which raises a man above small motives and vulgar passions and petty ambitions, makes him careless of criticism and indifferent to popular applause, which not only enables him to withstand a thousand influences that sway meaner natures, but in the absorption of his mind with larger objects, renders him absolutely insensible to them. Lastly, to name no other quality, I would add that the highest order of greatness cannot be reached save by those who combine with more or less of the foregoing elements that supreme quality which brings the human spirit into immediate communion and converse with the divine—pure and ardent religious earnestness. It is this which gives the highest touch of sublimity to all the other elements of human greatness. It is this which lends to genius the character of a divine inspiration, which transforms the poet into the prophet, the hero into the saint. It is this which infuses into morality an infinite elevation, exalts virtue into the aspiration after an eternal righteousness, and gives to duty the consecration of devotion to the will of God. It is this which enlarges for its subject the petty incidents and affairs of life into the events and stages of an infinite moral order, throws a more than tragic interest around the drama of history, and to the nature that is profoundly swayed by it communicates an exaltation and grandeur which is the very climax of human greatness.

These, then, and such as these, are the elements which, separately or in combination, enter more or less into the character which the instinctive judgment of the world designates 'great.' And now let us see whether and how far the principle of the text applies to the character so defined. "Whosoever will be great among you, let him be your minister; and whosoever will be chief among you, let him be your servant." Christ here contrasts the true greatness of which he speaks with that of the "princes of the Gentiles." The despotic powers of the world gain their greatness and authority at the expense of their fellow-men— by subjugating and enslaving their wills, dominating their minds, extracting the materials of a base splendour and elevation out of the lost freedom and ruined happiness of mankind. But it shall not be so, says our Lord, among you. Your greatness and mine, the Christian ideal of greatness, is attained, not by depressing, but by elevating others, not by rifling them of their freedom and happiness, but by ministering to and promoting it.

Is this, then, a true account of the matter? Is the great man of necessity the world's minister? Is it of the essence of greatness that it is attainable, not by subjecting and dominating, but by elevating, ennobling, and blessing mankind? That this principle is true will be seen if we consider successively these three points—what great men *are*, what great men *teach*, and, finally, what they *suffer*.

In the first place, great men serve the world simply by being great. Leave out of view for a moment what a great man is led consciously and intentionally to achieve for others, and consider what he does for the world simply in virtue of what he *is*,— and there can be no question that the very existence of a great and original nature, especially if it rise to the highest region of moral and spiritual nobleness, is of incalculable service to society. It is to the ordinary mass of men an embodied specimen of the hidden possibilities of their nature.

There are many things which lead us to think meanly of the nature and destinies of man. When we contemplate the spectacle of the misery and degradation, the sorrow and sin of the world, when we think of the multitudes who are sunk in the slough of animal desires and appetites, scarce one remove above the brutes that perish, there is little room for wonder that the paralyzing creed of the pessimist should seem to some so plausible. Or, again, when we reflect on the vulgar aims and satisfactions, the poor and petty ambitions that compose the life of so many more, on the all but universal scramble for money, ease, comfort, social position, the absence of ideal aims or of any aspirations that rise above the conventional standard of social respectability,—are we not tempted to pronounce that disdain of human nature, the contemptuous pity of the cynic, the bitter, biting scorn of the satirist, is no indefensible attitude of mind?

Now, it is this tendency to measure man's nature by its moral failures, or by its more ignoble specimens, that creates the need for great men, and constitutes their unspeakable value. For these, starting up ever and anon out of the dead level of spiritual mediocrity, are a revelation of nobler possibilities, a rebuke to our cynicism and sloth, a rousing call to higher things. In the midst of our false contentment they disclose to us that human nature contains in it the stuff out of which something immeasurably greater than this may be made. Apart from anything they *do* for us, their very existence stirs the moral stagnation into which we should otherwise settle down. To come into contact with a very original nature, a mind of marked individuality, a life full of great impulses and devoted to pure and noble ends—even to hear of such a man or to read the record of his life, is a most salutary experience for us. It lifts us out of ourselves, makes us ashamed of our pettiness and littleness, brings us into a new and bracing moral atmosphere, furnishes a salutary stimulus to thought and action, and enables us to catch at least a glimpse of the splendour of that future which is God's ideal for us. And now, passing by all other and lower examples of moral and spiritual greatness, I will ask whether in the person and life of Jesus Christ we cannot see the highest example of the principle of the text—"The Son of man came not to be ministered unto, but to minister." And it was just in *being* Son of man, in living a life which, with all the splendour of its spiritual beauty, was still truly and simply human, that Christ's greatest service to mankind was rendered. However men may differ in their theological views of the constitution of Christ's person, all Christian men will agree in this, that in this one human life there was presented to the world a new and transcendent ideal of human goodness, a type of moral and spiritual greatness such as the history of the race has never paralleled; and further, that by this one human personality there has been awakened in his own and all succeeding ages a new sense of the hidden grandeur of man's nature, a new and boundless love and veneration for what is good and holy and fair.

Leaving aside for the moment all other aspects of Christianity, consider simply what the world has gained from the character and life of Jesus Christ, from the fact that this one personality has entered into its history. Reflect on the minds it has quickened, the new ideas which, even outside of the sphere of religion, it has called forth, the imaginations it has kindled into a new creative power, the lips to which it has communicated a loftier eloquence, the great books that owe their inspiration to it, the immortal productions of art that have originated from it. And then, turning from these, think of its moral and spiritual power. Recall what since Christ lived and died, the experience of countless thousands in all lands and ages has owed to the thought of him, the sweetness and light and purity and peace which it has infused into men's hearts, the strange mingled love and reverence, awe and tenderness it has created, the meanness it has elevated, the great deeds it has prompted, the patient, sustained fortitude and courageous endurance in life and death of which it has been the source; and, finally, reflect on this, that it has introduced into the family of mankind a new bond of union, solving distinctions of class, melting away individual and national hatred and exclusiveness, constituting the germ and prophecy of that universal brotherhood of humanity which is God's ideal for the race. Consider this—consider, I say, what the world has gained from the fact that this one supreme life has been lived in it, and say if he is not himself the highest fulfilment of his own declaration, "Whosoever will be great among you, let him be your minister."

We have seen, then, that the highest greatness makes its possessor a minister and servant of mankind, in virtue simply of what he *is*. But the same thing will be seen more fully if we consider, not merely what he is, but also, in the second place, what he *teaches.* What is the source of the influence of great thinkers? If we reflect for a moment on this question I think we shall see that their extraordinary influence is due to this, not simply that they communicate truth to us on their own authority, but that they enable our own minds to see it; not that they arbitrarily announce to us what is true, but that they quicken in us, bring to the birth in our own souls the power to grasp it and to claim it as our own. Their influence, in other words, is due to the response and recognition which their words and ideas awaken within us. Their word is a word of power because it stirs in our hearts the dormant susceptibilities for what is true and fair and holy, because at its magic touch the hidden springs of thought and feeling within us are unsealed. A great original mind subdues and dominates other minds, not by forcing them to accept and blindly follow his teaching, not by crushing their intelligence under the weight of authority, but by giving voice and expression to ideas which, though few are gifted with the power of discovering, sooner or later all can recognize and appropriate. Great men do not think for us, but they think before us, as the mountain peaks catch first the light of the morning; but it is a light that is soon to flood the world. Thus a great master mind, a mind that leads other minds, becomes, from the very nature of the thing, their minister and servant.

There is indeed an inferior kind of greatness which may be said to be the caricature of that of which I now speak, and which is by no means to be confounded with it. Great men, I have said, rule men by becoming the mouthpiece of their moral consciousness; but influence and power of a sort are always to be got by the clever ready-witted exponent, not of the truer and deeper thought, but of the transient, surface notions and opinions of men. Study the drift of the popular mind, stoop to become the mouthpiece of its passing beliefs, the organ of its unreasoning tendencies; and a cheap popularity and power will be your reward. Embody and plausibly express the narrow notions of a sect or clique, give intensified utterance to the prejudice or passion of the hour, the feeling that for the moment sways and surges in the minds of the multitude; and a clamour of voices will syllable your name and a crowd of admirers flock to your standard. For men are ever ready to lend their suffrages to him who gives vivid utterance to their own dumb prejudices, who shows himself vibrating with intensified sympathy to the excitement that stirs them, or whose clever pen and ready tongue can give a dress of rationality to their own contracted ideas or their sectarian arrogance and animosity. The demagogue who flatters by formulating the class jealousies and passions of the mob, the ecclesiastical leader who can make even the foul spirit of fanatical rancour and uncharitableness look pious and respectable, will never fail of a kind of power.

It scarcely needs to be said, however, that true greatness is not for such as these. The influence they get is at best limited and ephemeral. Either the notions and feelings on which their power is based are merely local—felt it may be intensely and sounding big within a little circle or sect, and nowhere else, like the brawling of a petty brook, which is deafening to the bystander but a mile off is lost in the silence of nature—and in that case the greatness of the idol of the sect is only a local notoriety and beyond its immediate sphere passes off into insignificance; or that which lends them power is an ephemeral excitement, a passing phase of opinion or sentiment, an epidemic fever-heat in the blood of a community or nation; and then when society cools down and reason and truth reassert their claims, he who forced himself into prominence as its organ sinks back into his normal obscurity, if even the public consciousness that has become ashamed of itself and him does not turn upon him with derision and contempt.

Now the difference between this and the higher order of minds to which the name of great truly belongs is, that while both serve men by becoming the interpreters of their thoughts, the latter rise above what is narrow and ephemeral, above man's evanescent interests and selfish passions, to appeal to the infinite side of his nature, to call forth and give realization to that in him which is universal and eternal. The great poets of the past, to name but one example, owe their power over us to this, that they appeal not to the conventional tastes of a class, still less to the meaner instincts and passions of man's nature, but to that eternal yearning for what is beautiful and pure, to those aspirations after an infinite, invisible perfection in nature and life, of which the forms of the highest art are the embodiment and expression. All succeeding ages have recognized their claim to greatness because they wrote for all time, because their words were addressed, not to the transitory passions of the hour, but to those deeper elements of our being which are universal and undying as the nature of man himself.

And now, turning from all other and lower examples, may we not find here too our highest illustration of the principle before us in the teaching of him who is greater than the greatest of the sons of men. "The Son of man came not to be ministered unto, but to minister"; and he is, as a teacher also, greatest of all, because more than all other human teachers, he is servant of all. The kingdom of Christ, the dominion he already wields over the highest portion of our race, the universal dominion to which he is advancing, are due, not to any arbitrary authority, not to any mysterious dogmas which by the very fact that they transcend the human consciousness are powerless to move it; but, above all, to this, that the ideas of which he is the source, the truths concerning God and man, and human hopes and destinies, which he taught by his lips and embodied in his life, have revealed man to himself, quickened into new life the latent spiritual intelligence, kindled the spiritual imagination by the vision of a fairer than earthly beauty, infused a new and boundless ardour into the spiritual affections, armed the will with a new and commanding power over the passions, breathed amidst the struggles and sorrows of life a serener peace into the heart, and shed over all the future the light of a diviner hope. When, for instance, through him, the new conception dawned upon the world of humanity as one with divinity —of a God who is not the distant and awful Monarch of the universe, but the inward principle dwelling in us, the light of all our seeing, the inspiration of our life, of our truest thoughts and purest affections, that infinite life which, when we truly live, lives and moves and breathes within us—what a new flood of light did not this idea pour upon our human experience, what a strange solution lay in it of the enigmas of human life, of the restlessness and self-dissatisfaction which perturb the noblest hearts, of the boundless irrepressible aims and aspirations which the noblest spirits feel. When, again, there came to man through Christ the idea of the universal love of the Father—a love transcending all distinctions of birth or rank, of class or country, transcending even the terrible barrier of human guilt and sin; a love which no ingratitude can alienate, no disobedience exhaust, no degree of infamy baffle—when Christ proclaimed it to be God's will that no human soul should perish, but that all men should be saved; when, finally, Christ brought life and immortality to light, lifted the veil that hides from man the awful future, and revealed the bright path of eternal purity and blessedness stretching away interminably before him,—when, I say, we consider how these and kindred ideas have taken hold of the human spirit, met its gropings after light, found a voice for its dumb inarticulate instincts, and communicated to it a new consciousness of spiritual power and freedom, may we not, again I ask, regard him, who first taught mankind to see and know them, as realizing in himself beyond all others the principle that whosoever will be great amongst men must be their minister?

One other and sadder characteristic of greatness yet remains to be named. The great man is one who must not merely serve men, but be ready to sacrifice himself for their good. "The Son of man came," it is said, "not to be ministered unto, but to minister, and *to give his life a ransom for many.*" These words obviously do not refer to any theological doctrine of substitution. For the self-devotion and sacrifice of which they speak is set forth as common to Christ with others, as an element of that character which all who aspire to greatness must possess. Whosoever will be great must be great in the same way as the Son of man,—*even as* the Son of man gave his life, so must he. It is the same thought which Christ had just before expressed in the words, "Ye shall drink indeed of my cup, and be baptized with the baptism that I am baptized with." For you as for me there is no crown without the cross. He who would share in the Master's joy must enter into the fellowship of his sufferings. Sorrow, struggle, sacrifice, self-surrender are the inevitable conditions of greatness. Long and weary is the way by which, if ever, the sun-crowned height is to be gained. The glory of a benefactor of mankind is only for him who counts all things but loss, and holds not his life dear for their sake.

To all kinds of greatness experience proves that this condition is attached, that its reward is not ease, honour, earthly advancement, but more often than otherwise the sacrifice of all that most men hold dear. In that greatest of England's temples, where rest side by side so many of her noblest and best, you will read the names of some, indeed, who have been laid there, rich in honours and amidst a nation's tears; but you will read also the names of not a few whose career was brief and broken,—of poets who "learned in suffering what they taught in song," and whose very music owes its thrilling sweetness to the anguish of the heart from whence it came; of philanthropists, discoverers, explorers, whose life was a life of lonely and silent struggle, or of baffled endeavour, ending, for aught they saw, in disappointment and failure; of great statesmen bowed down by the burden of office, prematurely exhausted by its cares and responsibilities, and who scarcely ever knew an hour of rest till they found it in the sleep that knows no waking.

And the reason of this is obvious. They who work for great ends are, beyond all others, liable to the bitterness of unfulfilled hope and of effort crowned by no immediate reward. For great ideas are slow of bearing fruit, great works and enterprises are long of accomplishment in proportion to their magnitude. Seldom is it given to the originator to see the full results of his thought and toil; often it is his sad fate to pass away while his work is yet in the stage of germination and struggle, in doubt whether anything is to come of all his labours. A great man devotes himself to some noble object, takes up some cause or enterprise, is fired with enthusiastic ardour for the putting down of some gigantic wrong, or the reform of some ancient and deep-rooted corruption or abuse that is preying on the peace and welfare of society, sees and flings himself heart and soul into the effort to realize some great project, say, the reformation of a religion, the emancipation of the enslaved, the restoration of a nation to freedom; and it is true that, if his counsel be of God, it cannot come to nought. Give it time enough, and it is sure in the long run to win the day. Yes, but that day may not be his. All that he can accomplish may be only to begin the work, to sow in tears what, in the far-off future, other men shall reap in joy. The day will come when the world will appreciate his work; but in his own time there may be few to recognize its value. On the contrary, the very strangeness and originality of his ideas rouses the hostility of the slaves of custom. The changes he would introduce interfere with men's familiar ways; a thousand interests of individuals and classes may be bound up with the evils he would rectify, or with the imperfect notions and opinions he would subvert. His ideas are before his time, and that time will have none of them. Men will build one day the tombs of the prophets and garnish the sepulchres of the righteous, but to-day the progenitors of those who will do so may be their betrayers and persecutors. And so for these, the nobler spirits of humanity, life has often a sternness, and death a bitterness unknown to other men—

the sternness of uncheered and unfriended toil, the bitterness of broken effort, of work unfinished, of passing away while the wavering issue of the fight is uncertain, while the aim of a life-time is still but a far-off goal.

And here, too, as our Lord himself declares, it is in the Son of man that the most significant example of this thought is to be found. His was a work, his beyond all others were ideas in profoundest harmony with man's nature, and destined to find recognition in the consciousness of the race. But for that very reason they brought him into collision with the ideas and the spirit of the age in which he lived. He was the Redeemer of all men, but the very universality of his mission made him both incomprehensible and hateful to those who looked only for a Saviour of the Jews. Had he been what his fellow-countrymen at first took him for—a mere national hero, the representative of national pride, and the redresser of local wrongs—there was a spirit abroad in the people that would have borne him on to power and greatness. But when he revealed to them a God who was not the God of the Jew only, but the Father of all men; when he taught a gospel which was to be preached among all nations; when he dared, surrounded by an atmosphere of fanatical national exclusiveness and antipathy, to assert that many from East and West should sit down with Abraham and Isaac and Jacob, whilst the children of the kingdom should be cast out; when he thwarted those hopes of revenge and conquest which had for generations been slowly nursing in the national heart and waiting only for the hour and the man to give them reality, and announced the coming of a kingdom which was simply the reign of truth and righteousness in the hearts and lives of men—a universal brotherhood of love and charity binding in its blessed fellowship all men and nations together,—then indeed he taught a gospel which rose above all limits, which had on its side the deep and silent force of the spirit of the future; but just because of that, it was out of keeping with the narrow spirit and the shallow prejudices and passions of his time. And that spirit met him with contempt and derision, deepening gradually into a fiercer and more fanatical hate; and at last, as if in most terrible irony of fate, he, the Lord of men, the crown and glory of humanity, destined to be the object of the unbounded reverence and admiration of coming ages, perished ignominiously in the petty outbreak of a Jewish mob. He saved others, himself he could not save. He "came not to be ministered unto, but to minister, and to give his life a ransom for many."

Be it ours, then, let me say in conclusion, to prize and profit by the glorious heritage which has descended to us in the lives, the works, the example, of those who have taught us what true greatness is. I have suggested in the course of this sermon some of the lessons we may learn from the lives of great men, and especially of those in whom greatness rose to its highest form, that of moral and spiritual nobleness. There is one other lesson, with which I leave the subject, and that is, the hopefulness for the future of humanity which such lives inspire. Amidst the pettiness and narrowness of common life, in the presence of human weakness and baseness, the lives of great men do something to meet the misgivings which death forces on our minds. If all men were what, alas! a very large portion of humanity is, strangers to high thoughts and pure and generous emotions and noble and magnanimous aims, living a life petty and mean, or foul and evil, it would not be difficult to think that a being so mean, a thing of such sordid desires and contemptible pursuits, a nature so little worth preserving is destined to extinction, when, as has been said, "its brief term of fretfulness and folly has run out." But when we turn to contemplate human life in its nobler representatives, its beautiful, heroic, saintly spirits, refined and chastened by the discipline of life, growing to the last in purity and nobleness, it is impossible to believe, unless the world is governed by a mocking Moloch and not a God of wisdom and love, that all this abruptly terminates in a little heap of foul and mouldering matter, and that the end of these men is that of the beasts that perish.

But the hope for humanity which such lives inspire is something more than this. Is there yet a better time coming for the world? **Has** the far future a Golden Age, a period of universal purity and happiness in store for humanity? Is the race destined to reach a glorious future? I answer, Yes. It is no wild and quixotic faith which inspires Christian effort for the regeneration of human **society**. The final emancipation of the race from imperfection and **sin, the era of** millennial purity and perfection is no baseless **dream of** religious enthusiasm. We are compassed about with a great cloud of witnesses to the suppressed splendour that lurks in this poor nature of ours. There are latent resources in the least **and** lowest specimen of humanity which make it brother, and might make it peer **and** equal, of the brightest spirit that ever breathed mortal breath. Yea, with reverence be it said, the **very** greatness of him who was emphatically Son of man was a greatness in which all men may participate. And if you would form some faint conception of what human society may one day become, think of a world in which the common life of all shall rise to the level of what the noblest and best of the sons of **men at their** highest moments of intellectual and moral **exaltation** have **ever** reached. Can imagination in its highest soarings surpass that, which I believe to be **a hope** based on most sober and solid grounds of fact—the hope of a future in which every human being shall be wise with the wisdom of the wisest and holy with the goodness of the best? Yea, for even that falls short of the sublime reality— the hope of an approaching time when, in words which, if they were not those of inspiration, it might seem daring presumption to utter: We shall "all come in the unity of the faith, and of the knowledge of the Son of God, unto a perfect man, unto the measure of the stature of the fulness of Christ."

THE PROFIT OF GODLINESS.

"Godliness is profitable unto all things, having promise of the life that now is, and of that which is to come." 1 Timothy iv 8.

St. Paul's words, if taken literally, would cut away the ground from what used to be a favourite argument with theologians for what they termed 'a future state of rewards and punishments.' Such a futurity is rendered necessary, it was maintained, in order to redress the unequal distribution of good and evil in the present life. Justice demands that goodness and happiness, vice and misery, should be invariably connected. In a perfect world, or under an absolutely just system of moral government, we should never behold such a spectacle as that of prosperous vice, successful fraud and knavery, profligacy flaunting in fine robes and faring sumptuously every day; or, on the other hand, that of virtue in poverty and rags, honest worth despised and downtrodden, saints and martyrs counted as the very offscouring of the earth, passing through life in misery and hardship and dying in dishonour and wretchedness. A moral system, therefore, is supposed to demand that there should be another world in which the balance swings the other way, in which the good are compensated by at least a proportionate excess of happiness for the sufferings of this life, and the bad subjected to penalties which outweigh all their present sinful joys. But if we take the words of the text in their most obvious sense, it entirely subverts this theological argument for a moral government of the world; for that argument is virtually that godliness or goodness will prove profitable hereafter because it is unprofitable here, whereas the Apostle proclaims that it is profitable here as well as hereafter—profitable all over the range of human existence, temporal and eternal, "having promise of the life that now is" as well as "of that which is to come."

But it needs little reflection to see that this liberal interpretation of St. Paul's words would not help us to solve the difficulty. For the great objection, from a moral point of view, to any compensation theory in a future life is, of course, that it is not really moral, not to say, religious. It does not elevate or transform the character and motives of the worldly-minded or irreligious nature, but simply transfers them, and that in a magnified form, to the sphere of religion. It exhorts men, indeed, to put a check on their passions and give up many kinds of self-indulgence; but the love of selfish pleasure is not subverted or turned into a spiritual motive by the fear of hell and the hope of heaven; it is simply the same motive, the same attitude of mind transferred to a future world—worldliness enlarged into other-worldliness. And if the 'profit' of which St. Paul speaks were anything of this sort, it would only intensify the unworthy nature of this appeal to selfish interest. For instead of deferring the promised advantages of piety to a future life, his teaching would be that they are to be got here as well as hereafter, and that piety is not only of the nature of a good investment, but of an investment with immediate payment of interest; or, as we might express it, under the same commercial figure, it is not simply an insurance to be paid at death, but a speculation with the prospect of immediate profits.

But to any such interpretation of St. Paul's words there is the obvious objection that it would make them essentially self-contradictory. For to induce a man to become religious out of regard to the ulterior advantages of religion, would be to base religion on a motive which destroys it. No man is even at the threshold of the religious life so long as he has an eye to anything to be gained or got by religion, nay, we may even say, till there is nothing else he would not be ready to sacrifice rather than renounce or prove faithless to it. Nor, if you think of it, does this imply any extraordinary or abnormal attitude of mind, any seraphic elevation impossible for ordinary human nature; on the contrary, it is an attitude common to religion with all noble and worthy objects of human desire. Knowledge, for instance, may lead to fame and fortune, scholarly and scientific accomplishments may bring a man great reputation, a lucrative position, social rank and influence; but not only is it possible, when engaged in study or research, to be utterly forgetful and unconscious of anything outside the subject which engrosses us, but I suppose we should agree that the scientific spirit is never genuine till the pure delight of thought, of investigation, of the contact of the mind with truth, glows in a man's breast and, apart from all ulterior results, is for him a sufficient satisfaction and joy.

The same is true of those pursuits which we include under the name 'art.' Painters, sculptors, musicians, poets are often keenly sensitive to reputation, and may be far from indifferent to money and the pleasures and comforts which money brings, and many who care only or chiefly for these things may follow the artist's vocation; but if there be not in a man's breast some spark of a genuine æsthetic inspiration, something of that inner creative impulse which makes artistic production its own end and joy, he is not a true artist, but only a day-labourer or hireling in the field of art.

Still more profoundly true is this principle in the sphere of man's moral and spiritual life. Hedonistic moralists may make elaborate attempts to prove the identity of the moral end with pleasure or the largest sum of pleasures, but the unsophisticated conscience will cling to the belief that integrity, purity, justice, goodness, are things we should choose, even if no pleasure or profit come of them, nay, at the cost and sacrifice of all the pleasant things of life. A conscientious man, at any rate, it unhesitatingly pronounces, is not one who does his duty because, or so long as, it promotes his interests. There are innumerable things in the world he may dearly prize; but when these and duty clash, when it comes to be a question whether he shall give up these or be a liar or a knave, can he retain the faintest title to the name of a good man if he be not prepared to sacrifice all the world holds dear rather than be betrayed into baseness and dishonour?

And if godliness or religion mean love to God, reverence and devotion to the infinite Truth and Righteousness, love and loyalty to him who was its highest manifestation on earth, must not this, above all others, be a principle which needs no prop of external profit to secure its dominion over the soul? Even in relation to man, we should pronounce that love impure and unreal which has regard only to the money or other benefits that can be extracted from its object. 'What am I to gain by all this expenditure of affection, why should I repair to the presence or reciprocate the tenderness of one who is dear to me?'

Would it not be an insult to love to ask such questions? Would not the instant answer be, 'Gain! reward! result! I seek none, dream of none. Love is its own most precious reward; the richest joy that love can give is more love, deeper love, love that grows with what it feeds on.' And so it is also with the love of God. Earth knows no deeper, sublimer emotion than that mingled awe and tenderness, reverence and aspiration, that absolute self-surrender which human hearts have felt towards the Father of spirits, the Lord, Redeemer, Lover of the soul. To hearts once touched by it, it is as much its own end and delight as light and beauty are the delight of the eye, and sweet melody the immediate joy of the ear. To seek something else by means of it, to cultivate this emotion for the sake of material or other benefits here or hereafter, is an impossible and self-contradictory notion; for love divine is false and tainted love—is, indeed, no love at all, till it becomes its own heaven.

But there is another way in which St. Paul's doctrine of the profitableness of godliness may be regarded. Though it may be unworthy when viewed as a motive, it may be true as a matter of fact. That religion may be spurious which springs only from the hope of outward advantages, yet it may be true that religion *is* the source of manifold outward advantages, present and future. He is not an honest man who is honest only from motives of policy, yet it is true, nevertheless, that honesty is the best policy. Though we cannot be religious in order to promote our physical and social welfare, yet in being religious we may be taking the surest way to secure it.

And unquestionably there is a point of view from which, even as regards the present and temporal welfare of mankind, this doctrine is true. The religion we profess claims to be the sovereign cure for every form of evil, for all the ills, outward as well as inward, material and physical as well as spiritual, to which flesh is heir. Its Divine Author was not only the Physician of souls, but the Saviour of the body. During his brief earthly ministry he was not only the Revealer of saving truth, but had he been nothing else, he was, as regards the outward and physical life of man, the first and greatest of philanthropists. Wherever he came, the cry of the wretched awaited him; wherever he went, the blessings of them that were ready to perish followed his steps. The hungry blessed him for food, and the sick and diseased for healing, and the sad and broken-hearted for consolation, and the toil-worn and heavy-laden for rest. Moreover, it was no partial victory over evil which he foretold as the result of his mission. The ideal future of the world which he himself and they who drew their inspiration from him proclaimed, was a kingdom of God on earth, from which not only sin but sorrow and every form of evil—pain and suffering and poverty, want and weariness, oppression and tyranny, slavery and bondage, war and bloodshed, shall for ever have passed away; in which the inhabitant shall no longer say, I am sick; in which no tear shall ever again be shed, and from which sorrow and sighing shall have fled away for ever.

And when we turn from this ideal picture of the final result, to reflect on what the influence of Christianity has already been, it is, I think, unquestionable, that of all the agencies that have contributed to the progress of what we call 'civilization,' the gradual amelioration of man's physical and social life, the advancement of individuals and nations in science, art, industry, commerce, material wealth, civil and political freedom, to the suppression of barbarism, pauperism, grossness of manners, to the multiplication and elevation of human pleasures and recreations,—it is, I say, beyond question that of all that has tended thus to the brightening and bettering of man's outward estate, Christianity, though not the sole, has been the most important agent.

It is true that, looking only to the individual life of men, it would be absurd to maintain that there is any invariable connexion between religion and outward prosperity and happiness, or that prosperous infamy and goodness crushed by poverty and misfortune, are sights seldom or never to be seen. It is easy to adduce

T

innumerable instances in which the relation between the spiritual and material is the very reverse of that of which I have spoken—in which health, wealth, worldly success, all the gifts of fortune seem to be showered on the selfish and base, and the life of the best and noblest is embittered by ill-health or grinding poverty, or darkened by care, anxiety, and disappointment. But the answer is that in judging of the ameliorating influences of religion—of what it could do for the healing of the diseased organism of society, or for the checking and extinction of the pernicious brood of social maladies that prey upon it—it is impossible to test its inherent power by looking only to the lives of individual men. For no individual, however good and holy, can isolate himself from others, or keep off from himself those outward ills that are the fruit not of his own but of other men's sins. The nervous and other diseases that have made many a good man's life one long misery have been the effect of parental or ancestral vices. Trouble and sorrow are the lot of many true and gentle hearts because of the misconduct or profligacy of those to whom they are linked by inseparable bonds. In a thousand ways the natural and inherent effects of goodness are arrested and counteracted by inevitable relations to those who are not good.

To estimate what that natural effect would be we must try to conceive what man's outward life would become if all men were good and holy, if the inherent ameliorating power of religion were allowed free play, unhindered and unmarred by anything that is traceable to the presence of sin and vice. Or, to put it more palpably, picture to yourself for a moment what would be the result, as regards man's outward life, if a single people or nation on earth were composed of those and those only in whose breasts the spirit of Jesus Christ reigned with a pure and absolute dominion. Would not such a nation become not only the holiest but the happiest and most prosperous on the face of the globe? All being temperate, pure, simple, self-controlled in their pleasures and enjoyments, the taint of hereditary disease would speedily vanish, and many of the causes that injure health and shorten human life would cease to operate. All being impelled by a sense of duty to God for the use of every power and faculty, sloth and indolence would be unknown, and the idle, frivolous class that spends existence in selfish amusement would, under the universal contempt and dishonour, become an extinct variety of the human species. Envy and jealousy of superior abilities, selfish ambition and rivalry, the sacrifice of principle to preferment, the base arts of the demagogue and place-hunter, the vices that crush the capable and elevate the incompetent into place and power would disappear, the wisest and ablest would by universal consent be entrusted with authority, and all measures for the common good would be devised and executed with the utmost sagacity and promptitude. Lawlessness and crime being impossible, no costly system of law and jurisprudence, courts and officers of justice, prisons, penal settlements, would need to be kept up. War too, with all its outward horrors and its drain upon the resources of the community, would soon be expunged from the records of such a nation's history, perhaps of that of all other nations. For these, if not induced by their own interests to submit to the control of a community so wise and good, would find it impossible to cope with its vastly superior power.

I need not draw out the picture into further details. It is, you may say, a pious imagination, the visionary picture of a state of things that has never been, and never can be, realized in this fallen world. Yes, it may be so; but surely the question is, Could that dream be realized, would it not bring to the test of experience the power of religion over man's outward life, would it not bring to light in its true significance the principle involved in St. Paul's declaration that, even as regards external blessings—health, wealth, power, happiness, social peace and prosperity, the blessings we mean when we speak of the progress of civilization and the well-being of society,—" godliness is profitable unto all things, having promise of the life that now is," as well as of "that which is to come"?

But I hasten to remark lastly, that whatever, under any such condition of things, we have supposed might be the outward and temporal results of religion, it is not mainly these which the Apostle contemplates when he speaks of godliness as being profitable for the life that now is. From all the constituents and surroundings of human life a higher and richer profit is to be extracted than that which pertains to our outward welfare and happiness. And that profit has not relation only to a future world and our preparation for it. It is to be got here and now. It is a harvest of inestimable good which is to be reaped from and amidst the life that now is. It is the good or godly men who make the most of life, who extract the richest profit out of life.

To see what this means, consider how much more some men make of life than others. "The life that now is" is common to all that live, but how much richer, fuller, its passing days and hours are to one than to another, how much *more* in the same space of time some men contrive to live than others. You cannot measure the amount of life either by its length or its outward surroundings. Rate it not by the beat of the clock but by the pulse of the spirit, by the play and vivacity of thought and feeling, by the range and variety of its interests, by the intensity of the emotions, the creative activity of the imagination, and the force and energy of will that is thrown into it; and you must recognize that there are men who live more in a day, an hour, than others in a year, or others still in a whole life-time. Is there not, for instance, a sense in which we might modify St. Paul's words, and say, 'Intelligence has the promise and the profit of the life that now is'? Place two men beside each other—the one, possessed of all the outward means of living, but destitute of that inner spring of intellectual activity which redeems life from dulness and stagnation, narrow-minded, unidea'd, uncultured, for whom nothing has any deeper meaning than meets the eye, any deeper joy than material satisfactions; and the other, one in whom the pulse of being beats quick with the life of thought, for whom science has rent the veil that hides the open secret of nature, or in whom imagination responds to her wonder and beauty, and who has learned to look on man and human life with an eye enlightened by the contemplation of the great drama of history and by communion with the ideas and principles that are enshrined in the literature of the past;—place, I say, two such men side by side, and who will hesitate to pronounce that, though the world and life are a possession externally common to both, to the one it is a thing bare and barren and poverty-stricken, to the other full of resource and enjoyment, deepened, elevated, expanded, intensified, enriched by the ever-accumulating profit and usury which thought can extract from all things?

But from St. Paul's point of view there is a life richer, fuller, deeper far even than this, of which not a few but all men are capable, and to the moulding and development of which all things in our earthly experience may be made tributary. The highest use and purpose of existence here has not been fulfilled when it has yielded us the largest amount of material satisfactions, nor even when it has dowered us with the gifts of learning, culture, intellectual elevation and refinement. To gain these last is indeed much: who could occupy the place I now do and speak slightingly of their value? But it is no mere pious truism to add, all this may be ours, and yet for us the true, the highest end and purpose of existence may remain unanswered.

There is a life which can lend new preciousness to the gifts of intellect if we possess them, yet which many and many who are poorest in these have lived and are living, and which gives new meaning, worth, sacredness, dignity to all that betides us here. For is it not so that the whole aspect of this our earthly life is invested with a new and higher significance when we recognize in all things, from the least to the greatest, a moral and spiritual purpose, a silent, ceaseless discipline of our spirits, drawing us daily, if we will but yield to it, into closer affinity and fellowship with God? It is a partial, but only a partial, expression of this truth to say that everything in life is an opportunity of moral action, that our common work and toil, our studies and recreations, our domestic and social relations, our speech and our silence, our converse with companions and friends, our gains and successes, our losses, sorrows, disappointments—all constitute a ceaseless, continuous, never-intermitted trial and discipline of character, moulding the moral temper and spirit of our being; so that we never pass through the events of a single day, scarce enter or leave a room, exchange a few words in the street with a passing acquaintance, without receiving some touch of moral discipline, becoming insensibly better or worse, gaining or losing in strength of will, in purity and nobility of nature. Our whole life down to its minutest events is thus charged with moral influence. Now and again there may befall us events which are more critical, great temptations and trials of principle, striking to the very roots of character, leaving for good or evil a deeper mark on the frame and temper of the soul. But for the most part our character is formed, not by moral catastrophes, but by the stealthy and ceaseless deposit of circumstances, by the circumambient moral atmosphere from which we cannot for a moment escape. We live and move and have our being in it, and there is scarce one slightest wave of feeling that passes over us but is leaving its imperceptible impress upon us, contributing to the process by which the final shape and complexion of our moral character is determined.

But St. Paul's conception is something more than this. It is not morality but godliness that, according to him, is profitable for all things. The high, the transcendent prerogative of our nature—that which was revealed to the world in Jesus Christ—is that by its very essence it is related to what is infinite and eternal, and that in the soul that is one with God the glory and splendour of the Infinite suffuses and shines through this gross and common life. The supreme motive of love to God in Christ lifts all the actions and events of a man's life into a higher plane, and sheds a new dignity and sacredness around its least and lowest details. We know how even human love breathing through our actions can make the meanest noble. It is not, for instance, the inherent value of any gift we give or receive for love's sake that makes it precious. There are, perhaps, in our possession things that to other eyes are trifling and worthless; but the old letter whose fading lines were once traced by a loving hand, the ribband, locket, the merest trifle, valueless in other eyes—these things we treasure up as priceless for us because of the tender thoughts and loving memories that gather round them.

Think again how the purest of human affections, parental love, can make the most insignificant actions beautiful, how every smile on the face, and every gleam of light in the eye, and every **touch** and movement of the caressing arm that embraces the child, has a meaning and a beauty which only love can lend **to** it. Or, think once more how the least and meanest offices of affection in the sick chamber—the touch that smoothes the sufferer's pillow, the placing of the cup to the parched lips, the gentle word that cheers his wakefulness, the very silence and stillness of the long hours of watching—how these things are ennobled by the love that inspires them. And in like manner the love that comprehends and transcends all earthly love, the supreme motive of self-surrendering, self-abnegating love and devotion to God in Christ, **lends a** consecration to the humblest, lowliest life on earth, and sheds an invisible glory over all the **acts** that spring from it, so that all the world and all life is a field from which love is for ever reaping its golden harvest of profit.

But even this, however true, does not exhaust St. Paul's meaning. Christian love is not simply love to God, it is the very life of God moving and throbbing in human hearts, it is the spirit of the Eternal breathing through this finite spirit of ours and making us partakers of a divine nature. "He that dwelleth in love dwelleth in God, and God in him." As the principle that binds two atoms of matter together is one and the same principle that holds the planets in their orbits and maintains the harmony of the universe, so all goodness, all love—finite love, infinite love, love human, love divine—is fundamentally the same, and every slightest movement and manifestation of spiritual principle in a human heart is one in essence with the life of the living God, with the eternal life that was manifest to the world in Christ. The little child, as in awe and reverence it breathes its earliest prayer at a mother's knee, is feeling the first throbbings of the infinite life within its breast; in the whispering of conscience prompting us to every slightest act of duty or resistance to temptation, the voice we hear is not simply our own, it is an echo of the voice of eternal truth and righteousness; and in every passing emotion of reverence or aspiration or sympathy with what is pure and good, every slightest act of self-denial for the good of others, every least sacrifice of inclination to duty, known but to God and your own heart, there is a breath of inspiration from the Infinite, a ripple of the boundless ocean of love that fills and floods the universe.

Surely in the light of this truth we can see that 'godliness' not merely contains in it the promise of a far-off future, but is a present and inestimable possession in every Christian soul; and we can discern the profound significance of St. Paul's assertion that "Godliness is profitable unto all things, having promise of the life that now is, and of that which is to come."

THE SPIRITUAL RELATIONS OF NATURE TO MAN.

"When I consider thy heavens, the work of thy fingers, the moon and the stars, which thou hast ordained; what is man, that thou art mindful of him? and the son of man, that thou visitest him? For thou hast made him a little lower than the angels (Revised Version 'a little lower than God'), and hast crowned him with glory and honour. Thou madest him to have dominion over the works of thy hands; thou hast put all things under his feet." PSALM viii. 3-6.

THE doubt as to God's mindfulness of man, which the contemplation of the material universe suggested to the writer of this Psalm, is perhaps not that which presses with greatest force on modern thought. It was the impression produced by the vastness of the visible creation as contrasted with the littleness, the seeming insignificance of man, which gave rise to the question, "What is man, that thou art mindful of him?" The apparent boundlessness of nature, filling the mind of the observer with the sense of the pettiness of himself and of the fret and fever of his passing life, has often awakened the doubt as to whether he can be, as religious doctrines would have us believe, the object of a divine interest or a supernatural interposition so disproportionate to his real importance. On this difficulty, however, I do not think it necessary to dwell. It is based on a very mistaken criterion of greatness and littleness, and on a superficial or anthropomorphic conception of the nature of God and of his relations to the world. It conceives of God as a magnified human potentate ruling the universe from some far-off celestial court or seat of government, and virtually represents him as so busied with the great affairs of his vast empire as to overlook the petty concerns of one who occupies so limited a space in it.

But there is another aspect of the physical system by which we are surrounded, which, even more than its vastness or magnitude, seems, especially to modern thought, to conflict with the conception of God's individual mindfulness of man,—I mean its unbending constancy and uniformity, the unvarying and unalterable character of its laws. Can an order which never varies, whose changes and revolution recur with the regularity of a machine, admit of personal sympathy or of adaptation to our individual character and needs? The form in which the difficulty to which I here refer has most frequently arisen, is that of the compatibility of prayer with the uniformity and unchangeableness of the course of nature. Is there not almost a contradiction in terms between the idea of benefits bestowed in answer to prayer, and the recognition of the world in which God has placed us as a vast system of fixed, determinate, unchangeable relations, in which every atom has its prescribed place and function, and every event is part of a chain of causes and effects in which the disturbance of a single link would imply the subversion of the whole?

And this special form of the difficulty is only a particular aspect of the question to which the text points, the question, namely, whether in the vast material order in which we are placed there be any indication of moral sympathy, or, on the contrary, whether it does not convey the overwhelming impression of moral indifference—of a system which goes its own way and works out its own fixed and predestined results, absolutely irrespective of the moral and spiritual character and exigencies of the individuals who are subjected to it. With the writer of the text I may believe in a Creator of the heavens and earth, ordering the movements of suns and stars and systems from the mightiest to the most minute, and determining all the processes of organic life, the simplest alike with the most complex; and in all this seemingly limitless and complicated system of things, in its unity, its harmony, its wondrous adaptations of means to ends, I may discern the signs of unbounded power and wisdom. In myself, as on one side of my being, a part of this physical system, I may perceive a relation and correspondence betwixt my corporeal organization and the power and will that ordain all material things. But the question that rises up in every human breast when the feeling of individual weakness and dependence comes upon us, or when we realize the fact of our perpetual exposure to physical pains, dangers, disasters which no human precaution or power can avert, and still more, when there is awakened within us the sense of our moral and spiritual needs, the longing amidst the darkness of the world for spiritual light and guidance and protection, for deliverance from the burden of guilt and the haunting memory of sin and the fears and forebodings which an awakened conscience projects into the future—the question, I say, of the Psalmist becomes one which cannot be met or solved by the recognition of nature as the manifestation of creative power and wisdom. "When I consider thy heavens, the work of thy fingers, the moon and the stars which thou hast ordained,"—when I contemplate the immoveable, unvarying order, stability, and permanence of the visible universe, can I discern there any indication that the Invisible Power that originated and underlies it has any care or concern for me, any interest in my individual career and destiny? Is there any gleam of moral sympathy in all this material magnificence, any sign of a personality that takes note of my sorrows and trials, my moral efforts and aspirations, or that cares whether I succeed or fail? In this calm and stately order is there any faintest suggestion of moral approval or condemnation, any indication that the Power that sways it hears the cry of my penitence, any response to my prayer for forgiveness and help? Or, in the perturbation and doubt and dread that rises within me when I look forward to or am called to face the mystery of death, is there any ray of hope piercing through the veil of nature and penetrating the darkness of the future? When I consider this vast, impersonal, mechanism of the universe, does not the irrepressible doubt arise within me which finds expression in the question, "What is man, that thou art mindful of him, and the son of man, that thou visitest him?"

If, then, we regard the problem I have now stated —a problem which in some respects advancing knowledge of nature has deepened and rendered more oppressive for modern than for ancient thought, as that which is expressed in the Psalmist's words—we shall find, I think, in the sequel of his meditation, suggestions for its solution. And these suggestions the writer of the Epistle to the Hebrews adopts, whilst at the same time he infuses into them the deeper significance they derive from the Christian revelation, and especially from the person and life of Jesus Christ. And the solution, as we shall see, is substantially this, that man is himself greater and nearer to God than nature. To human nature as made in the image of God, as only in its finitude "a little lower than God," and, above all, as that nature is seen in its ideal glory in the person of him who was at once Son of Man and Son of God, there pertains by its very essence the potentiality of an inner elevation and nobleness transcending far all the grandeur of the material creation. Regarded in his intelligent, and, above all, in his moral and spiritual nature, man is no longer the helpless slave, but the lord of nature, made to have dominion over it, to subdue and subordinate it to the ends of his higher being and destiny. If he only realize and lay hold of his spiritual birthright, he need no longer remain the bewildered spectator of an awful and impassive material order, no longer feel himself in the grasp of a blind necessity, abandoned to the power of indiscriminating forces and laws. As related to God and the things unseen and eternal, he is in a sense enfranchised from the dominion of nature, sharer in a life that transcends the sphere of time and sense, possessor of a freedom which rises above all material limits, crowned with an immeasurably greater than all material glory. "Thou crownedst him with glory and honour, and didst set him over the works of thy hands: Thou hast put all things in subjection under his feet."

The two points, then, which this passage of Scripture brings before us, and to which I will now briefly direct your thoughts, are, first, the doubt which nature suggests as to God's individual moral sympathy or mindfulness of man; and second, the solution of that doubt which is found in man's own spiritual nature.

Is nature so poor in manifestations of moral sympathy as the text seems to imply? What the writer seeks is, as we have seen, not a proof or proofs of the existence of God and of his power and wisdom. *That* his words already presuppose when he speaks of the heavens as the work of God's hands, the moon and stars as ordained by him. But what he craves for, as he gazes on the wondrous spectacle of the material universe, and what, as his words imply, he fails to find there, is some proof or indication of moral sympathy, of interest in his career and destiny as a spiritual being, in one word, of God's mindfulness of man.

Now, from this point of view, is the world in which God has placed us so barren of the indications of moral sympathy as would seem here to be implied? Are there not, indeed, other parts of the Scriptures both of the Old and New Testament in which the visible material world is clothed with moral significance, and the invisible things of God are declared to be clearly seen, being understood by the things that are made; so that even those who were ignorant of any supernatural revelation are declared to be without excuse if they lived without God in the world? "Let the heavens rejoice, and let the earth be glad; let the sea roar, and the fulness thereof. Let the field be joyful, and all that is therein: then shall all the trees of the wood rejoice before the Lord: for he cometh, for he cometh to judge the earth: he shall judge the world with righteousness, and the people with his truth." "Sing, O heavens; and be joyful, O earth; and break forth into singing, O mountains: for the Lord hath comforted his people, and will have mercy upon his afflicted." When the rapt vision of the ancient prophet thus beheld all mute and material things instinct with a spiritual significance, replete with living sympathy or the joys and sorrows, the moral career and destinies of humanity, is there not here the recognition in nature of something more than dead material power and blind material forces and laws? So when our Lord spoke of moral lessons to be learned from the lilies of the field, what was it that he saw and would lead his hearers to see in so common and seemingly insignificant an object as a wayside flower? Not simply what the senses perceive—form, colour, motion, physical organization and growth; no, but far deeper than that, a spiritual meaning which the thoughtless eye might easily miss, a thought of boundless, unwearied care and watchfulness, of tender, condescending love, of ceaseless beneficence shedding from its inexhaustible stores a beauty with which human art could not vie, on the meanest thing that lives. And in the whole tenor of our Lord's parabolic teaching is there not a tacit recognition of the principle of the moral and spiritual significance of nature?

If, again, we turn from sacred to secular literature, there is surely something more than a mere poetic illusion in that communion with nature, and that elevation of spirit in the contemplation of the glory and splendour of the material world, which finds expression in the noblest imaginative literature of modern times. Surely this attitude of mind cannot be without a basis in the nature of things. When men of profoundly contemplative spirit profess to hold a communion with an invisible Spiritual Presence in nature, in some respects as deep and real and more elevating and ennobling than that which they hold with their fellow-men, is there not something in our common experience which makes the assertion by no means an extravagant or indefensible one ? For how is it in our ordinary experience that mind communes with mind, spirit with spirit ? What is that process by which at this moment thoughts, ideas, feelings, emotions are passing over from my mind to yours ? It is not by any immediate contact, so to speak, of soul with soul; but it is through matter and modifications of matter, through sounds, gestures, movements; by the recognition on your part of the spiritual significance of purely material forms. How, it has been asked, does the child in the mother's arms know that a living, loving personality is present to it ? It is not that in any immediate way soul touches soul; no, but it is by the light in the eye and the smile on the face, by the touches, gestures, caresses, manifold physical movements of the human frame, by the intuitive apprehension of the spiritual significance of material signs, that in its helplessness, clinging dependence and weakness, the child knows, and rests in the knowledge that a living, loving human spirit is holding converse with it. So, may we not say, through the forms and movements of material nature, and the instinctive recognition of their spiritual significance, it is possible for the finite dependent spirit of man to hold communion with the Father of spirits, in whose image it was made?

Nor is this merely the experience of men of high and uncommon imaginative sensibility. There are few of us who have not in some measure felt the power of material things to awaken moral emotion, the power of nature to calm, to elevate, to subdue, to gladden, to console. Consciously or unconsciously there have been moments in the life of most men when they have experienced something of the strange charm, the healing, soothing, medicating influence over the human spirit that lies in the sights and sounds of the visible world; how the silence of the hills and the stillness and repose of woodland solitudes, and the fading effulgence of the evening skies, and the shimmering brightness that plays over the vastness of summer seas—how these and similar aspects of nature have a power to steal us from ourselves, to breathe into our souls something of their own calmness and rest, to allay the feverish restlessness of passion, rebuke the meanness of unworthy pursuits and aims, and lift off the burden of worldly care; to bring to us suggestions of boundless benignity, of pathetic tenderness, of serene, majestic patience, of lavish, inexhaustible bounty, of abiding, eternal purity and righteousness amidst the incessant changefulness of earthly things.

Yet when all this has been said, allowing the utmost for the spiritual suggestiveness of material and visible things, there is an obvious limit beyond which the moral significance of nature cannot pass. There is a sense in which the material system of things presents to us an aspect, not of sympathy, but of stern indifference and irresponsiveness to our individual feelings and needs, in which nature wears a mask through which no gleam of pity or compassion can penetrate, and preserves a silence unbroken by any faintest sign of interest in our good or ill. A well-known modern writer has expatiated on what he designates the "pathetic fallacy"—the fanciful egoism that reads into nature's movements a reflexion of our human joys and sorrows, that sees in her ever-changeful face a look of responsive grief or gladness, that hears in her many voices, now the wail of sorrow for our calamities, now the sound of jubilant rapture for our successes and triumphs, that makes her wear for us now the wedding garment and anon the shroud. Nature never really individualizes, never discriminates. Her changeful aspects are absolutely irrespective of our changeful fortunes. The same serene sky overarches the house of mourning and the scene of festivity and revelry, and if it seem to be in sympathy with the one, it seems also to mock the misery of the other; but in truth it neither mocks nor mourns, it is coldly apathetic alike to misery and mirth. Go to nature in your hour of sorrow, when ruin, disaster, bereavement befall you, when your home is desolate and your heart is breaking, and there is not a whisper of sympathy in her many voices, not a sign that the Invisible Presence is moved by your distress. Go to nature in your times of spiritual darkness and trouble, when an awakened conscience perturbs you, when the haunting memory of sin fills your soul with anguish and foreboding, and with the same unmoved and unpitying aspect she confronts your wretchedness.

Again, the moral indifference of nature is indicated by the seeming impartiality with which her forces and laws lend themselves to the service of good and evil. If "man is one world and has another to attend him," the latter is a world which is absolutely indifferent to the character of its master. As a machine will go on working whether it be the purest or the vilest of mortals that employs it, and wholly independent of the ends to which its results are to be devoted, so is it with the wondrous mechanism of the universe. The forces of inorganic nature, the laws of gravity, light, heat, electricity, chemical affinity, and so on, constitute a vast and exquisitely contrived mechanism which is at the command of the base and evil alike with the good and holy. The luminous ether brings its messages from furthest space to the eye, the medium of sound carries the sweetest melodies to the ear of the impure and vile with the same precision as to those of the saintly and pure; or they will convey the angry or lascivious glance or the words of blasphemy and malice as readily as the look of pure affection and the voice of compassion or the rapt accents of prayer. The organic laws and processes of brain and nerve and muscle that convey the mandate of the will to arm and hand will operate with the same certainty and rapidity whether it be stretched forth to perform an act of charity or a deed of ruthless violence.

So again, in what we call the beneficent or destructive agencies that produce health and happiness or carry ruin and devastation simultaneously to multitudes, there is the like utter absence of moral discrimination. The same revolving seasons pour the harvest treasures into the lap of folly and selfishness and into that of beneficence and virtue. The winds that waft the vessel, the storm that brings shipwreck and death to the voyager, make no selection of those who are to be benefited or destroyed. When the epidemic disease visits a community, the poison germs attack and work out their destructive results in the bodies of the best and most useful alike with those of the most worthless members of society. When the pent-up forces of the volcano or earthquake burst forth and carry wild havoc over fair field and smiling homestead, they act with blind regardlessness of innocence or guilt, passing by and exempting without love, injuring and destroying without hate, careless whom or what they exempt or destroy. No cry from sainted any more than from sinful lips will arrest the engulfing flood, or stay on its career of destruction the descending rock or avalanche. The laws which these agents obey take absolutely no account of the moral greatness or meanness, the preciousness or worthlessness of the beings they encounter in their exterminating career.

I need not dwell further on this line of thought, but the considerations I have adduced leave on the mind the general impression of what I have termed the moral indifference of nature, and of a vast system of irresistible material forces which go their way and work out their results in absolute indifference to the character and the moral and spiritual exigencies of the beings who are subjected to it. They seem absolutely regardless of the happiness or misery they bring to us. Whether they bless or ban, hurt or heal, bring health and happiness, or pain and decay and death, we can neither resist nor modify them. In the hands of nature, and of the Power that is behind nature, we seem to be in the grasp of an awful, inexorable necessity. And it is this aspect of things that lends profound significance to the question, "What is man that thou art mindful of him, and the son of man that thou visitest him?"

And now let us turn for a moment to the answer to his own question which the Psalmist suggests. It is in substance this, that viewed in his true nature, in its essence, its capacities, its boundless possibilities, man is not the slave, but the lord of nature. With all their vastness, their resistlessness, their unbending uniformity, there is that in the spirit of man which, even when he submits to them, makes him immeasurably greater than the forces that subdue him. By God's decree he is sharer in a life that transcends the sphere of the visible and material, and can subordinate it to its own higher ends. "Thou hast put all things in subjection under his feet,"— 'as endowed with an intelligence and, above all, with a moral and spiritual nature akin to thine own, thou hast set him over the vast material empire of nature'; "Thou crownedst him with glory and honour."

In the first place, man is greater than nature, for there is a sense in which it may be said that he creates nature. Conceive for a moment such a thing as a great library or museum, a repository of the treasures of literature and art existing in a world from which every human observer had for ever vanished, in which not one solitary intelligence was left or should ever re-appear to be the inheritor of this intellectual wealth and beauty. The greatest books, the most exquisite productions of human genius, would be but dead material lumber, meaningless marks and scrawls, modifications of matter worthless as the dust into which they are destined to crumble, if never again mind should come to quicken the dead symbols into the life of thought, never again a living sympathetic intelligence should return to recreate inanimate shapes into colour and form and beauty. And so is it, may we not with reverence say, with the productions of a greater than human wisdom and art. All the glory and splendour of nature, her forms and colours, her sounds and movements, her order and harmony, are what they are, not in themselves, but in relation to the eye that sees and the ear that hears, and the intelligence that apprehends them.

The unreflecting observer, indeed, may seem to himself the mere passive spectator of a world which exists in all its reality apart from the organs of sense and the intelligence that informs them. He thinks of the hues and colours as spread over earth and sky, over mountain and meadow and forest and flower, of the woods as ringing with song, and of the multitudinous music of winds and waves and brooks and streams as ever sounding and reverberating as they do now, even when no ear is listening and no mind responding to them. But the slightest advance beyond this crude realism teaches us that what the senses convey to us is at most only the raw material out of which the world is to be created, and that what we ascribe to nature has no existence save in relation to the sensitive consciousness of the observer. It is mind, it is the intelligence that works behind the senses, by which the dark and silent world—material motions, vibrations of ether—is transfigured into shimmering light and ringing sound, into the radiant, coloured, vocal world of our outward experience. But for that wondrous chemistry with which mind is endowed, the heavens that are the work of God's hand would be but a black and lightless vault, the moon and stars which he has ordained, the suns and stars and systems that roll through the distant realms of space but a congeries of whirling atoms. Nay, we may go still further. For all that we speak of as the beauty of nature, the 'splendour in the grass and glory in the flower,' the sweet light of each returning dawn, the fading effulgence of evening, the mantle of glory with which earth and sky and sea are invested; or, again, as the presence of law, order, design beneath seemingly orderless confusion; still more the suggestions of unseen benignity, of infinite thought and love, of a loveliness which eye hath not seen, nor ear heard, of an eternal presence of which the grandest material objects, the everlasting hills, the boundless sea, the immeasurable, star-strewn realms of space, are but the shadow and reflexion,—let, I say, the conscious, constructive, idealizing intelligence be extinguished, and over all this invisible glory a black curtain would drop, and the infinite thought that reveals itself in them would remain unrecognized and unknown. Let there be no finite intelligence to read, after God, God's thought in nature, to become alive to that spiritual element which everywhere lives and breathes, not only through vast cosmical movements, but in every minutest organism, every trembling leaf, every fragile flower, every least and meanest finite object on which the eye can rest, which in its seeming insignificance is encompassed and instinct with the presence of eternal laws—let finite mind cease to exist, and this vast volume of creation would be as if it were not, an unopened book, a work of exhaustless intelligence which has never found a reader. If it be mind in which creation lives, if it be in knowledge, admiration, reverence, responsive intelligence and love, that the material world culminates and is recreated, surely we have here at least one answer to the question, "What is man that thou art mindful of him, and the son of man that thou visitest him?"

Lastly, man can not only think nature, there is a sense in which he is independent of nature. In his moral and spiritual life it is possible for him not only to rise into a region which external forces cannot touch or affect, but in which he can master and subdue them, and make them tributary to his higher destiny. In his physical nature he is but a link in the chain of necessity, his activity infinitely surpassed by the power of external causes, a single minute force encompassed and determined by the endless multiplicity of external forces which he has no power to alter or resist. He is dependent for his health, his happiness, his pleasures and pains, his very existence, on the vast material order in which he is placed, a mere waif in the impetuous current of outward influences, worn and wasted by their attrition, and destined soon to succumb to their disintegrating and destructive power. Viewed on this side of his being, the whole history of man and of the human race is but a sombre record of weakness and evanescence, of races and generations appearing successively on the stage of life only, one after another, to swell the triumph of that calm, relentless power which, itself unchanged and undecaying, makes havoc of human hope and happiness.

But this, blessed be God, is not the last word that can be spoken of the nature and destiny of man. In that nature which God has made in his own image and of the ideal greatness of which Christianity is the supreme revelation, there is at least the possibility for all men of a life which transcends the world of time and sense, and in virtue of which in his seeming weakness he can triumph over all external forces and limits, and claim affiance with God and the boundless realm of the infinite and eternal. In the moral and, above all, in the religious life, lies the secret of a spiritual power and freedom, an ideal perfection which nothing in the universe can hinder or arrest. When in any human soul there has been awakened by God's grace a response to the imperative of duty, to the voice that sounds on the inner ear the command, 'Be true, be pure, be just, be good,' there is at least here the revelation of a law which we feel and know to be absolute and unconditional, the authority of which is supreme over all external conditions and circumstances, over all the impulses, desires, passions that link us to the outward world. 'Thou shalt not speak the false word, thou shalt not do the base deed,'—when there comes to me such an irresistible demand of the divine law of duty, this at least I know, that against it no physical or material consequences are for a moment to be counted, that at all hazards, through pain, suffering, disaster, at the risk or cost of dear life itself, I am bound to obey. Yea, it is no exaggeration to say—though all nature should be armed in hostility to it, though the heavens should fall, I am bound to obey. Above all, when religious principle, when the supreme motive of love to God, of faith and devotion to him who is the highest manifestation of the infinite love and goodness, takes hold of a human spirit, then is indeed the final "victory that overcometh the world"; for then my hope, my happiness, my deepest life and being are identified with that which now and for ever is beyond the sphere of change and accident.

I may forego this spiritual birthright, I may let myself be implicated, soul and body, with the world and the things of the world, with the lusts of the flesh, with pleasant sensations and gratified appetites and sensuous pleasures, with that side of my being whose bliss is to bask in the sunshine of material enjoyment; and then I am at nature's mercy. At any moment of my brief existence, by the slight turn of her forces, by sudden accident or swift-working disease, I may be rendered bankrupt of all on which my life is staked, torn away from every element or ingredient of my happiness. But the life of love, of purity, of self-sacrifice, of holy aspirations and sweet affections, of that faith in God which links and blends the life of the soul with the very life and being of the Eternal—if this life be mine, then amidst a world of change and accident, through all sorrow and pain and decay, amidst the rushing stream of time which, as the years pass on, bears everything else away, my feet are planted on a rock; for though "the world passeth away, and the lust thereof," "he that doeth the will of God abideth for ever."

ART AND RELIGION.

"O worship the Lord in the beauty of holiness." PSALM xcvi. 9.

THE text would seem to indicate that the attitude of religious worship is one not only in which beauty and goodness are closely related, but in which the two things we so designate are united or blended with each other—in which goodness clothes itself in a form of beauty or has beauty as its characteristic quality. Is this idea one which reflection verifies? Is there a point of view from which the conception of what is good or holy identifies itself with the conception of what is fair or lovely? If we conceive of religion as the lifting up of the human spirit into union and communion with the divine, the self-surrender of the soul to God, is there any affinity between this attitude of mind and the feeling with which we gaze on the glory and splendour of nature, or stand in rapt admiration before some noble masterpiece of art, or listen, thrilled with delight, to some exquisite piece of music, or read the works of the great poets of ancient and modern times? Or, if we think of religion as manifesting itself in our moral and social relations, is it literal truth or only the language of metaphor when we speak of the beauty of a heroic action or the loveliness of a pure or self-devoted life? Or when we contemplate the one human life which is to us the perfect ideal of moral and religious excellence, can we with strict propriety of language pronounce it to be not only holier, but more beautiful, than that of any other of the sons of men?

Now there are, doubtless, many devout persons to whom there would seem to be something unmeaning in the identification of goodness with beauty, or in speaking of an essential relation between religion and art, in whose minds even a painful feeling of irreverence is aroused by the attempt to identify the æsthetic with the religious emotions, or to trace any essential connexion between the feeling for beauty and the experiences of the spiritual or religious life. Nor can it be questioned, I think, that there are many considerations which seem to justify the dislike, even the Puritanic hostility, to the intrusion of art into the sphere of religion.

For one thing, may it not be maintained that the two things we so designate appeal to different, independent, often antagonistic susceptibilities in the nature of man? Religious affections, it may be urged, may be experienced in all their depth and reality by minds that are incapable, either naturally or from lack of culture, of any sensibility to artistic beauty; and, on the other hand, the keenest appreciation of the beautiful in architecture, sculpture, painting, music, and in imaginative literature, may be felt by minds for which religious ideas and experiences have no interest or attraction. Even moral goodness and purity of life are wholly independent of the capacity for æsthetic feeling. The domestic and social virtues may attain their fullest development in the lives of men who would stand unmoved and apathetic before the noblest production of ancient or modern art. And, on the other hand, experience shows it to be by no means impossible for the highest genius for art and song to be associated with much moral laxity or even with sensuous excess. Nay, the admirers of genius in poetry and art are sometimes heard claiming an exceptive indulgence for the objects of their admiration on the very ground that the artistic temperament is not to be judged by the rigid canons of morality, and that the emotional mobility, the finely-strung nervous susceptibility, which are the condition of artistic excellence, give rise to an impatience of conventional restraints, a tendency to aberrations from the strict rules of morality, to which men of less impulsive and excitable temperament are not exposed.

Again, it has been sometimes urged, that the danger of a too close connexion between religion and art finds ample verification in the history of the Church. Has religion, it is asked, been purest, has the spiritual life been deepest in times and places where it has allied itself most closely with art, where the ritual of the Church has been the most sumptuous, and the resources of artistic genius have been most lavishly expended on the rearing and decoration of its temples and the imposing beauty and pathos of its services? Is there not some ground for the assertion, that if we seek for the periods of the Church's history in which religion has exerted its most powerful influence over the spirit and life of man, where it has prompted to the highest manifestations of heroism and self-sacrifice, where it has best resisted the blandishments of worldly pleasure or the terrors of persecution and suffering for the cause of Christ, we shall find that these have been the times when the spirit of religion in its naked simplicity has owed nothing to the sensuous attractions of art, and everything to the inherent power and grandeur of the facts and doctrines of the Christian faith? And the reason for this, some will urge, is plain. Spiritual objects can be grasped only by the spirit. "Eye hath not seen, nor ear heard, neither have entered into the heart of man, the things which God hath prepared for them that love him." Can all the resources of art furnish any shape or form or picture of material beauty that will be an adequate representation of him whom heaven and the heaven of heavens cannot contain? Do we not shrink almost with a sense of something blasphemous from the representations of the infinite object of worship which we find in the religious art of mediæval times? Or can we accept even the pictures by the greatest artists of the Man of Sorrows, or of the crucifixion and the agony, as an adequate expression of the sacrifice of the Cross and the infinite sorrow of the Redeemer of the world? "God is a Spirit: and they that worship him must worship him in spirit and in truth." To reduce spiritual realities to what can be apprehended through the medium of the senses is to lower and falsify them, and to deprive them of their boundless influence over the heart and life.

But now, when all this has been said, I think that there is, nevertheless, a point of view from which it may be seen that the best and highest art lies in essence very close to religion. Though it is true that religion may exist in all its reality and power in minds that are almost wholly destitute of artistic sensibility, yet it may be not uninstructive to point out that not only is there no antagonism between them, but that there is a sense in which there is an intimate analogy between the end or aim of the highest art and the end or aim of religion. They agree in this,—and I shall confine myself to-day mainly to this point of view,—that they both seek, each in its own way, to unfold to us the hidden meaning and the true grandeur of human life. They disclose to us—the one by imaginative representation, the other by spiritual insight and aspiration—the ideal of a fairer, nobler, more complete and harmonious life than the common eye can discern in the world of our ordinary experience. Neither the one nor the other ignores the facts of real life, but both reveal to us a deeper reality shining through them—the facts of life illumined and transfigured into that ideal perfection which is, after all, their real significance. They appeal and give voice to the unextinguishable yearning after a life no longer marred and distorted by sorrow and sin. Amidst the low-thoughted cares, the mean and selfish aims, the baulked and disappointed endeavours, the miserably imperfect attainments, the confusion and trouble and strife of the world of our actual experience, the longing for a better, fairer, more blessed existence is the deepest and most irrepressible thing in the human breast. And art in its own way, under the forms of imagination, religion in its infinitely higher and more adequate way of Christian faith and hope, show that to which this longing points to be no mere dream or illusion, but the real meaning of the world and the end to which all things are working. Let us reflect for a few minutes further on this conception of the analogy of the ends or aims of religion and art.

First, as to the end or aim of art. It is not the function of art simply to copy nature and life. Incompleteness, unloveliness, deformity, as well as moral imperfection and evil, exist everywhere around us. It is not the office of true art merely to reproduce these things, but rather to show or suggest the deeper beauty and harmony which underlie and are struggling through the outer form of things. Realism, as it is called, either in painting or poetry, is only at best an inferior and uninspiring, sometimes an unwholesome and degrading, kind of art. What we want the artist to do for us is what, in another way, we want the man of science to do for us, namely, to help us to interpret nature, to look on nature with larger, other eyes than our own. As science discerns order and law where ordinary observation finds only the play of accident, so the poetic imagination sees in the common face of nature a beauty which the eye of sense is unable to discover. And to the idea which, by the intuitive force of imagination the great artist has divined, he gives shape and expression through the medium of sensuous forms and images, borrowed indeed from the actual world, but more speaking and significant than to the common eye they can ever be. That which arrests and holds the appreciative mind in the great work of art is not nature slavishly copied and reproduced, but the idea, the inspiring conception speaking to our soul from the soul of the artist, and causing nature to shine for us with a new, a spiritual significance and glory.

It is indeed the true **mission of art to reproduce our** common life, but so to reproduce it that we shall see **it replete** with spiritual significance, that we shall **discern the** pathos, the beauty, the secret rhythm and harmony that underlies it, the moral meaning that is too often obscured and lost amidst the perplexing confusion of its accidents, the triviality, vulgarity, and often the ugliness and repulsiveness of its outward details. And there are two ways in which the great imaginative artists, and especially the great poets of ancient and modern times, have revealed this ideal meaning of human life. Sometimes they accomplish it by creating characters and scenes replete with an ideal nobleness and perfection; in other words, by carrying us away by the spell of their genius into a region where the possibilities of greatness, after which in our highest moments we yearn, have become realities, where the unuttered longings of the human heart have found fulfilment, and the breath of a purer atmosphere floats around us. Like the great poet, whose loss England has recently been called to mourn, they lift us above ourselves to dwell in a past, even though it be an imaginary past, an age which this world never knew, when love was unselfish and honour unstained, and all noble impulses and affections filled the heart and ruled the life, when it was deemed no fantastic thing in men

> "To reverence ... their conscience as their king,
> To speak no slander, nor to listen to it,
> To lead sweet lives in purest chastity,"

and

> "Through all this tract of years"
> To wear "the white flower of a blameless life."

But art fulfils its function, not simply or mainly by elevating the mind by the contemplation of a visionary beauty either in the past or future, but rather by opening our eyes to the beauty that lies scattered on our daily path, the infinite moral interest that pervades even the humblest human life. For the hardness, unloveliness, and vileness that darken the outer life of man are often, to the keener and more comprehensive insight of the great artist, but the veil of a soul of goodness that is present in and struggling with things evil, and which is for him the silent prophecy of its own triumph over them. The great tragic poet does not leave out of his picture the darker tints of human life, its vice and malice and cruelty and crime; but he never depicts moral foulness for its own sake, or so as to call forth in the mind of the reader only the feeling of repulsion and disgust, or to lead him to look on human life only with a sense of hopelessness or despair. If he paints vice in all its horror, if he sometimes discloses in the human heart a very abyss of evil, there is ever some gleam of a heavenly light, some star of hope seen rising on the darkness. If in the brief epitome of human life which in fiction or drama he presents to us, the catastrophe be one in which baseness and crime go unpunished, or malign passions, hate and revenge, lawless lust or ruthless ambition, seem to triumph, and if the issue of the plot might seem to leave on us the impression of a world that is the sport of blind fate or the scene of lawless accident and disorder; there is ever in the greatest efforts of genius an undertone of moral purpose, a suggestion of the working of a law of right with which it is vain and suicidal to conflict, against which the individual who refuses to be its instrument can only wreck himself; of a principle of love and goodness that transcends sorrow and disaster and death, of a larger drama of human history in the issue of which the seeming disorder and chaos, the broken harmony of life will find its restoration.

And now, turning to the sphere of religion, let us ask if there is anything here that is analogous to what I have described as the function of art. And to this question the answer, I think, is an obvious one. Christian faith can glorify human life and invest its hard, external facts with a beauty far transcending the fairest visions of imagination. Before the eyes of Christian faith, too, there rises an ideal of human perfection transcending the noblest creations of art, appealing, as no production of human genius has ever done, to our deepest emotions of admiration, tenderness, aspiration, awe; lifting us, as we contemplate it, above ourselves and the conditions of our transient life; softening us by its pathos, stirring us by its sublimity, touching all the springs of passion and power within the breast. But religion immeasurably transcends art in this, that it is not through the poor material of form and colour, not on the canvas or the marble that it seeks to embody its ideal, but in actual, living, breathing human souls, moulded into the likeness of the Infinite; that its aim is not to transport us into an imaginary world, but to transform the world of our daily experience into a world freed from all deformity and degradation, and on which "the beauty of the Lord our God" is resting. It bids us discern in every human spirit, the meanest even and the vilest, a nature made in the image of God, having in it boundless possibilities of knowledge, goodness, happiness, capable of sharing in the very being and blessedness of the Eternal. And its high and ennobling aim is, by a diviner than human art, to realize this ideal in the individual life and in the life of the world. To obliterate the taint of selfishness, to erase the deformity and ugliness of vice and sin, it regards as no impossible endeavour; for in these things it sees not man's true nature, but foul and foreign excrescences that mar and deface its inherent nobleness. In its efforts for the regeneration of man's social life, for the coming of a kingdom of God on earth, it is inspired by no Utopian dream of a perfect society; for it is but the realization of God's ideal for humanity that his will shall be done on earth as it is done in heaven. For that faith, which is the "substance of things hoped for," the foul mists and exhalations that have long brooded over the world have rolled away; the disharmony of selfish passions, the jarring strifes and enmities of classes and communities, of warring interests and ambitions that have rent asunder the fair symmetry of the moral world, have yielded to the transforming touch of a diviner than human art; and the universal life of man, in its restored harmony and beauty, is seen reflecting a glory caught from the realm of the Infinite and the Eternal.

I can well conceive that to many ears what I have now said may seem only the language of extravagance and unreality. When we think, not merely of the multitudes of human beings who are sunk in the slough of ignorance and vice, scarcely one remove in their desires and passions above the brutes that perish, but also of the dull routine of common-place respectability which is the best that most of us can boast of, it seems the very paradox of fanaticism to talk of man's nature as allied to the Infinite, having in it boundless possibilities of moral beauty, of a latent heaven of spiritual perfection as present in every human soul, and of the destiny of the race in God's design as one of a glory and splendour of which the beauty of nature and the fairest achievements of art are only the faint and inadequate type. But ere we dismiss this idea as absurd and fantastic, let me ask you to reflect whether this or something like this be not the very essence of our Christian faith. If you are tempted, as you look on the poverty and meanness of human life, on the vulgar aims and poor ambitions, and sordid cares and selfish indulgences, which make up the life of so many of us, to think meanly of human nature, and to ask whether a future of ideal perfection for such beings is not a dream of romance, the answer of Christianity is, 'Know what humanity is capable of by what it has actually become. Learn from the height of moral elevation it has actually attained what by its very make and structure is God's design for it, the true birthright of humanity which in our moral sloth and selfishness we are renouncing, and which all, the least and lowest of us, may hope to regain.'

It is not by the poor and imperfect specimens that we know, in the case of any product of creative power, what it is capable of becoming. You do not know the potentiality of loveliness that lies hid in seed or germ by looking at some specimen of imperfect or arrested growth, but only by observing the full grown plant in all the luxuriance of its summer beauty. You do not know the true nature of the wild free bird by what you see in the poor caged creature, with dull eye and drooping wing and crouching feebleness of aspect; but rather as you watch it cleaving the air on outstretched wing, in unfettered liberty and the fulness of animal strength and joy. You do not seek your type of man's physical nature and capacities in the low-browed, stunted Australian savage; but rather in forms such as those from which Greek art drew its representations of human symmetry and strength. And so when we would form a conception of what humanity is capable of, of the moral perfection and beauty for which God designed it, shall we seek our type in the marred and imperfect lives which for the most part men are content to live? Shall we not rather seek it in its noblest representatives, its minds of rare and piercing intelligence, its beautiful, heroic, saintly spirits, exalted above all lower motives and ambitions, and doing deeds at the recounting of which our hearts thrill with involuntary admiration? Shall we not seek it, above and beyond all others, in Him, the one stainless, flawless, only perfect realization of God's ideal for humanity, sharer of our finite nature, our common life, our cares and toils, our sorrows and trials, our temptations and struggles; yet through whose earthly lowliness shone the glory and beauty of the Infinite? Yes, it is here, when our sense of human degradation is keenest, when pessimistic doubts and fears paralyze us, that our hope for humanity is rekindled. Since Christ lived on earth, human nature has been lifted out of its meanness and become invested with a new sacredness and splendour; a profounder sense of the degradation of sin, and of the possibility of deliverance from its guilt and power, has been awakened in us, and it has become no vain dream to think of humanity as capable of an infinite perfection and blessedness, no impossible and extravagant ambition to respond to the exhortation, "Be ye therefore perfect, even as your Father which is in heaven is perfect."

It is this, then, let me say in conclusion, that constitutes the link between religion and art, between material and moral and spiritual beauty,—that both point to an ideal perfection beyond all that is ever realized in the present and actual experience of man; and further, may we not add, that the highest end and use of material and outward beauty, and the secret of its power over us, is mainly in this, that it is the symbol and type, the unconscious expression of a beauty deeper than meets the eye, the beauty of love and purity and truth and goodness. If we try to conceive why it is that this strange, indefinable thing we call beauty exists, or why the hand of God has scattered it with infinite prodigality over the face of the visible world,—why it is that beyond mere material form, and ordered sequence of material phenomena, and adaptation to the uses of man, far and wide over heaven and earth, over mountain and forest and stream and sea, suffusing, insinuating itself into all the processes of nature, the dawn and the sunset, the spring, the summer glory, the fading splendours of autumn woods and fields, the softened play of light and shadow, the infinitely varied wealth and harmony of colour and form, into all fair scenes and sweet sounds, —if we ask why God has so made the world that this strange element of beauty is everywhere added to use, and what is the secret of its power over us—its power not merely to awaken admiration, to charm and thrill us, but, at least in some minds, to stir in them inexpressible longings and aspirations that transcend the range of experience,—if we ask such questions as these, I think the answer must be that the highest end and use of all this material glory of God's world lies in its power to carry us beyond itself, to be the suggestive type and symbol of a beauty which eye hath not seen, nor ear heard, nor imagination conceived.

The ideal of our life, the conception of a life of perfect moral beauty and harmony, is in this world ever only a future and distant one. For most of us, in the struggle with manifold temptations, every attainment in goodness is of the nature of a hard-won conflict. Even here, indeed, in this life of ours, brief and broken though it be and darkened by the shadow of evil, there are some lives which, in their transparent purity or their absolute unworldliness, or their nobility, their heroic fortitude, their saintly elevation, we can characterize not simply as useful, upright, conscientious, but by no other epithet than 'beautiful.' But even such lives are valuable, not chiefly for what they are, but for the prophetic glimpse they afford us of the better life that is yet to be. Even those of whom we thus speak would be the first to acknowledge that they have not attained, neither are already perfect. Our best, fairest, loveliest souls are most of all those to whom life is a broken and unfinished plot; they pass away with boundless capacities still unexhausted, and far, immeasurably above and beyond all they have attained rises before them the ideal of spiritual perfection, bathed in ineffable light and glory. Yet though they know not what they shall be, though finite imagination cannot fill up the picture of that glorious future which is the destiny of Christ's redeemed, they can at least think of it as a world from which imperfection and evil, doubt and fear, shall have disappeared for ever, where all hearts are moved with a deeper, purer love, and eternal truth shall be seen no longer through a glass darkly, but long-delayed hope shall be crowned with fruition, and the peace of God which passeth understanding, and which is never more disturbed by earthly passion, shall fill all hearts and minds. Then at last shall come the satisfaction of our highest hopes and aspirations, the realization of what is now only our fairest dream of perfection. Then shall come the fulfilment of that ancient prophecy, which speaks of the passing away of earthly glory and beauty, and the coming of an eternal radiancy of which it is but the type. "The sun shall be no more thy light by day; neither for brightness shall the moon give light unto thee: but the Lord shall be unto thee an everlasting light, and thy God thy glory."

THINGS NEW AND OLD.

> "Then said he unto them, Therefore every scribe which is instructed unto the kingdom of heaven is like unto a man that is an householder, which bringeth forth out of his treasure things new and old." MATT. xiii. 52.

OUR Lord here speaks of the qualifications or characteristics of a true scribe or teacher of religious truth. Of these the text specifies two. He must be a man "instructed unto the kingdom of heaven," having insight into that spiritual world or divine order of things, that kingdom of eternal truth to which our Lord tells us he himself had come into the world to bear witness; and in the second place, and in consequence of this insight, he is one who is endowed with the capacity of appealing at once to men's reverence for the past and aspiration after the future, to the faith that clings to unchangeable truth, and the hope that is ever yearning after higher and better things. He is one who "bringeth forth out of his treasure things new and old." Omitting for the present what might be said as to the former of these characteristics, I shall ask you to reflect for a few minutes on what is involved in the latter.

There are tendencies in human nature which often set the old and the new in opposition to each other, but the opposition is not a necessary one. It is possible to love both, and for both the love of the old and the love of the new much may be said. The love of prescription and antiquity is from some points of view a respectable and even noble sentiment, and it has often much to urge in defence of itself and of its resistance to change. It may aver, for instance, that it has experience on its side. The institution that has stood the test of time, the theory that has been long verified by practical results, the doctrine or system of truth which has come down to us with the prestige of ancient authority, which has resisted a thousand assaults of scepticism, which has on its side a consensus of generations of men who have found in it intellectual satisfaction or moral strength,—these are examples which show that veneration for what is ancient and established is no irrational attitude of mind. Nay, the mere poetry and sentiment which gather round and consecrate for us things ancient and time-hallowed, have a root not in mere instinct, but in some measure in truth and reason.

It is no false sentimentality which makes us feel that there are things which have gained a glory and sacredness simply by age. The grey old tower or keep, standing lone and grim on moor or mountain side where for centuries it has stood; the ancestral home from whose walls the faces and forms of bygone generations—warriors, statesmen, courtiers, and divines—look down on the living inheritors of their name and fame; the ancient minster or abbey to whose original architectural grace and nobleness, decay has added a tender, pathetic beauty that is all its own,—the love that clings to these things, though it never thinks of justifying itself, is no irrational or indefensible emotion. It might plead on its own behalf that even mute and material things are ennobled when they bring up before us the vanished ages, and awaken in us the thought of those who, though they have long passed away and their very existence is but the shadow of a name, are yet linked to us by the tie of a common nature—of those joys and sorrows, hopes and fears, which once for them were as real and absorbing as our own. It might urge, too, that apart from their own use or beauty, there is that in these monuments of antiquity which gives material embodiment to the lesson of permanence amidst change, to the thought that there are things which the ever-flowing stream of time cannot wear away; and that there is a side of our being on which we, the children of a day, are yet related to that which is invisible and eternal.

Thus it is obvious that, as against the mere levity

of nature which wearies of the old because it is old and is ever restlessly craving for what is new, the instinct which clings to that which time and tradition have consecrated has at least something to say for itself. The mere discontent that comes from familiarity; the instability of nature that never sticks long to one pursuit or study, that is easily attracted for the moment by some new enterprise, and then, impatient of its difficulties, or of the steady application and toil which it demands, flies off from it to some other employment whose attractions will be sure to prove equally illusory; the love or friendship that never can be trusted to last a day after the flush of novelty has worn off; the superficial intelligence that drops its opinions and beliefs as lightly as the fashion of one's garments, and for which the latest paradox in science or philosophy, the last brand-new canon of criticism in literature or art, the most recent nostrum for the cure of all social or political ills, the pretentious religious theory that has just issued from the brain of some popular writer, possess an irresistible attraction—this temperament is one which betokens a very feeble and shallow nature, a habit of mind in comparison with which the most stolid, unintelligent philistinism is respectable.

Yet, on the other hand, in all fields of attainment, secular and sacred, the aspiration after what is new has also not a little to urge in defence of itself.

The history of secular knowledge, as we all know, is, on the whole, one of continuous and ever-accelerating progress. Each succeeding age is the inheritor of the intellectual wealth of all preceding ages, and the inheritance it has received it hands on, enriched by its own contributions, to that which comes after. And it is this characteristic of human knowledge which constitutes the inspiration and ever present stimulus of intellectual effort. Without its quickening influence, thought and research would lose half their charm.

But science,
> "like every gift of noble origin,
> Is breathed upon by Hope's perpetual breath."

It is just because of its progressiveness, because it is continually discovering new lines of enquiry, opening up new fields for the exercise of man's intellectual and practical faculties, and suggesting new means for the improvement of man's estate, that it kindles such persistent enthusiasm in its votaries.

And there is another consideration. We might admit all that is claimed for old and long-established institutions and systems of beliefs, whether in matters sacred or secular, if the being for whom these institutions and systems have been devised were himself always unalterably the same. If human nature stood still, what has long been found to meet its needs would not fail to meet them now and in all time to come. If man's body never grew, the size of his garments would never need alteration. If his mind stood still, the same outward institutions, secular and religious, would suffice for it from age to age. But the spiritual nature of man does not continue ever the same. Society changes like individuals, and the same institutions can no more suit or affect in the same way society at an earlier and at a more advanced stage of civilization than the same clothes fit the child and the man.

Moreover, if institutions must be adapted to those for whom they are intended, they cannot remain stereotyped, if for no other reason than this, that they themselves, if at all efficient, tend to modify the nature that is subjected to them. The medicine that heals supersedes itself. The school discipline that educates in self-command and self-restraint, by its very success makes itself no longer necessary. Its rules and restraints have not achieved their purpose, unless they have fitted us for that mental and moral freedom which makes them useless. In like manner the laws, institutions, forms of civil and ecclesiastical government, the educational and religious systems, even the books inspired or uninspired, the creeds and formulas, the whole order of external agencies for the intellectual, moral and spiritual education of mankind, if they fulfil the ends for which they are intended, create the necessity for their own modification, sometimes for their own entire reconstruction.

And even religion and religious ideas and organizations are no exception to this law. Through all past ages religious systems, patriarchal, legal, prophetical, have been perpetually superseding themselves. And a time will come when even inspired books, prophets, evangelists, preachers of divine truth, will have served their day and become no longer necessary. "Would God," said an inspired prophet, "that all the Lord's people were prophets, and that the Lord would put his Spirit upon them!" Would God, that is, that the office of all authoritative heaven-inspired teachers were rendered obsolete by the very fact that through such teaching the spirit, not of one man here and there, but of all men, has been raised into communion with the Infinite Mind, and so that vision of God and divine truth, which was once the exceptive gift of a few, has become the common possession of all. And a New Testament writer tells us of a period when this prayer shall be fulfilled, when it shall be no longer necessary for any special agent of heaven to say to other men, "Know the Lord"; for the gift of divine insight, the immediate intuition of heavenly things, shall rest on every human spirit, and all men shall know God "from the least of them unto the greatest." And the greatest of Christ's Apostles in a well-known passage speaks of a coming era in the history of the Church, when not only miraculous gifts of tongues and prophecy, but even that knowledge which is got by **supernatural revelation**, will be regarded as but the leading-strings of childhood, which are discarded as soon as the independence and freedom of manhood have been reached.

If all this be so, then, even more than the reverence for what is old, does the aspiration after what is new, the longing for change, renewal, advancement, receive its justification from the nature of man and the divine order under which we live. For all men, but most of all for Christian men, there is a poetry of hope as well as of memory and retrospection, a beauty that is of the dawn as well as of the evening. If the whole basis of our spiritual life connect us with the past, if the legacy of ideas, books, institutions that have come down to us from the ages that are gone, constitute a treasure which only the fool would despise or fail to appropriate; yet, on the other hand, that very treasure will ill serve its end if we hide it in the field or make it not the capital for new acquisitions, that the Lord of all may at his coming receive his own with usury. If, therefore, we need teachers who will bring out of that treasury things that are old, who will recall to us the wondrous story of man's life in the past, who will tell us of the great deeds that were done in the old time that was before us, who will lead us to contemplate that providential order which remains steadfast through the events of human history, and, above all, that redemption from evil which God has wrought out for mankind through the Son of his love; so too, on the other hand, do we need teachers on whom rests the spirit of prophecy, of high hope and aspiration, of faith in the inexhaustible nature and immortal destinies of man, in whose breast all that humanity has attained in the past only awakens the belief in the immeasurably greater things that are in store for it in the future; so too do we need those whose voices rebuke our indolence, our apathy, our self-complacent recollections and unavailing regrets, and bid us "forget those things which are behind," and with unresting endeavour reach "forth unto those things which are before," our eye fixed on the far-off "mark for the prize of the high calling of God in Christ Jesus our Lord."

The two tendencies of which I have spoken may be conceived of as existing independently or even in reciprocal antagonism. But it is to be observed that the text speaks of them as existing in the same mind and in perfect union or harmony with each other. The scribe instructed in the kingdom is one who brings "out of his treasure things new and old." It is not that he brings out, now things new and again things old, but that the things he brings out are, at once, both new and old. And that this combination is no impossible one we may help ourselves to see by considering, for one thing, that there is a sense in which it may be said that the old is ever new.

There are things that never grow old in the sense

of losing their freshness, their fertility, their suggestiveness, their power to evoke new interest and wonder and delight. To the lover of nature age does not wither nor custom stale her infinite variety; never a new morning dawns in which the old world does not repeat the marvel of creation and start into being from the hand of God, with a glory and beauty as unexhausted as when the morning stars sang together and all the sons of God shouted for joy over the new-born earth. So again, it is one test of a great book that it bears reperusal. Of the books, indeed, which issue year by year from the press in perpetual flux there are many which we should no more think of opening a second time than of re-reading old account books or railway time-tables. But there are others whose interest is not exhausted on a second or even a third reading; and far beyond even these, there are a few great books of ancient and modern literature, in philosophy, in history, in poetry or fiction, whose transcendent excellence is attested by the fact that the appreciative reader turns to them again and again with unsatiated appetite, each time to find not only the old charm of profound thought or exquisite beauty of form and expression revived, but to derive from them new elements of enjoyment—to see new lights, unseen before, breaking out on the same intellectual horizon, new wine at the miraculous touch of genius filling the old vessels.

And, need I say, there is one book which beyond all others meets this test—one book which, regarded simply as literature, much more as the revelation of divine and eternal truth, the repository of guidance, instruction, consolation, of the things that touch the deepest springs of thought and feeling, has proved itself, whether in the experience of the race or of the individual, inexhaustible as the Mind that inspired it, "a well of water springing up into everlasting life." And, I may add, that in the individual experience also, as some at least who hear me will attest, this book has often over us the power both of what is old and new. It is new, for its blessed truths are ever bringing to us fresh consolation and hope. It is old, for a thousand undying associations are intertwined with it. They can recall the wonder and awe with which they listened to its lessons at a mother's knee. They can associate with its pages the great sorrows of life to which it brought consolation, the hours of doubt and darkness on which its words shed light and hope. And as they now read the old familiar words, it is as if the unforgotten music of the past mingled with the thrilling strains of a melody unheard before.

Once more, the idea of the text may be illustrated by considering that often what is new to us is so only because of the quickening of our discernment to see the true meaning of what is old. One function of the true scribe is to help us to read the open secret of the universe. What we call originality is often, not the creation of new materials, but simply the capacity to see old things in a new light. The whole world, all nature and life, are full of wonders of which men never catch a glimpse, because they "seeing see not, and hearing they hear not, neither do they understand." It is so, for instance, with what men call the progress of science. The extraordinary advance of human intelligence in the realm of nature, which began in the fifteenth and sixteenth centuries, and has been going on with ever increasing results down to our own day, arose, not from any change in the objects known, but from a change in the point of view of the observer. Men had gazed for ages upon the heavens above and the earth beneath, on sun, and star, and sea, on a vast organized system, every portion of which, from the revolution of planets to the falling of a withered leaf, or the glittering of a drop of rain or dew, was instinct with the play and operation of laws of exquisite beauty and harmony. But though the treasure of knowledge had been always there, it had lain locked up and unused, till an age came when some foremost searcher found the key, and all at once a hitherto undreamt of and unappropriated wealth lay open to men's view.

The same principle applies to spiritual things. If we think of what we mean by 'revelation,' we shall see that the function of even inspired teachers has ever been not to create or reveal what is new but to bring to light what is old. When, for instance, inspired writers teach us the spiritual significance of nature; when one ancient seer speaks of the heavens as declaring the glory of God and the firmament showing his handiwork; when he writes thus, "When I consider thy heavens, the work of thy fingers, the moon and the stars, which thou hast ordained," and proceeds to deduce from a contemplation of the material world ideas as to the nature and destiny of man and his relations to God, the verbal revelation he utters is indeed new, but the real revelation to which it points, the revelation of the glory of God, and of man and human life at once in its greatness and littleness, was one which the heavens had been preaching since the dawn of human consciousness. Only to many, or most, their voice was unheard, till a spirit endowed with a new insight into nature and man arose, and then creation broke its silence, and the ears of men heard, and their hearts were thrilled by its long inaudible voice.

So again, inspired history and prophecy is in one sense a revelation of new truth, but it is true because it is a record of that anterior and older revelation of the mind and will of God which is unfolded to us in the life of nations and the course of human history. The principles of the divine government, the inherent might of right, the prevalence in the long run of good over evil, the tendency of selfishness and wrong to sap the vitality and undermine the fair prosperity of nations,—these and the like are principles which, though an inspired writer points to them, have been from the beginning of history inwoven into the life of humanity. They are not announced for the first time in the pages of an inspired book, but they are proclaimed and have been ever of old, now in the vivid language of peace and prosperity and power and greatness following on the steps of national virtue and integrity, now in flaming characters of disaster and ruin, of anarchy and impoverishment, of paralyzed energies and exhausted resources that are the awful, providential retribution for national corruption and sin. The verbal revelation is new, but the real revelation is that everlasting law of righteousness and retribution which is both old and new, which is inscribed by the finger of Providence on the history of England and France and Germany, alike with that of ancient Israel or Egypt or Assyria, in the destinies of modern Europe as in those of ancient Asia.

But passing by all other examples of this principle, we find its highest illustration in that revelation of eternal truth which was vouchsafed to mankind in the person and life of Jesus Christ. Here too we have a revelation of what is at once new and old. It was new, because never such a life as this had been lived on earth; because it embodied in a mortal form a glorious idea of moral loveliness, such as the most soaring imagination in its dreams of human perfection had never approached—a human mind the pure medium of infinite intelligence, a human heart devoid of the faintest pulsation of selfish emotion, throbbing in absolute unison with the Infinite Love, a human existence suffused by the Spirit of the living God.

But in all this, and just because it was all this, what Christ revealed was old as well as new; for it discloses to us the latent possibilities of that nature which was made in the image of God. It reveals to us what, according to God's design, lay hid in the very make and structure of the spirit of man, the true birthright which in our guilt and wretchedness we are renouncing, and which all—the least and lowest of us—may hope to regain. It points back to that germ of infinitude, that relation to what is divine and eternal, that potentiality of ever-advancing greatness and blessedness, which was stamped on the nature of man when God breathed into him the breath of life and he became a living soul.

And it is this last thought, let me say in conclusion, which makes Christianity, above all things, the religion of aspiration, of hope, of progress, of unresting endeavour after a perfection that is yet to be. If there be views of life which lead to reaction or stagnation, to a false consecration of the past or despair of the future, it is not to Christ's teaching they can appeal.

If there be those who are disposed to regard the misery and degradation, the sorrow and sin that crush down vast masses of mankind with a weight heavy as frost, as incurable evils, who turn away from the present life and transfer their ideal of goodness and happiness to a world of visionary bliss beyond the grave,—to none of these, to no form of the paralyzing creed of pessimism, does Christ's conception of life afford the faintest sanction. For not only does Christ proclaim that there are no forms of evil, material or moral, poverty, disease, pain, sorrow, suffering, or even those darker, deeper ills that oftenest baffle human healing—guilt and sin, unholy passions, evil desires, impenitence, remorse, and despair,—no forms of evil, however deep-seated and inveterate, to the victims of which he may not address the invitation, "Come unto me, all ye that labour and are heavy-laden, and I will give you rest"; but he goes far beyond this, and proclaims the coming of a kingdom of God, a universal reign of light and love, an era of perfect goodness and blessedness, as the predestined future of humanity.

Nor is this future merely that of another world, a celestial region beyond the grave, to which, in despair of this world, the pious imagination may fly away, to depict it in whatever glowing colours of supernatural splendour it will. The kingdom of heaven which Christ announces is indeed an ideal, transcending in its moral and spiritual beauty every vision of a perfect state, every dream of a paradise restored, or island of the blessed, or heaven of unfading beauty and ecstatic joy, which ever visited the imagination of poet or seer. But the one thing which distinguishes his ideal from all others, is that it is an ideal which he declares to be realizable on earth. If you ask where in God's universe is this home of the blessed, in what region of space lies this land of ineffable purity and happiness, the answer of Christ is, "The kingdom of God is in the midst of you." Here on this familiar earth is its seat. The materials out of which it is to be constructed, the means by which it is to be brought about, are within and around us, in our hands and in our mouths. In the nature of man, made in God's image and redeemed by the Son of his love, are contained the hidden capabilities of this heaven on earth, the latent forces by which all the foul incrustations of evil are to be thrown off. No miracle is needed to bring it near. Live as God made you capable of living, renounce all that is false and foreign to your true nature, be true to yourselves and to that purpose of God which is stamped on every element of your being, and this earth will become the heaven you seek. And if to any this seem only the language of enthusiasm and extravagance, let us remember that Jesus Christ, whom we regard as having touched the very summit of moral exaltation, is not a monstrosity but a man, and that the materials of a hidden Christ are in every human breast. Think of this earth of ours as it would be if all men rose to "the measure of the stature of the fulness of Christ," and then, for you, a kingdom of heaven on earth will be no fantastic dream. Nay, rather, we shall know it as an ideal that is ready at any moment to break through the veil of earthly things. Let men but lay hold of the hope set before them, rise to their true destiny, be what they may become, and the heaven we seek, not far away but underlying this common life of ours, would reveal itself. The common air and earth and skies, our daily work and toil, our coarse cares and common-place trials would be transfigured by the celestial light that gleamed through them; earth itself would become heaven, because the prayer which Christ taught us to pray would be fulfilled, "Thy kingdom come. Thy will be done in earth, as it is in heaven"; and the words of Christ's great Apostle would receive their perfect fulfilment, "Old things are passed away; behold, all things are become new."

I cannot bring these services to a close without referring, however briefly, to an event which, whilst it may be regarded as nothing less than a national calamity, has come upon the members of this University with a sense of personal loss. The reflections in which we have been engaged have only an accidental relation to the event of which I speak; but surely of the great man[1] who has passed away it may be said that he was one of those who make us think better of our common nature, who raise our ideal of humanity, and reveal to us what possibilities of high and noble things it contains. He was one in whom the best qualities of head and heart were beautifully combined. He was a leader of thought, a master in his special department of science, a statesman, wise, far-seeing, judicious, moderate, practical. But he was more than that. One who now hears me, and who knew him long and well, has described him to me as a man brave and true as the day, full of all generous instincts, resolute and courageous in the face of difficulties, scornful of all baseness, yet simple, gentle, and tender-hearted as a child. In the fiery heat of political warfare he so bore himself as to win the respect and even the affection of friends and foes alike. No rancour or foul recrimination ever embittered his relations to those from whom he differed, no stain of selfishness ever rested on his blameless integrity. In the words of the friend to whom I have referred, "he was one who kept himself unspotted from the world."

Life is more or less a struggle to all of us, and its best prizes are those which are gained by the con-

---

[1] Professor Fawcett, Lord Rector of the University of Glasgow, who died on November 6, 1884. This sermon was preached on the Sunday following.

quest of difficulties. But to him the struggle came in a form which would have tried the fortitude of most men. Who of us has not been touched by the pathetic words of our great English poet, when he speaks of himself as old and solitary and blind? But if the loss of sight be sad to the old, it is an even greater calamity when it comes to one entering on a career of honour and usefulness, cramping his powers, limiting his activities, laying an arrest on fair hopes and aspirations. How this brave soul met it, with what fortitude he refused to let it weaken his manhood, with what long patience he strove with its difficulties and embarrassments, with what marvellous success he overcame them, I need not tell you. Surely, as the mystic veil drops and the shadows of the invisible gather round him, ere we turn again to the pursuits and cares of the world, we,—the oldest as well as the youngest of us,—may well pause for a moment to gain from the story of his life some fresh ardour of resolution, some new inspiration and strength for duty.

THE TEMPORAL AND THE ETERNAL.

"Our light affliction, which is but for a moment, worketh for us a far more exceeding and eternal weight of glory; while we look not at the things which are seen, but at the things which are not seen: for the things which are seen are temporal, but the things which are not seen are eternal." 2 Corinthians iv. 17, 18.

The idea which in this text St. Paul brings before us is that the contemplation of invisible and eternal realities has in it a power at once to shorten the duration and to lighten the force of suffering. He was coming to the end of a long life of labour and sorrow, he was looking back on the many years in which suffering had been his daily companion, of which restless toil, want, poverty, persecution, were the almost constant conditions, and yet he had that within his spirit in virtue of which he could pronounce this protracted career of pain and hardship brief and easy to bear—a light affliction that was but for a moment.

And if we try to enter into St. Paul's attitude of mind, paradoxical though the words, literally construed, may seem to be, perhaps a little reflection may enable us to realize their simple, unexaggerated force and significance. When he declared that the long years of his troubled life seemed to him a light affliction which was but for a moment—was he not expressing a principle the truth of which has been often experienced? Is it not literally true that there is, for many, another measure of time than that which is furnished by the beat of the clock or the vibration of the pendulum? It is no mere poetical hyperbole which finds expression in such words as these:

> "We live in thoughts, not breaths;
> In feelings, not in figures on a dial;
> We should count time by heart-throbs."

Or again,

> "Our noisy years seem moments in the being
> Of the eternal silence."

Who is there, indeed, whose familiar experience has not taught him, in some ways at least, the power of thought to master time, of feeling to lend wings to the leaden hours, or, what is relatively to us the same, to render us unconscious of their flight? Absorbing employment, intense excitements, critical emergencies, things and events that deeply affect or move us, often, as we all know, make hours to vanish unnoted and unmeasured, whole days to contract almost into the brevity of hours. When the flow of composition urges the writer's rapid pen, when the inspiration of a congenial subject kindles the artist's mind and lends deftness to his touch, when the orator is borne onwards on the swift tide of successful speech, when the trial is proceeding on whose issue life or death is suspended, when the decisive engagement, big with the fate of nations, is being lost or won—these and such as these are occasions on which time is not reckoned by physical measures, on which intensity of thought and feeling quickens the rate at which life moves.

Now perhaps, even on this lower ground, we might find at least a partial explanation of the way in which St. Paul could speak of his long and troubled career as if it contracted itself into the brevity and evanescence of a passing moment. We might even carry the same kind of explanation further, when we consider the power of thought to master or modify, not only time but trouble, of the tone and temper of a man's mind to create a kind of insensibility to suffering. There is a sense in which, up to a certain point, bodily pain and toil, the outward ills and calamities of life, have no absolute and uniform intensity, but are altogether different to different men, or to the same man in different states of mind. Buoyancy or elasticity of temperament will make all the difference between severity and slightness in the same external troubles. Things that harass and weary one man, waste his energies and fret and darken his mind, pass over another as lightly as the summer cloud over the sky. In mere sport, again, on the playground, in a journey of relaxation, men will often, almost without the sense of fatigue, go through an amount of hard labour, which, if demanded for some piece of uncongenial work, would have all the feeling of painful and protracted toil. And not only is this alleviating power experienced on particular occasions when our heart is thrown into our work, but it is capable of extending its influence over the whole complexion of our lives. There is nothing, for instance, which tends so much to brighten or darken our life as the measure in which we are at one with the calling or career we have chosen. When a man has mistaken his vocation, or has been forced by circumstances into one for which he has no aptitude, all the labour demanded by it, all its incidental difficulties and hardships, fall with double force upon him; whereas a strong natural bent, and the self-forgetfulness which congenial work diffuses over life, render him superior to a thousand cares and vexations, enable him to brush them off with disdain, or make him almost unconscious of their presence.

So, may we not say, was it, almost beyond all other men, with him on whose words we are commenting. If intense interest in life and its objects can lighten the force of outward ills or lessen the space they seem to fill, surely in a singular degree was it so with St. Paul. From that hour when the consciousness of a vocation to Christ's service came upon him with a vividness which lent to it the character of an immediate call from heaven, life became to him instinct with the significance of a great purpose, and all its details were lifted up into a new elevation and unity. His whole subsequent career, as we read of it, is that of a man self-concentrated, losing all thought of self, all sensibility to meaner motives, in one absorbing aim. To win the world to Christ, to diffuse over its darkness the light and life of the gospel, to subdue the powers of falsehood and sin, to hasten the predestined triumph of the kingdom of truth and righteousness—this was the object which arrested his mind and kindled his imagination, and became the dream and passion of his life. Henceforth dulness and stagnation were gone from life. Every day and hour of it were quickened with a new and subtle intensity. To cold and unsympathetic observers he seemed as one beside himself, as a man whom much brooding on a single object had made all but mad. The atmosphere of elevated feeling into which other men rise only on rare occasions, was that in which he seemed perpetually to breathe. The words that fell from his lips or his pen seem, as we read them, to glow with latent passion: "To me to live is Christ"; "I am determined not to know anything among you, save Jesus Christ, and him crucified"; "I count all things but loss for the excellency of the knowledge of Christ Jesus my Lord." The incidents of common life seemed to him raised into the eventful interest of a great drama: "We are made," says he, "a spectacle unto the world, and to angels, and to men." The rapid hours of life seemed only to mark his progress to a goal that grew ever nearer to his sight: "I press toward the mark for the prize of the high calling of God in Christ Jesus." When we try for a moment to imagine a state of mind of which such words were the natural and habitual expression, to conceive what life was for a nature such as this—the quickening of the pulse of existence, the absolute insensibility to personal discomfort, weariness, toil, which came to him from consecration to a great beneficent purpose—perhaps we may be able to discern in his case something of that mastery of thought over time and trouble of which I have spoken, and to see something more than a mere outburst of enthusiastic feeling in the words, "Our light affliction, which is but for a moment."

But it may be said that, in attempting thus to account for St. Paul's making light of the hardships of his long and troubled life, the explanation we give amounts only to this, that in so regarding them, he was labouring under an illusion. The absolute length of life, the afflictions to which he was subjected, as a matter of fact, remained the same, however he contrived to speak of them. Life was not really shortened by a single hour, nor its ills and sorrows lessened of their pitiless severity, though by a trick of the imagination, or in the illusory excitement of feeling, he could look on them as brief and light. But if any one be disposed so to argue, I think he will find an answer to his objection in the words which follow. How could St. Paul look on sufferings, long protracted, and of almost unexampled severity, as light and evanescent? The answer is contained in the words, "We look not at the things which are seen, but at the things which are not seen; for the things which are seen are temporal, but the things which are not seen are eternal."

To understand this answer let us consider what a complete difference it must make in our estimate of what is great or small, important or unimportant, if we accept the principle that it is the things we see and touch and handle that are unreal and transient, the things we perceive only by the mind and spirit that are real and lasting. For very many men the criterion by which all things are estimated is just the opposite of that which St. Paul here avows as his standard of judgment. The outward material world, the solid facts that appeal to our senses, these seem to us the most stable and enduring realities; whilst the things of the mind and spirit—opinions, thoughts, ideas, convictions, seem fluctuating and evanescent, airy unrealities that come and go with the state of our minds or the varying temper and fashion of the hour. Amidst all these fluctuations in us, the solid facts, the actual realities without us, remain what they are, and, as they confront us in their fixed and permanent existence, supply the infallible corrective of men's merely subjective notions and conceits. "One generation passeth away and another generation cometh, but the earth abideth for ever," were the words of one of old, who thoroughly accepted and applied this criterion of reality. "There is no remembrance of the wise," he tells us, "more than of the fool." The time comes when the wise man's ideas, opinions, vaunted treasures of thought, vanish away alike with the vagaries of the fool; human ignorance and folly are but shadows that play and flit on the surface of things; but, meanwhile, the earth, the solid material world, remains in its stability, to mock both alike—"the earth abideth for ever."

Now, undoubtedly, there are many things which would lead us to think that this view is the true one, that which has the sanction of experience and common-sense. When we ask which of the two, the things seen or the things unseen, are the most enduring, there are times when we seem irresistibly led to pronounce that it is the former. There are times when we have all felt the force of that contrast between the evanescent thoughts and feelings of man, and the solid permanence of the outward world which presented itself with such overwhelming power to the writer whose words I have quoted. The one thing that often seems to us in its calm and changeless stability to stand in striking contrast with the mutability of human thought and the incessant fluctuations of human feelings and desires is, the earth that "abideth for ever." A man comes back, say, after long years have come and gone, to some spot or scene with which in earlier life he was familiar, and he is struck perhaps with the contrast between the seeming constancy of nature and the change that has passed over that inner world of thought and feeling which we call 'ourselves.' There stands the old familiar scene as if he had left it but yesterday. Something of change there may be in the things which the agency of man can alter; but the hills, the woods, the streams, the bolder features which nature's hand impresses on the face of things, remain the same, or with changes too faint to strike the eye. Still the old hills, with their well-remembered outline, girdle the plain as if they had never felt the touch of time, and the shadows lie softly on their sloping sides, as if their rest had been unbroken by the lapse of years; still the summer sun sheds its mid-day brightness or its evening softness on woodland and field and homestead, and the stream by whose banks the memory of many a boyish feat still lingers, dashes downwards through copse and glade to where the river still rolls its unvaried course to the sea. But whilst through the long years nature has continued the same, he is conscious, perhaps, that of all that once constituted the inner world of mind— ideas, opinions, desires, hopes, aspirations, ambitions, scarcely one vestige remains to remind him of what once he was. His views of life, his youthful enthusiasms, his dreams of success and happiness, his principles of judgment, his crude ideas of men and things, have vanished as completely as the incidents of a forgotten tale. Or if, by touching the springs of memory, the external scene recall to him some faint image of his former self, it is only to awaken in him the sense of the marvellous transformation of mind he has undergone, it is only to force on him the feeling that, as to all that constitutes the character and complexion of our mental and spiritual being, we are "such stuff as dreams are made of." It is thus the things that are unseen, the elements of the invisible realm of mind, that are transient; it is the things that are seen, the material world and its contents, that constitute our only anchorage to reality.

And yet, plausible as this representation may be, second thoughts may suggest hesitation as to whether St. Paul's standard of judgment is not the wiser and truer of the two. Even outside of the sphere of religion, if we ask what, in the realm of observation and experience, are the things to which we can attach the notion of reality and permanence, is there not much to be said for the view that the things that are seen are temporal, whilst the things that are unseen are eternal? We do not need to go beyond the rudest elements of physical knowledge to learn that the seeming constancy and invariableness of the outward world is but a vulgar illusion, and that even in outward nature the things that abide are not those which the eye sees or the senses can grasp. The sameness and permanence which our supposed observer, returning after the lapse of years, ascribes to external nature, is no real sameness. The streamlet, for instance, that dashes from the hills, or the river winding onwards through the plain, though you speak of it as the same as in the distant years, is obviously, in anything that sense perceives, never, for ever so brief a space of time, the same.

But there is here something that does remain unchanged. The hidden force which regulates the velocity of the ever-changing particles of matter, the laws which determine in relation to surrounding objects the course of the current, the form and colour of the rushing waters, the vibrations of the air which bring to us the impressions of light and sound,—these are the things which no eye can see, but they are things that never change: these constitute a hidden, invisible element constant through the passing years and the ceaseless mutation of all that meets the eye. Or if you turn from the inorganic to the living elements of the scene, in them, too, it is what is seen that is transient, what is invisible that alone is permanent. It is not merely that the grass which clothed the fields, the plants that waved in the woods, the flowers that blossomed and died in successive summers and autumns, have perished; but there has not been one infinitesimal fraction of time in which a single living organism has not been undergoing that ceaseless process of change—of growth, development, decay—which is the essential characteristic of its being. But here again there is something which has continued the same, and here too it is something which does not, and never can, meet the eye, namely, that constant operation of undeviating laws which determine the structure, form, functions, of every springing blade and every plant and tree in a thousand forests. These are the invisible realities, inapparent, impenetrable to sense, which never for one moment intermit their operation, and yet which, not merely through all the years wherein the individual observer can note them, but through all the ages of the past, have never by one hair's-breadth varied from what they were when animate nature began to be.

And though it is true that there are other parts of the visible world of which to the outward eye material change seems to be less predicable, yet we know in point of fact that the most stable portions of inorganic nature—the solid earth beneath our feet, the rocks and cliffs that resist for ages the assailing sea, the hills and mountains which we speak of as everlasting, and over which the storms of a thousand years seem to pass ineffectual—all alike are affected by innumerable agencies which never suffer them, either in external form or inward condition, to abide for two successive moments the same, all are undergoing a process of change as real as that of the materials in the crucible of the chemist. But here, once more, and throughout the whole visible cosmos, that which never alters is an invisible presence, a power which no eye can see, which only thought, penetrating beneath the flux of sense, can apprehend—the presence of those vast, all-comprehending laws which the Creative Mind originated, which are the expression of immutable wisdom, and whose existence is, in one sense, as eternal as the Mind from which they sprang. Even, then, as regards this outward realm of nature, may we not say with St. Paul, "The things which are seen are temporal, but the things which are not seen are eternal"?

But now, let us turn for a moment, in conclusion, to that higher realm of moral and spiritual life to which his words specially relate. And here too may we not find much to convince us that the standard from which St. Paul drew his estimate of human life, and of the greatness and littleness of the things that compose it, is profoundly true? What are the objects of human desire, the things in which, at this moment, we take delight, and which constitute the sources of our happiness? Consider them and ask to which, if to any of them, it is possible to ascribe the character of permanent, unchanging reality. What are those of which we can be sure that they will never vary, and that we shall never cease to care for them? Can we pronounce of any of them, in contrast to others, that neither in themselves nor in relation to them, can any change ever come which will deprive them of their charms, or us of the happiness they bestow? Is it possible for any man to say, 'Here I have found a secure and abiding satisfaction; whatever changes or accidents fate has in store for me, I know that the joy, the bliss I now find in this object, in all the future of my earthly life I shall never cease to find'? Nay, can we go further still, and aver that, amongst the objects of human desire and delight, we have at last found any, or even one, of which we are certain that its capacity to satisfy outstrips all limits of place and time, that not merely here and now, but through all the ages, it will be a joy to us, that its nature is such that "neither death, nor life, nor things present, nor things to come," will separate us from it, or dry up the blessedness it brings?

Now if we try to answer this question, we find that there are many things of which the briefest experience of life tells us that they at least possess no fixity or permanence as sources of enjoyment. It is one of the tritest of moral common-places that we are all through life being perpetually undeceived of our illusions of pleasure and enjoyment; so that we sometimes look back with a kind of contemptuous pity on our former selves, or at any rate with the consciousness that the things in which we once took delight have utterly and for ever lost their capacity to please. The things that stirred the emotion of the child, the slight and trivial objects that were capable of making for us whole days a dream of delight, the pains and troubles that could cause us bitter distress,—the loss of a plaything, the denial of a holiday, a slight bodily pain or sickness,—these things which were once to us so real, fruitful of a thousand eager desires and regrets, are less than nothing to us now; they were relative to a state of feeling which has vanished for ever. And the same lack of continuity or permanence notoriously applies to many of the interests, pursuits, enjoyments of our riper years. There is no one here who has not in some measure experienced the fact that many things which once stirred our passions and absorbed our thoughts, on the gain or loss of which we even felt as if our whole happiness were staked, we have long ceased to care for, and we now look back with mingled wonder and disdain on the amount of interest they called forth. The days and nights of anxiety, the feverish unsettlement and perturbation of mind, the bitter pangs of disappointment we once experienced, if they ever recur to our recollection now, it is only to think of them as utterly disproportioned to their objects, as a foolish waste of feeling, as light afflictions which were but for a moment.

And if we go on to ask, what are the things which engross us *now*, the objects that fill our thoughts, the ideals that fascinate us, the ends and aims of our present life, and whether we shall not one day undergo with respect to them a similar process of disenchantment—whether it be not conceivable that these, in their turn, will in the retrospect be regarded as the childish things of a bygone stage of our history, and all the mental force we are expending on them seem to us a chasing of shadows and illusions—if we ask this question, I think the only answer to such a question is that which is involved in the words of St. Paul, " The things which are seen are temporal; but the things which are not seen are eternal." There are some pleasures of which we can see at a glance that they have no inherent permanence, that they depend on conditions which are local and temporary; so that it is quite possible that what delights us here and now may hereafter or elsewhere become barren of enjoyment or turned into a source of pain and misery. The pleasures of sense and appetite, the enjoyments that spring from gratified desire or passion, from the lust of the flesh and the lust of the eye, of these at least we can pronounce that they depend on conditions which are essentially variable, and of which the slightest alteration would leave the man who lives for such pleasures bankrupt of happiness. Let there be a slight change in the organs of sense, and the agreeable sensations that pour in upon us from our material surroundings would be arrested; a slight modification of our physical organization, and the garniture of colour and beauty would vanish from the earth's face, every sight would become repulsive, every sound agony, the things that please the palate and gratify the appetite would become nauseous and revolting, the thrill of sensuous enjoyment would be turned into dull insensibility or acute pain. Even if they held out to the last moment of our earthly existence, there are innumerable elements of enjoyment which are purely relative to the present conditions of things. Let these conditions cease, let the man whose happiness depends on them pass into a scene where they no longer obtain, and the capacity of enjoyment which relates to them would become useless and vain. The satisfaction they can give is not commensurate even with the term of man's life on earth; there are those who, to their bitter cost, have found that far less than threescore years and ten have sufficed to exhaust it. So true is this, that the sense of weariness and vapidity has sometimes overcome the animal instinct that clings to life; and men who have lived the life of the flesh, who have implicated their happiness with sensuous pleasures or worldly enjoyment have found even this brief life too long, and in the intolerable sense of vacuity and exhaustion have been fain to cut it short.

But, on the other hand, there is another side of our

nature in which we are related, not to what is material and transient, but to what is infinite and unchangeable. There are enjoyments possible to us which from their very nature transcend all limits of place or time, which no lapse of years can wear out and no change of circumstances can be conceived to affect. Search that nature which belongs to you as spiritual beings, made in the image of God, and you will discover there something more and larger than pertains merely to the things of time—capabilities which have in them at least the potentiality of a life that is common to all worlds, of a blessedness which no lapse of ages can exhaust. Whatever doubts we may entertain as to the range of physical law, there can be none as to the universality and permanence of those great moral and spiritual laws on which our existence and happiness as spiritual beings depend. Whatever else is local, truth and justice and goodness are common to all worlds; whatever else is transient, charity never faileth. To whatever mutations organic life may be subject, of this we may be sure, that the life of love and purity and goodness shall never in God's universe find a scene where it cannot flourish. Live for the world and the things of the world,—for pleasure, money, ease, comfort, earthly honour and enjoyment—and even here your happiness is at the mercy of a thousand accidents, and you have not a shadow of security that that dread transition that is fast approaching will not dissipate your dream of enjoyment for ever. But while the world passeth away and the lust thereof, there *are* things—holy thoughts, spiritual convictions, sweet affections, pure feelings, gentle charities, inward possessions and prerogatives of thought and spirit—which even here retain their preciousness through all the changes and losses of time, and which must, from their very nature, survive the shock of dissolution and the transition that shall carry us away from all earthly things. "The world passeth away, and the lust thereof"; on the rushing stream of time everything we love and trust seems to be borne away from us, but there is one rock on which we can plant our feet—" he that doeth the will of God abideth for ever." You may suppose another or a hundred different worlds, but you can never suppose a world in which truth and benignity and self-sacrifice are no longer capable of existing, no longer the sources of supreme satisfaction and blessedness. You can conceive a time to come when a thousand earthly ideas shall be shattered, a sphere of existence where our earthly standards of honour and admiration shall be all subverted; but you can never conceive, in all the ages of the illimitable future, a time, in all the boundless immensity of God's universe, a place, where the ideal of moral and spiritual loveliness which the life of Christ presents, the splendour and sacredness which have drawn to that one life the homage and the love of human hearts, shall have ceased to be an object of veneration and affection. When the day comes that we must quit this old familiar world and be torn away from much that we have known and loved on earth, we may pass into regions and worlds unknown, where all besides shall be strange and new, where many of the powers and acquirements of the past shall be superseded, where tongues shall cease and knowledge vanish away; but the soul which loved and lived for Christ, and imbibed the spirit of his life, in which the divine fire of love to God and man has been enkindled, that soul is free of God's universe. In that moment when the tie to earth and earthly things is severed, and it must pass a naked, solitary thing into a world unknown, wherever its destiny may be, unless it can go where God is not, the atmosphere in which it breathes, the elements of its happiness, will still be there, fresh as when it drew the first breath of spiritual life, welling up with inexhaustible fulness from the eternal springs of thought and joy. For "the things which are seen are temporal, but the things which are not seen are eternal."

THE LAW OF HEREDITY IN THE SPIRITUAL LIFE.

> "He that reapeth receiveth wages, and gathereth fruit unto life eternal: that both he that soweth and he that reapeth may rejoice together. And herein is that saying true, One soweth, and another reapeth. I sent you to reap that whereon ye bestowed no labour: other men laboured and ye **are** entered into their labours." JOHN iv. 36-38.

WHATEVER we may think of the justice of such an order of things as these words indicate, of the fact of its existence there can be no question. It needs little reflection to see that, as respects the religious as well as the other conditions of our life, the world is not ordered on the principle that each individual shall get only that for which he laboured. It would be nearer the truth to say that heredity rather than individualism is the principle according to which the blessings of life are dispensed to mankind. We are living witnesses to the enormous advantages which accrue to the generation to which we belong from the fact that it is heir to the moral and spiritual as well as to the intellectual wealth of the ages that are gone. The youngest student at the present day begins his career with opportunities of knowledge which would have made him the envy, not merely of the learners, but of the sages and philosophers of the past; and the humblest member of a modern Christian Church, born and bred at a time when Christian ideas have penetrated into the general intelligence and formed the public conscience, is familiar with and has had his spiritual being unconsciously moulded by religious facts and principles which "many prophets and righteous men" desired, but were not permitted, to know.

In so far as intelligence and goodness depend on our outward surroundings—and, from one point of view they do depend as much on these as the growth of a plant on soil and climate,—that any one of us attains to a high measure of intellectual and moral advancement and not merely to a stunted and arrested inward growth, is due to this, that we are born amidst the better influences of the present rather than under the feeble light and in the depressing moral atmosphere of an earlier time. And if we ask to what or to whom, under heaven, we are indebted for these benignant influences—this bright and genial light of Christian civilization, this soil rich in the fertilizing energies of intelligence and virtue—the answer is, 'Other men have laboured, and we have entered into their labours.' To produce this rich and varied life —its science, its art, its philosophy, its civil and religious freedom, its widely diffused culture, and, above all, its high standard of moral excellence and its spiritual beliefs and hopes—the hands and brains of a hundred generations of buried workers have been busy. Ideas which are familiar to us as the air we breathe have been slowly wrought out by the thought and toil of a long succession of searchers after truth. Moral principles and ideals that come to us as if in our sleep, are the final result of the long travail of the ages, the precious spiritual product into which the struggles and conflicts of individuals and nations through the long lapse of the vanished past, have been distilled. Privileges and blessings that we have only to put forth our hands to grasp as easily as the wayfarer the wildflowers on his path, are the very things which, seen only dimly and far off, kindled the eager hopes and aspirations of the very noblest of our race, and for the attainment of which they were willing to spend their very lives. Truly may it be said to us, "I sent you to reap that whereon ye bestowed no labour."

And then, along with this comes that other thought of the text, that not only is this splendid heritage one for which our own hands have not wrought, but one in which those who wrought for it are not permitted to share. In one sense the whole order of things in which we live is so constructed that it is precisely the greatest benefactors of mankind who are least permitted to enjoy the fruit of their labours. Life is long enough to gratify to the fullest the men of meaner aims and ambitions, but it is miserably inadequate to fulfil the aspirations of those who live for the highest ends. For the creature of mere animal and sensuous desires there is time enough to drain out to the last drop the satisfaction which such desires can yield. But it is when we turn to contemplate human life in its nobler representatives that the sense of unfulfilled hope and unrewarded effort forces itself upon us. Its minds of rare and piercing intelligence, filled with the ever-growing thirst of knowledge, catching glimpses on all sides of unexplored regions of thought, and still after the labour of a lifetime seeming to themselves to be only standing on the outskirts of the realm of truth; its great moral and religious teachers, capable of leading mankind into higher thoughts of God and the things unseen, or of discerning the wants of society and framing comprehensive plans for its amelioration and progress—it is in the case of such natures as these, filled with great designs, fired with a noble enthusiasm for the advancement of mankind in knowledge and goodness, that we perceive the most striking contrast between desire and satisfaction, effort and reward.

A great scientific discovery, for instance, may be fraught with the most splendid results, economical and social. It may be destined not only to extend incalculably the range of human knowledge, but to give to man a new command over nature, to create new industries, communicate a new impulse to trade and commerce, to multiply the means of human enjoyment, or by increasing the facilities of intercourse to bind the members of the human family together in new bonds of mutual intelligence and sympathy. But the life of the discoverer is numbered by years, the results of his discovery it takes centuries to develop. Or, again, a new and loftier conception of man's spiritual nature has dawned on the mind of some solitary thinker and awakened in him a noble enthusiasm, say, for the reformation of a religion, for the emancipation of mankind from the bondage of error and superstition, for the salvation of human souls from ignorance and sin. The whole life of the religious or social reformer has been devoted to it. His whole happiness is implicated in its success. It would be the dearest reward of his efforts to witness its triumph. But in no such case is it given to the originator to see and enjoy the full results of his thought and toil. Future generations may look back on him as a benefactor of the race, his name may be revered and honoured as that of one of the great contributors to human progress, but the success or the gratitude may come only when the ear has been long deaf to human applause and the generous, benignant heart has long ceased to beat.

Thus in these and other ways the order of things under which we live would seem to be one in which the principle of justice expressed in the words, "**Whatsoever a man** soweth, that shall he also reap," gives place to the strangely different principle of our text, "One soweth, and another reapeth." The inevitable conditions of life would seem to be such that **its** richest rewards are kept back from those who **have**, in order to be bestowed on those who have **never,** earned them; that unrequited and thankless **toil must** be the lot of those who bear the burden **and heat of** the day, whilst those who come in when the day is far spent reap where they have not sown, and gather where they have not strawed.

Such, then, is one of the great problems of human life which the text brings before us. Let me offer one or two suggestions, directly or indirectly implied in our Lord's words, for its solution.

' One obvious consideration is that **the** moral worth of our work is to be measured, not by our actual attainments, but by our opportunities. Men are to be judged by their opportunities,—we of this later time by the splendour and affluence of ours, **they of other and** less favoured times by the scantiness of **theirs.** We see at once the truth of this principle in its non-religious application. In science, **in** philosophy, in politics, in the experimental arts, we do not measure intellectual greatness simply by the amount and range of men's positive achievements. If we did, a scientific student of average diligence in our day would be intellectually greater than many whose names we venerate as the greatest of the past—greater, say, than Archimedes or Euclid, greater than Galileo or Kepler, greater than Bacon or Descartes. The former knows many things which these great men never knew. He knows that the earth goes round the sun; the whole hierarchy of scientific intellects prior to the sixteenth century believed that the sun goes round the earth. He has a fair acquaintance with the science of geometry; Pythagoras is said to have offered up a hecatomb to the gods for the discovery of the proposition as to the square of the hypotenuse. He is sure that alchemy and astrology are mere pseudo-sciences; many of the profoundest intellects of past ages wasted their thought and toil in casting nativities and trying to discover the philosopher's stone. He has, or with ordinary diligence may acquire, a far more comprehensive knowledge of the facts and principles of astronomy, of chemistry, of biology, than was possessed by some of the great men I have named, and he knows at least of the existence of other sciences of which they were in absolute ignorance. Nevertheless, we see at once that the mere range and extent of knowledge affords no accurate criterion of intellectual power. If we estimate men not by the contents of their knowledge, but by the intellectual power implied in it—by keenness of insight, by the capacity to rise from the known to the unknown, by the originality and force of mind which enable them to assimilate and transcend the knowledge of their time—then we perceive the incomparable superiority of the mind that, in an early age and with imperfect and slender resources, could carry on, if only a single step, the progress of human knowledge, as compared with one whose acquisitions, far greater in amount, are merely the appropriation of other men's earnings, the gathering of the ready-made harvest which other hands have sown. To enable a man to claim equality with the great discoverers of the past, he too must by fresh discoveries increase the sum of human knowledge; and even then his greatness is not due to the fact that he knows more than his predecessors in bygone times, but to this, that with vastly greater resources at his command he has made proportionately greater advances than they.

And in religion the same principle holds good. Here, too, in the eye of reason, or, what is the same thing, in the judgment of God, the decisive question with regard to each of us is, not absolutely what is the measure of our moral and spiritual attainments, but what they are relatively to the opportunities we possess. The average goodness and respectability which is almost a matter of course in one age or state of society may mark the supreme height of excellence in another. The point of moral attainment which is the cheap product of convention and public opinion in our day may in other times have been reached only by a life-long struggle with depressing conditions, and by an agony of moral aspiration and effort. When he goes back to the Old Testament the simple reader of Scripture is sometimes puzzled to notice the strange blemishes and imperfections, judged by the Christian standard, which are to be discerned in the lives of the best, and apparently in the inspired writer's view, the holiest of men. In its sacred hymns he finds on the same page and from the same pen the loftiest aspirations of pious ardour and the fiercest utterances of personal hatred and revenge. Patriotism, dauntless courage, magnanimity, tenderness, unswerving trust in God, and heroic devotion to what was deemed the cause of truth and righteousness, are found united in the same personages with sensual vices which in our day would banish the perpetrator from decent society, or with deeds of cruelty and ruthlessness which would expose him to the penalties of the criminal law. Can the modern evil-doer palliate his vices by the example of these Scripture worthies? Or if not, must we remove the latter from their pedestal of sanctity and reverence? I answer, No. Ere we find excuse for our sins and imperfections in such precedents, let us ask ourselves how much our moral respectability costs us, how far our fair and stainless conduct is due to the artificial props of conventional propriety, to the repressive force of public opinion or the dread of losing caste; and, on the other hand, let us bethink us how far the moral blemishes we read of in lives otherwise noble were due to the spirit of their time, and the moral conditions under which they lived; and whether in such a moral atmosphere as theirs the virtues that shine through all the errors of these Hebrew saints and heroes do not indicate a force of character, or even a moral grandeur of nature, which leaves most of us, with all our modern advantages, little to boast of.

But these men, some one will perhaps answer, lived under a special divine dispensation, and were raised up by God to play their part in it. What shall we say, then, of those who, having no such supernatural aid, shine as lights amid the darkness of the ancient heathen world? What shall we say of those seekers after truth whose names are here familiar to our lips, on whose thoughts we, of this late Christian age, still feed, and whose teaching forms no slight element of our Christian civilization? What shall we say, to name but one example, of him who, in his own day, well deserved the name of wisest of men, who through a long life of noble simplicity and self-denial, gave himself to the work of teaching men to be wise and good, whose voice was ever heard amidst the political ambitions and strifes, the fanatical bigotry, the worldly scepticism of his time, awakening the youth of his day to reflection upon the principles of morality; and whose tragic death, in its serene cheerfulness, its disdain of unworthy concessions and unswerving fidelity to truth, set the seal to the reality of his convictions and the nobility of his life? What shall we think of him and others such as he who, amidst the spiritual darkness or the seething moral corruption of the ethnic world, felt, and felt not unsuccessfully after God, if haply they might find him? No doubt, measured by the Christian standard, their best. was imperfect. No doubt the picture of heathen virtue contains much from which the eye, accustomed to a nobler ideal, turns away with pain. But when, ever and anon, we light on touches of genuine moral beauty, when fairer forms and softer lights meet the eye, and our hearts thrill with involuntary admiration, shall we suppress such emotions, shall we sophisticate our consciences, and say that because the impossible motive of faith in Christ was lacking to them, these heathen virtues were at best only 'splendid sins'?

Nay, rather, before we presume to do so, let us ask what use we of this age of advanced Christian civilization have made of the larger opportunities at our command, of the ideals of excellence that have encompassed us, of the impelling, accumulating force of moral influence that has been acting on us from the beginning of our life till now.

Many centuries have passed since a new ideal of human excellence—an ideal actually realized here on this earth in the life of Jesus Christ—was first revealed to the world, and we profess to believe in it as that on which our life should be moulded. Instead of dimly groping after the light, and finding a lifetime of enquiry rewarded only by faint gleams of knowledge breaking through the darkness, the light of the knowledge of the glory of God in the face of Jesus Christ has, from the first hour of our conscious existence, been pouring full-orbed upon us. This is the light in which we live, this the faith and hope by which we profess to be inspired. Who shall picture the elevation, the high endeavour, the unresting effort, the sustained moral excellence which might well be expected of those on whom this splendid heritage has descended? And if, in answer to the question, 'What have we made of it?' the utmost to which many of us can point be a life of conventional propriety, of surface decorum, of refined self-indulgence or respectable worldliness—if this, so far as we are concerned, be the ripest fruit of ages of moral and spiritual development, the last, finest growth on the stem of Christian civilization —who are we that we should compare ourselves with those who in other days, though it may be with stumbling and uncertain steps, followed the "true light which lighteth every man that cometh into the world"? Measure them by the meagreness of their opportunities and ourselves by the magnitude of ours, and may not many of us be constrained to pronounce that the very least amongst them was nobler and better than we?

One other consideration which may serve to throw light on the order of things described in the text is, that it is an order which calls forth and cultivates in us the highest moral and spiritual attainment. The very greatness of the work to which Christ calls us lies in this, that it points to a future—to an end or goal, that far transcends our individual life. It is, as you know, the doctrine of a certain school of thinkers in our day that the Christian hope of immortality is an essentially selfish motive, or at least one which is marred by the taint of selfishness. The highest virtue, they tell us, is that which does good with no hope of future reward. Benevolence or philanthropy reaches the supreme height of moral greatness when the lover of his kind not merely rejoices in good deeds that can be reciprocated—in beneficence that will bring him back a return of honour, gratitude, affection; but is content to spend his life for the advancement of society in knowledge and virtue, and for the happiness of countless multitudes in future ages, long after he, their benefactor, has passed away. It is something to fight for a good cause cheered by the assurance that ours shall soon be the victor's joy, with the shout of predestined triumph already ringing in our ears; to sow the good seed of truth, to which the world is ready to respond, knowing that society is prepared to welcome it and to honour its teacher, and so that the reaping-time of joy will speedily come ; but does not its nobility pale, they ask, before that of the man who knows that his must be the strife, but to others shall come the success, that the fruit of his labours shall be reaped only when he shall be for ever beyond the reach of earthly honour or reward ?

Now, over-strained as in some respects this so-called altruism is, I admit and maintain that it contains an element of truth ; and I say, further, that if a man's good deeds are prompted mainly by personal fears and hopes, even if it be the fear of hell and the hope of heaven, then the motive of the altruist morality is higher and purer than his. Does any one answer me that the former, the desire and hope of personal salvation, is, at least for most men, a practical and powerful motive, whilst for the great majority the latter is not ? Can, it may be asked, any more distant hope for humanity surpass or subdue in the heart of man the more intimate fear as to the approach of death and what comes after it ? The securing of their own salvation is a motive which all men can feel; but is it not the fantastic dream of a theorist to think that men can be induced to care much for the state of the world after they have done with it, or to care more for it than for what is to become of themselves in that awful, inevitable hour which is approaching for each of us? I reply, Be your own judges. Look around you and say whether the motive of which I speak, care for those who shall come after us, be it nearly or more remotely, is not only one of the motives that bespeak more inherent nobleness in the nature that can feel it, but also one of the most practical and potent of human motives? No doubt there are those who are utterly insensible to it. "I perceive that there is nothing better, than that a man should rejoice in his own works; for that is his portion: for who shall bring him to see what shall be after him?" And again, "Behold that which I have seen: it is good and comely for one to eat and to drink, and to enjoy the good of all his labour that he taketh under the sun all the days of his life, which God giveth him: for it is his portion"—this is the philosophy of life which the writer of the book of Ecclesiastes records as the result of prolonged experience of the world. Yes, but it is put into the mouth of one whose better nature had been petrified by selfish and sensual indulgence, of an effete and sated voluptuary. "After me, the deluge": there was at least one human being so lost to shame as to give utterance to this sentiment; but is it not the instinctive judgment of every healthy conscience that a meaner thought was never uttered?

On the other hand, to begin at the lowest point, is there not abundant proof that those who are actuated only by that measure of beneficence which **belongs to** the natural affections, do not feel it to be an impossible or fantastic motive to care for the welfare and **happi**ness of others in which they themselves shall have no part or **lot**? What personal share shall any one of the many who are toiling hard to leave a provision **for** their families have in the comfort and happiness which will be enjoyed only when the hand and brain that toiled for it are turned to dust? If you say, 'A man's family is only a kind of magnified self; care for the future of those we have seen and known and loved is only a prolongation of the interest **we feel in them** now'; and if you ask what proof there is that men can be much influenced by regard for the future of society or the permanent and progressive good of a world they are soon to leave; again I answer, Be your own judges. Are the objects which appeal to the best and noblest natures, and which call forth their deepest interest and their most incessant activity, those which are limited by the horizon of their own passing lives; or are they not rather those which transcend it, and call forth all this high and even enthusiastic interest, just because they far transcend it? Is it only for the existing generation that **such men** interest themselves in schemes of education, in philanthropic enterprises, in plans for the subversion **of** ignorance, pauperism, crime, for the putting down of social abuses and the abrogation of evil laws, for the promotion of the health and happiness of mankind, physical, intellectual, and moral? Are not these, rather than the pleasures and pains, the gains and losses that extend no further than the individual life, the things which are not only recognized by men in general as worthiest objects to work for, but which actually do create the largest interest of the largest minds, and give birth to emotions, conflicts, passions, enthusiasms, transcending in depth and intensity all merely personal and individual interests? And when we think of those whom the universal verdict of mankind places on the highest range of moral elevation—the philanthropists, patriots, heroes, saints, and martyrs, who have counted not their lives dear for the good of their kind, who have struggled and bled and died for the emancipation of the oppressed, for the diffusion of truth, light, and liberty, for the advancement of the cause and kingdom of Christ in the world—is not the one fact, which lent wonderful power to such men and which has exalted our conception of them, that their work was not for their own day and generation, but for all time, and that ages after they have passed away their words and deeds live as imperishable agents in the life and destiny of mankind? And if we pass from all lower examples, what was it that constituted the supreme, absorbing aim of Him whom all Christians regard as the highest ideal of goodness? What was that blessedness of which it was said that "for the joy that was set before him," he "endured the cross, despising the shame," and in the anticipation of which he saw of the travail of his soul, and was satisfied? What but this, that from his life and death was to go forth to mankind through all coming ages a redeeming, saving power, never to be arrested till the human race should grow up to the divine ideal of perfection, to "the measure of the stature of the fulness of Christ"?

And now you see the force of the conclusion to which these considerations tend. If the order of things of which the text speaks be one which elicits and cultivates spiritual elevation and nobility of nature, is not that the highest proof, if proof were needed, of its wisdom and equity? You may say that preparation for another and better world is the supreme interest of every individual man, and that regard for the future and permanent good of mankind cannot and ought not to suppress or supersede in a human breast the profound interest each man must feel in the question, 'What is to become of me after death?' You may urge that the ideal perfection of the present world is at best a distant thing, but that the world to come with all its awful mystery is near and close at hand; that it is almost certain that some one who is now listening to me will not be living when another year has elapsed, and that it is always a possibility that a week, a day, an hour, may solve for us in our own person the dread secret, the meaning of the mystery of death. I answer that I admit all this. But if our destiny hereafter be not an arbitrary one, if it be determined by what we are and have been here, if heaven be "a character and not a locality"; not the baby-dream of white robes and palms and crowns, of rapturous sensations and material splendour, that floats before the sensuous imagination, but the home of perfect purity and goodness, where the long strife with selfishness and sin shall be ended, where hope and faith shall be triumphant and purity shall be unsullied, and the light of eternal truth and love shall fill all minds with its ineffable radiance and blend all hearts in one blissful communion of spirit,— if this be the heaven we seek and for which we are here to prepare, then I ask what conceivable preparation for it can be better than to live and labour for the fulfilment of God's purpose for the redemption of this world from evil? If heaven be for the good and holy, for the unselfish, the true, the loving, the likest to Christ, where can these virtues find a better or ampler discipline than in the endeavour to hasten on the reign of goodness and righteousness, the kingdom of God on earth? Where can love and self-sacrifice, fortitude and self-devotion, find a better means for growth, or a better field for training, than in the great battle against wrong which the elect of all time have been waging? Where is there to be found for hope and faith a more inspiring purpose, or ampler room to exercise their might, than in hastening on that final triumph over wretchedness and wickedness and death which the religion of Christ is to bring at the close of the long battle? Of the place or state into which death shall usher us we can form not the faintest conception. From behind the veil that hides it and the myriads who have passed beyond it, no whisper has ever broken the awful silence that reigns over it. But this at least we know, that, be heaven what or where it may, they will never find themselves unprepared for it who, filled with undying faith in Christ's promise, have in life and death identified their own happiness with the cause for which he lived and died, the final triumph of the kingdom of light and love, the kingdom of Christ in the world.

I close these reflections in a single sentence, with the thought on which I cannot dwell but of which we have in our Lord's words the clearest and most emphatic declaration, that a time is coming when all who work for Him shall see the fruit of their labours and participate in each other's joy. When or how or where it shall be accomplished we know not; but our deepest spiritual instincts respond to Christ's promise that they who have sympathized with his joy—the purest, sweetest, which human hearts can feel, the joy of living that human souls may be rescued from sin and death and brought back to God—shall one day with him see of the travail of their souls and shall be satisfied. The end of all noble work is one, and one too shall be the reward. The holy and good of the past, the succession of true and noble and beautiful souls, whether known or unknown, whether blazoned on the roll of the Church's saints and apostles and prophets and martyrs, or passing their lives in lowliness and obscurity—all who have identified themselves, or in the ages yet to come shall identify themselves not with the interests of the fleeting moment, but with the glory of eternal righteousness and the good of their fellow men, all who have shared in the work of the world's redemption—the Lord shall bring with him in the day of his second and glorious advent to share in its consummation. Many a summer sun has risen and set since the first seed of truth was cast into the field and the early sower rested from his labours, many a day of earnest toil may come and go ere the last sheaf shall be gathered in; but in the great harvest-home that is surely coming, not the first sower in the far past dawn of history, not the last belated reaper when the autumnal sun shall be setting on the field, shall miss his share in the common harvest joy. In that predestined hour to which the whole history of the world is pointing, both he that soweth and he that reapeth shall rejoice together.

The thought that the labourers in the great field of

human thought and effort pass away in swift succession, and leave their place and the fruit of their labours to others, may well at this time come home to us of this University with singular emphasis. Since last we met in this Chapel two of our most eminent teachers, and a third who had only recently retired from the duties of his office, have been taken away from us by the hand of death.[1] I cannot to-day attempt to delineate the individual character and career of those whom we have thus lost. I content myself with saying in a single sentence that they were, one and all, men of no little intellectual power, of great scientific attainments, of enthusiastic devotion each to his special department of knowledge, and that whether as teachers or as original enquirers they have done notable service to science, and brought no little honour to this the scene of their labours. I will add that, one and all, they were men of pure and elevated character, who drew to themselves not only the respect and admiration, but the affection of all, whether colleagues or pupils, who were brought into contact with them. We who have been for long years associated with them in the work of this place can never cease to cherish their memory as that of able coadjutors and of friends revered and beloved; and to you, my younger brethren, they have left an example

---

[1] This sermon was preached in November, 1894, the year of the death of Professors Nichol, Veitch, and Leishman.

of great gifts devoted to noble ends, of untiring and unflagging application, of fidelity to duty, and of pure and blameless lives. Can such lives be lost for ever to the world? Are they and such as they only shadows and phantoms appearing for a little and then vanishing away for ever? Has all this treasure of lofty intelligence and noble endeavour and achievement been created, only after a few short years to be flung recklessly away? Can we hold fast at once to our belief in God and to such a thought as this? I will believe it when I can believe that man is wiser and more merciful than God, and human affection more trustworthy than divine. Then and not till then will I believe that He spake falsely who declared, "I give unto them eternal life; and they shall never perish, neither shall any man pluck them out of my hand."